CREATING KILLER WEB SITES

QUALITY   BREVITY   BANDWIDTH

CREATING KILLER WEB SITES

The Art of Third-Generation Site Design

David Siegel

Hayden
Books

CREATING KILLER WEB SITES

This book is sold as is, without warranty of any kind, either express or implied. While every precaution has been taken in the preparation of this book, the authors and Hayden Books assume no responsibility for errors or omissions. Neither is any liability assumed for damages resulting from the use of the information or instructions contained herein. It is further stated that the publisher and authors are not responsible for any damage or loss to your data or your equipment that results directly or indirectly from your use of this book.

Trademark Acknowledgments

All terms mentioned in this book that are known to be trademarks or services marks have been appropriately capitalized. Hayden Books cannot attest to the accuracy of this information. Use of a term in this book should not be regarded as affecting the validity of any trademark or service mark.

Library of Congress Catalog Number: 96-75903
ISBN: 1-56830-289-4

Printed in the United States of America
1 2 3 4 5 6 7 8 9 0

HAYDEN BOOKS

The staff of Hayden Books is committed to bringing you the best computer books. What our readers think of Hayden is important to our ability to serve our customers. If you have any comments, no matter how great or how small, we'd appreciate your taking the time to send us a note. You can reach Hayden Books at the following:

Hayden Books
201 West 103rd Street
Indianapolis, Indiana 46290
(800) 428-5331 VOICE
(800) 448-3804 FAX

Email addresses:

America Online: Hayden Bks
Internet: hayden@hayden.com
Visit the Hayden Books web site at: http://www.hayden.com

Publisher:	*Lyn Blake*
Editor-in-Chief:	*Michael Nolan*
Publishing Manager:	*Laurie Petrycki*
Managing Editor:	*Lisa Wilson*
Development Editor:	*Steve Mulder*
Publishing Coordinator:	*Rosemary Lewis*
Cover and Book Design:	*Studio Verso*
Manufacturing Coordinator:	*Brook Farling*
Production Team Supervisor:	*Laurie Casey*
Production Team:	*Joe Millay, Christine Tyner, Karen Walsh*
Indexer:	*John Hulse*

Contents at a Glance

Acknowledgments and Credits

This book was written, designed, produced, and shipped (including the design of four web sites) in two months. The team that built this book and the companion site is the most dedicated, good-natured group of people I have ever worked with. Although the book is written in first person, almost everyone at Studio Verso wrote a part of it. They designed most of it. They illustrated all of it. They were a step ahead of me every day, pulling rabbits out of hats and performing miracles of production magic. Special thanks go to David Cullinan, whose pursuit of quality has lasted unfailingly from preproduction in November to May, and also to Russell Brown of Adobe Systems for help providing the software that made this book possible.

I want to thank Steve Mulder for his many encouraging email messages and relentless pursuit of the finer points of HTML. His interest and willingness to try the examples provided a perfect test environment for many of the new concepts I present. Michael Nolan deserves credit for having the vision of *Creating Killer Web Sites* as a design book above all else. His fanatical concern for the design community guided the table of contents and steered the overall direction of the book. Finally, my deepest thanks go to designer and mentor Gino Lee, for being my alter ego as the book took shape. Gino served as the spiritual guide for the entire group, keeping us on course and focused. It is a privilege to be a part of the Web with these remarkable people during these remarkable times.

Development Editor:	*Steve Mulder*
Copy Editor:	*Louise Galindo*
Readers:	*Henry McGilton, John Giannandrea*
Special Contribution:	*Todd Fahrner*
Illustrators:	*David D. Cullinan, Todd Fahrner, Robert Frank, Matthew Johnson*
Divider Illustrations:	*Michel Milano*
Production Coordinator:	*David D. Cullinan*
Production:	*Todd Fahrner, Matthew Johnson, David Siegel, Ilsa VanHook*
Contributors:	*Ray Guillette, Hussein Kanji*
Layout/Design:	*Todd Fahrner, Gino Lee*
Cover Design:	*David Siegel*
Book Site Team:	*David D. Cullinan, Brian Dame, Robert Frank, Matthew Johnson, Hussein Kanji, Gino Lee*

The principal typefaces used in this book are FFScala, Meta, and Matrix Script.

Contents

*This book is dedicated to the surfers from around the world
who visit my web sites regularly. Keep the cards and letters coming!*

Introduction

The Book Site:
http://www.killersites.com

New software emerges on the Web daily. Any CD-ROM included with this book would be hopelessly out of date before pressing.

My company, Studio Verso, maintains a site, http://www.killersites.com, which serves as an up-to-date companion reference to this book. There you will find all the files you need to follow these chapters from your own desktop, as well as pointers to books and software useful for making third-generation web sites.

It is generally referred to as the "Book Site" throughout the text. We hope it will serve you well!

About this Book and its Contents

This is not a first book on HTML. In addition to a good book on basic HTML, I recommended the following books on design principles:

The Form of the Book by Jan Tschichold, edited by Robert Bringhurst (Hartley & Marks, Vancouver, BC, 1991.)

The Visual Display of Quantitative Information by Edward R. Tufte (Graphics Press, Cheshire, CT, 1983.)

Envisioning Information by Edward R. Tufte (Graphics Press, Cheshire, CT, 1990.)

WE DON'T MAKE WEB SITES the way our parents did. The typical "Welcome to my home page," menu-driven, icon-encrusted model is fast being replaced by a model I call *third-generation site architecture*. Though third-generation sites rely heavily on today's browser technology, the difference is not technology *per se*. The difference is design. This is the first book about the conception, design, and construction of third-generation sites.

I have written this book in three parts. Part I covers the nuts and bolts of making third-generation sites, from theory and structure to implementation and tools. Part II contains case studies that take you through the design and construction of five third-generation sites, ranging from introductory to advanced. This section ends with a chapter that showcases several real-life design solutions from around the Web. Part III introduces Adobe Systems' Portable Document Format (PDF) with a primer and a case study. Finally, I discuss issues beyond HTML as we know it today, presenting a vision for the future of on-line design.

Although this book is more than a survey, it is far from complete. I have tried to cover graphic design as applied to the Web, and that necessarily involves a great deal of technical detail. There is much to know and learn about information design, form design, internationalization, and user interfaces. I touch on these subjects briefly. These are substantial subjects, too big for any one person to put into a single book.

We must start somewhere. The days of paper used frivolously are over. The Web is here to stay. I hope this book helps designers to make the transition. In her essay entitled *Electronic Typography,* Jessica Helfand, a brilliant designer who has turned her modem into a design tool, wrote:

Here is the biggest contribution to communication technology to come out of the last decade, a global network linking some 50 million people worldwide, and designers – communication designers, no less – are nowhere to be seen.

With the freedom of the Web comes new responsibility; it will take new thinking to make the Web more visually rewarding as it continues to grow more interesting.

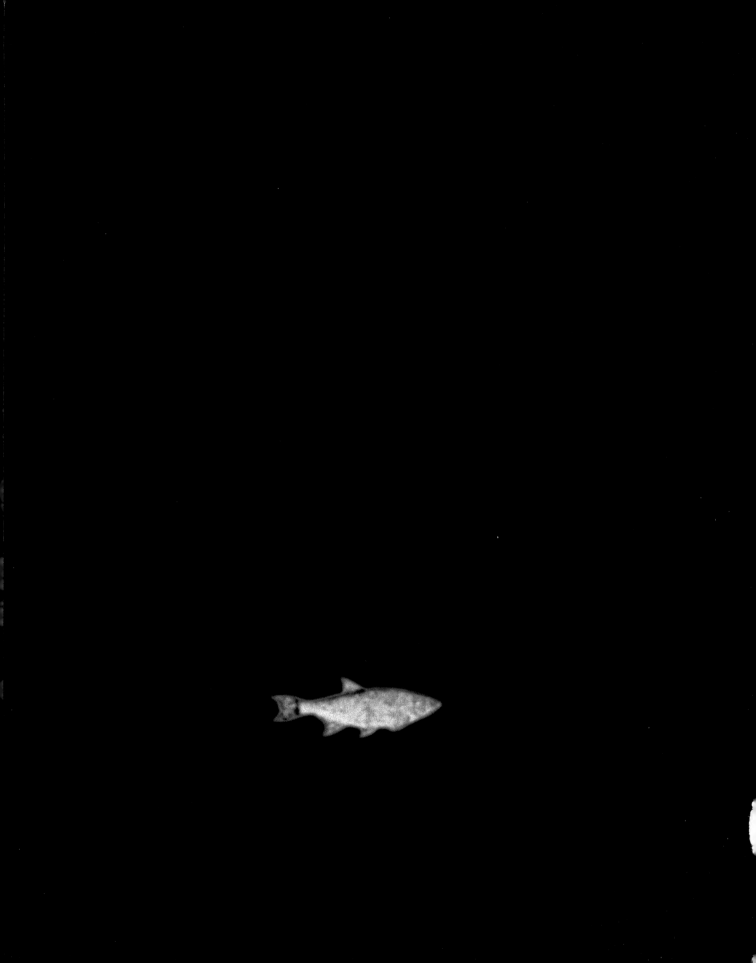

Part I

## CHAPTER 1

Form versus Function

The World Wide Web Consortium

The World Wide Web is the universe of network-accessible information. The World Wide Web Consortium exists to realize the full potential of the Web.

W3C works with the global community to produce specifications and reference software. W3C is funded by industrial members but its products are freely available to all. The Consortium is run by MIT LCS and by INRIA, in collaboration with CERN where the web originated. Seed funding for W3C was provided to MIT LCS by DARPA, and to INRIA by CEC. Please see the list of members to learn about individual members and visit their World Wide Web sites.

- W3C Activity areas and directions
- How to contact W3C
- Frequently Asked Questions about W3C
- W3C meetings, newsletter, mailing lists [W3C Members only]
- Help

In this document:

- News and Updates
- Web Specifications and Development Areas
- W3C Software
- The World Wide Web and the Web Community
- Getting involved with the W3C

News and Updates

- Fifth International World Wide Web Conference: 06-10 May 1996 in Paris, France: The preliminary program is now available.
- Distributed Indexing/Searching Workshop will be at MIT, 28-29 May 1996. New!
- **17 April 96**: CommerceNet and W3C Announce Initiative to Standardize Payment Method Negotiation for the Web (JEPI)
- Workshop on High Quality Printing from the Web, Cambridge MA, 25 Apr 96. One day technical workshop on issues relating to improving the quality of printing from the Web.
- Joint W3C/OMG Workshop on Distributed Objects and Mobile Code, Boston, June 24-25, 1996
- Fourth International World Wide Web Conference: 11-14 December 1995
- Several new W3C Tech Reports are available.
- Press Releases and Press Information
- News and Updates Archive

WELCOME TO MY CASBAH!

Here I am
on a good
hair day.

This isn't my home page. This is just the **casbah**, otherwise known as the blonde bombshelter. When you are done visiting here, follow this link to my **vestibule**.

1.1 A, B Information (ABOVE) versus Design (BELOW): Who will win?

The first time I saw the same web page through two different browsers at the same time, a feeling of panic swept through me. Why should the pages look so different? I knew various systems had different color spaces and resolutions, but these programs actually presented the pages in different ways. As a graphic designer, how could I design web pages if I didn't know how they would look? Could I let browsers reinterpret my work as they wished?

As it turns out, that is precisely what the Framers of the Web had in mind. They saw browser differences as beneficial. Because every document is marked with structural *tags* (headlines, list items, captions, and others) they believed users should control the presentation of documents they see. html (HyperText Markup Language) lets the visitor choose how her browser displays the page.

That's like telling the artist how to hold the brush! I wanted more control. It was either toss in the mouse and go back to print design, or jump into the Web and color outside the lines.

I threw my HTML book in the trash and started from scratch. I built my own tags and made pages the way I wanted them to look. I began using images to lay out pages in two dimensions, rather than one. When tables became available, I poured columns of text in them. I reduced the colors and made the file sizes small and – guess what? – people came! The numbers actually broke my access counter.

I started teaching others what I had discovered. Those of us who broke the rules challenged each other with every new page we made. Like the painters of Russia's avant garde in the Twenties (Rodchenko, Malevich, Popova), we felt like pirates. I received flaming threats from people who said I didn't understand the Web, I was ruining the information, and I should go back where I came from because I didn't understand the power of the medium. I fired back with more pages. I made it clear we were not going to go away. If the Puritans wanted a fight, we would give them one [1.1 a, b].

Structural Markup versus Layout

Print and on-line design are very different. As a print designer, I use programs like Adobe PageMaker and Adobe Illustrator – programs that write PostScript to describe pages. PostScript is a page-description language. As a web site designer, I am required to use HTML rather than PostScript to make my sites (although this is changing, as you will see in Chapters 12 and 13). Designers want to make web pages with the same degree of control they have over paper. Designers must have layout capabilities if they are to design pages for artistic, entertainment or marketing purposes. To quote hypermedia visionary Ted Nelson:

Multimedia must be controlled by dictatorial artists with full say on the final cut.

html is a *structural markup language.* It has no ability to display a fixed-size page or a fixed-size text container. Standard html gives the author almost no formatting control. It is meant

mainly to describe the *structure* of information in a document, rather than its *appearance.* In theory, html browsers are responsible for handling display and layout. In practice, browsers make standard html look about as compelling as tax forms.

Structure has its uses. Structured documents can be fed into databases and searched easily. Their formatting can improve as html becomes more capable, enabling companies with large sets of documentation to enter information only once, then present it many different ways. This is of critical importance to people publishing large reference works, databases, searchable indexes, and documents for people with visual disabilities. As Tim Berners-Lee, the inventor of the Web, states:

Information to be published on the Web must also be formatted according to the rules of the Web standards. These standardized formats assure that all Web users who want to read the material will be able to view it.

Different audiences have different needs. In a perfect world, markup and layout would be in balance. Instead, they are at polar extremes. Today, html is under heavy pressure from designers to be more visual, even as PostScript is being pushed to carry more structure.

What will happen in the future? Is the Web on a collision course with disaster? Will visually unimpaired designers battle against academic library scientists in a winner-take-all contest for the eyes and minds of web surfers everywhere?

Surfer Software

The browser wars are over – Netscape's *Navigator* and Microsoft's *Internet Explorer* are the only two left standing.

Now we have *feature wars*. Even though third-generation sites are distinguished by design, they will also be made differently when everyone has the next generation of browsers (Explorer 3.0 and Navigator 4.0).

I design web pages for Navigator and Explorer, Macintosh and Windows. That's not everyone, but it is 90 percent of the market. (I don't design sites for people who use other browsers or who surf with images turned off.) If a client needs a text-only version of a site, I'm happy to provide one, but third-generation site design is about competing for surfer mindshare and bringing in results.

Surfer Hardware

Consumers have come to the Web. According to Mary Meeker and Chris DePuy, authors of *The Internet Report*, "We believe consumers will begin connecting in earnest during 1996-1997, and that the rate of growth in American Internet connectivity will continue at a near 100% annual rate until the late 1990s."

Most consumers surf the Web on their lunch hour, which means they want to be entertained. They have 640 × 480 screens, but more are starting to log in with 800 × 600 screens, which will be the new entry-level standard. Consumer systems can see only 256 simultaneous colors, because they don't have sufficient VRAM to see more.

The answer to that question may surprise you. I'll return to it in the final chapter, after I've had a chance to make the case for using visual layout principles on your web pages today. For now, think visually! Throw away your old html tags. Replace them with the concepts and techniques that follow.

Summary

As the Web mutates and evolves, site designers find themselves in the middle of a roaring debate on standards and tools. Although this book mostly covers techniques of visual layout control, its real emphasis is on design. When the techniques become obsolete, good design endures.

Web Surfer Demographics	July 96	1998	2000
Number of US web surfers	7.5 m	60 m	95 m
	Percent	*Percent*	*Percent*
Modem (dial-up) users:	70	90	?
Surfers at 14.4KBPS	30	3	—
Surfers at 28.8KBPS	40	80	10
Surfers with ISDN (128KBPS) or better	3	12	80
Female (US)	30%		
Male (US)	70%		
Netscape Navigator Users	70%		
Internet Explorer Users	9%		
PC Users	68%		
Macintosh Users	20%		

Source: Interpolated from *The Internet Report*, by Mary Meeker and Chris DePuy (Harper Business, New York, 1996).

Third-Generation Sites

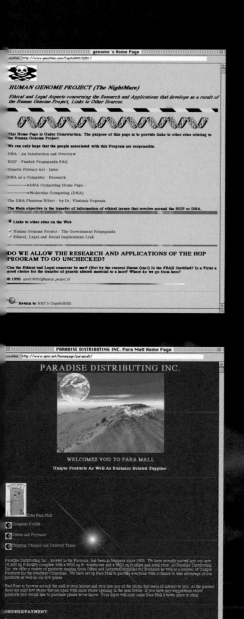

2.1 A, B First-generation sites: horizontal rules
(ABOVE) and wall-to-wall text (BELOW) are the
norm.

WHAT IS A THIRD-GENERATION web
site? A third-generation site uses typographic and visual layout principles to
describe a page in two dimensions.
Third-generation site designers carefully specify the position and relation-
ships of all elements on the page,
retaining fine control of the layout.

Third-generation sites use metaphor
and visual theme to entice and guide.
They strive to make a site feel familiar
and easy to navigate, with clear typography and high production values.
This chapter covers the evolution of
third-generation sites and discusses
their structure in relation to well-
known models of consumer behavior.
This chapter also addresses the design
needs of information-based sites.

First-Generation Sites

The Framers of the Web designed
HTML to look good on ASCII (text-only)
terminals, black-and-white monitors,
and low-resolution color displays. It
needed to be functional, so scientists
around the world could share their
findings.

First-generation sites are linear.
Looking at a typical first-generation
page, you can see the restrictions
imposed by slow modems and mono-
chrome monitors. The page displays
a top-to-bottom, left-to-right sequence
of text and images, interspersed with
carriage returns and other data-stream
separators, like bullets and horizontal
rules. All the initial HTML constructs
were designed around this teletype
model for laying out pages.

First-generation sites were gray
[2.1 A]. Some sites had banners and

were well organized; most had edge-to-edge text that ran on for pages, separated by meaningless blank lines [**2.1 B**]. At best, they looked like slide presentations shown on a cement wall.

Second-Generation Sites

In the spring of 1995, Netscape announced a set of extensions to HTML. People played with the extensions and had fun with the <BLINK> tag. Second-generation sites began to sprout [**2.2 A-C**]. Second-generation sites are basically first-generation sites with icons replacing words, tiled images replacing the gray background, red and blue borders around the images, and banners replacing headlines. They use a top-down, home-page model to present a hierarchy of information [**2.3**]. Although first-generation sites still dominate by volume, second-generation sites are more popular because they have more graphics. Somewhere along the way, legibility went completely out the window.

Technology has always driven the Web. Exciting new capabilities appear weekly, urging designers to try them. Second-generation site design continues to be menu-, icon-, and technology-driven. These sites tend to follow the

A

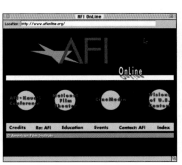

B

C

2.2 A-C Second-generation sites push visitors by using simile and hierarchy.

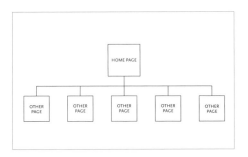

2.3 First- and second-generation sites start with a home page and a list of options.

The Restaurant Model

I use a restaurant metaphor when thinking about sites. You hear about a restaurant from an advertisement or a friend, or discover it while passing by. You check out the daily specials chalked on a board out front and smell the aroma in the doorway.

Once through the door, you make a quick stay-or-bail decision. In a popular restaurant, you might have to wait for a table. If you stay, someone shows you to a table and hands you the menu. You make your selection.

When the food arrives, you have no urge to rearrange the various items on the plate. The food and presentation are the creations of the chef. You sample the various items, skipping among them, mixing flavors and textures.

When you are finished, you have dessert, ask for the bill, and pay. You leave a tip, pick up the card next to the cashier, and maybe exchange a few pleasant words with the owner. Later, when you are hungry again, you return or you don't, based on the quality of that first experience.

2.4 A, B Early third-generation sites.

2.5 Third-generation sites pull people in the front door and guide them through.

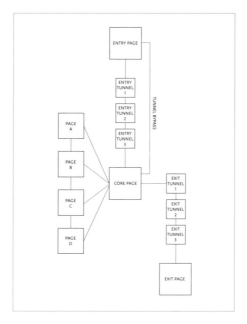

home page model, where the first page you see is adorned with icons and 3-D graphical representations of buttons, windows, and pictures. At worst, noisy backgrounds and interminable waits for sound files make these sites unbearable. At best, they are nice white sites with color-coordinated icons.

Third-Generation Sites

A third-generation site is wrought by design, not technological competence. Third-generation sites give visitors a complete experience, from entry to exit. Design makes the difference. Creative people have made third-generation sites with all generations of graphical browsers [2.4 A, B].

Third-generation sites pull visitors through using metaphor and well-known models of consumer psychology. Just as retailers spend a lot of time tuning their environments to the customers passing by, third-generation site designers spend hours and days making their pages enticing to the audience they seek. Third-generation sites form a complete experience – the more you explore, the more the entire picture of the site comes together. *Third-generation design turns a site from a menu into a meal.*

Browser version numbers do not compare! Netscape renamed a small upgrade to Navigator 2.0 as its 3.0 version, while Microsoft's Internet Explorer 3.0 is a giant step forward. Third-generation site *design methods* have nothing to do with third-generation browser versions. Navigator 4.0 will be the next major release from Netscape, promising to match

a good portion of the Explorer 3.0 feature set and take the Web in new directions.

Site Structure

Millions of people surf the Web. You don't need all of them in your site. You want to reach a select group and turn window shoppers into customers who will take some action that benefits you both (send e-mail, order a product, give feedback, etc.). Telling people to order your products doesn't work. You must ask them nicely to come in and make them feel at home in your site. Most third-generation sites have an entry, a center area with a core page for exploration, and a well-defined exit [2.5].

Third-generation sites pull visitors through by tantalizing them with something exciting on every page.

Entry

An entry to your site tells people where they are without serving your whole smorgasbord of delights at once [2.6 A, B]. More and more sites have *front doors* for just that purpose. A front door – also known as a *splash screen* – loads quickly and tells people what's going on inside. A good front door should be hard to walk away from. Present an image that grabs your audience and pulls them in.

Above all, splash screens should load quickly. Your first screen should take no more than 15 seconds to load at prevailing modem speeds – faster if possible. Present your visitors with a tedious download, and they'll be at

Case Study: Sobek Mountain Travels

Baiting the hook means giving something away. With the commercialization of the Web, fish food is nearly *de rigueur*.

One of the best gimmicks I've seen is the digital postcards of Sobek Mountain Travels. Visitors can send a postcard to a friend, and the site then sends that person an e-mail message saying there is a postcard waiting for them at the site.

They take the special number back to the site's virtual postmaster, who then shows them the picture and text from their friend who visited before. Once there, they are drawn into the rest of the site, where they learn about their tours and send postcards to all of *their* friends. This is a great example of how to give before you receive.

Yahoo! before your access counter can tell you what happened.

Fish Food

As people wander by your site, hold out a basket of goodies to tempt them. Gossip, news, sports scores, weather information, stock quotes, promotional sales, package-tracking services, pictures of Marilyn Monroe, free software, recipes, and sound files routinely lure potential audience members to third-generation sites.

This is what I call *fish food*. If you want to attract investors, put up either current stock prices or some lively, timely investment advice. If you're looking for dog owners, put up "The anatomy of the flea," or have a "name that breed" quiz. You want a gimmick that reaches out to the people you hope will form your community.

The technical term for fish food on the Web is *free stuff* [2.7 A–C]. Give visitors free stuff and a percentage of them will wander into your site. Use your imagination. Think of something your crowd would like to hear about, tell each other about, and go see. When people send your URL to their friends, you know you're serving something they want.

As any advertiser knows, there are no rules for getting people's attention. Use any means at your disposal, even

Java. Put up games, stunts, live video feeds, soap operas, a club for left-handers – anything that generates a buzz. Vandalize your own site, challenge another site to a contest, ask people to vote on something. Things like this work better than filling out forms and asking the search engines to list your site because of its great content.

Entry Tunnels

As visitors enter my sites, I like to give them the option of taking a little ride rather than going straight into the site. I call these rides *entry tunnels*. They help build anticipation [**2.8**] as people approach the heart of the site.

Entry tunnels are most appropriate for consumer sites [**2.9**]. Limit them to about four or five screens and make them entertaining. *Think of the Web as a cozy little town with a half-million restaurants.*

The Core Page

The ultimate goal of most web sites

A

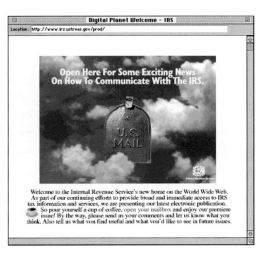

B

2.6 A, B A front door targets your audience.

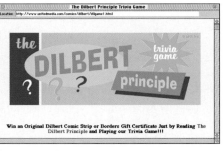

A

B

C

2.7 A-C The goal of free stuff is to generate a buzz on the Web.

2.8 Entry tunnels build anticipation.

2.9 The Joe Boxer entry tunnel.

Barriers to Entry

Third-generation sites lure, seduce, coax. New visitors might not wait for a lengthy download on a high-bandwidth front page. Even the entertaining free stuff will irritate serious, re-peat visitors if alternate points of entry or direct links to the core of the site aren't easily accessible. The best sites hook an audience before the audience even knows it.

In entry tunnels, it's no longer practical to ask people to register. Some entry tunnels say "Register here – free!" Who wants to register for free? If you really want people to regis-ter, you'll have to give them something major in return. Registration is a barrier to entry – be sure you need it before putting it in.

New approaches to registration will replace today's pleas for marketing information from surfers. The Web is advertis-ing-driven. The advertisers will figure out a way to get what they want to know. In the future, your browser will automati-cally tell sites much more about you than they do today.

is to create a community. A good site pays off when people return again and again to purchase or participate. Core pages make this process enjoyable.

In contrast to the second-generation concept of a home page, third-genera-tion sites can have either one or several core pages to organize and present the contents. Core pages direct and guide the visitor by providing links to relevant pages and other core pages. Core pages hold content while continuing to entice the visitor through the site [2.10].

Don't be afraid to guide your audi-ence. Give them choices, but also make suggestions. Give them lots of intrasite links and few external links. Put some-thing interesting on every page.

Traditional home pages easily degen-erate into an endless vertical list of links. Core pages use content to lure and tantalize. Use details of images and excerpts of text to guide your visitor – otherwise, your work remains buried behind flat, uninformative links.

Take the example of a mail-order site, where the goal is to get your user to call an 800 number or fill out an order form. A direct link to that order form or the 800 number itself should be avail-able on almost every page. Most people won't click the first time they see it, but clicks are a function of exposure. Put the links to these final action pages ev-erywhere, and your audience will get there when they are ready.

Exit

Paradoxically, a well-marked exit entices visitors to stay. Showing visitors the door to an exit tunnel informs them that this is the way out of the site. If they come to an area that doesn't hold their interest, they shouldn't just type in "www.cirquedusoleil.com" and surf on. They should visit any areas that might be interesting before taking the exit.

Announcing the exit builds a sense of expectation, like announcing the names of the guests on the talk show at the beginning. It's worth your time to make an interesting exit. Cap their visit with a bang, but don't over-advertise it. Links to your exit should be subtle and constant, without enticing people to leave before seeing the rest of the show.

The exit page is a good place to ask for something from your visitors. You might want to have them fill out a form, call your 800 number, make a purchase, sign your mailing list, or take some other action. They are willing to work with you at this point, because you've rewarded their expectations.

The big finish may be as simple as a list of related sites on the Web, or it may be as fancy as an e-mail interface to an electronic billboard in Times Square (www.joeboxer.com).

Exits often include a chance to send comments or feedback, see a special image or movie, solve a puzzle, visit a random link, enter a drawing, etc. Free stuff can work as well at the end of a site as at the beginning.

Net Equity

If people talk about your site, if they come back often, if your metaphor starts a buzz and the front door is enticing, you will be on your way toward

building *net equity*. Simply put, net equity is audience mindshare.

Change Is Good

You have a site. You want bookmarks. People don't need to bookmark the entrance to your site – they can probably remember that. But if you have a compelling core page, they just might bookmark it. The free stuff gets them there, but they come back regularly to the core of the site to see what's new.

If your site changes every month, it might as well be static. If it changes weekly, people might bookmark the pages with interesting things going on. If it changes daily, you could be in for

2.10 A core page with content on the left and a magazine metaphor on the right.

Case Study: Klutz Press

John Cassidy, owner of Klutz Press, asked me to create a web site for his company, a leading publisher of children's books. He wanted to put a few of the books' chapters on the Web, to illustrate how much fun they are. My original design for Klutz included a long entry tunnel, a dark room with a light switch, then a four-walled room. Each wall had a book on or near it. When you clicked on a book, you found yourself at the book's title page. Clicking on the title page took you to the book's table of contents, from which you could finally begin to play.

People loved the site, but few even reached the books. Most left after the entry tunnel. The book chapters were 14 clicks from the front door! Our redesign for Klutz is much more direct, without sacrificing fun.

As you arrive at the Klutz treehouse, an animated GIF automatically opens the door and beckons you in. On the second screen, you're in a room that contains a book, with its table of contents below. Selecting a chapter takes you right into the content on page three. We used a Perl script to randomize the books, so you get to a different book every time you enter the treehouse. This eliminated the need for another directory page – another layer of HTML with no content.

The moral of the story: put content on your pages as you guide your visitors.

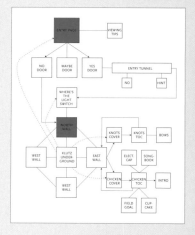

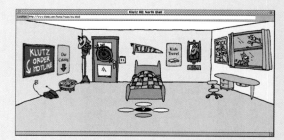

The first sequence (ABOVE) and the revised sequence (BELOW).

some big numbers on your access counters. Make sure to provide links from your active pages to more static areas, especially if you are trying to drive visitors to a particular page.

How many sites have "What's New!" on the front page? We don't need to know how to get to what's new. If it's new, and it's important, it should be in our faces. Put some content on your core page – don't bury it under a "What's New!" link.

Give Before You Receive

Third-generation sites hand out free samples, feed their visitors as they make their way through the site and reward them for coming back. The more you give, the more you must keep giving **[2.11]**. If you keep at it, visitors will give back when they are ready.

Attention to the details of making a third-generation site will create a place where people like to hang out, and hanging out translates into net equity. The more net equity you build for your audience, the more you'll be able to ask for later.

Metaphor: Vehicle of Exploration

Third-generation sites often make efficient use of metaphor. A strong metaphor can guide a visitor and glue a site together. Metaphors must be familiar, consistent, and appropriate for the modem speeds of the Web. Metaphors pull in visitors, make them feel at home while giving them features to explore. Examples of metaphors include galleries, comic strips, television

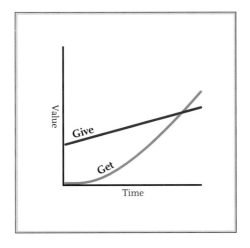

2.11 Only a constant effort to give people what they want can reap rewards later.

2.12 The FAO Schwarz site has a good mix of metaphor and content.

35

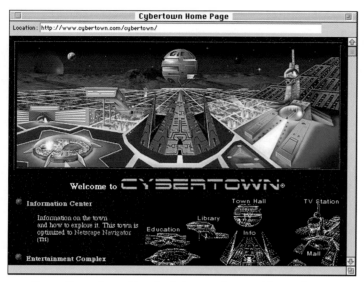

2.13 Some sites get caught up in their metaphors and forget the content.

2.14 A good metaphor is simple and well executed.

channels, magazines, tabloids, store environments, museums, postcard racks, amusement parks, inside things (computers, human body, buildings, ant farm, and so on), safaris, cities, and cupboards. These can be done well [**2.12**], or they can be overdone [**2.13**].

Metaphors are vehicles of exploration. Make it simple, consistent, and easy to get around. A good metaphor puts the switch where you expect it. A bad metaphor makes you learn a whole new set of commands to enter. Well-executed metaphors make it difficult to get lost.

Some sites try to present arcade-like interfaces or physical-space metaphors that rely heavily on 3-D graphics. You find yourself wandering down hallways, through doors, up staircases, and so on. These can work at high bandwidth or on CD-ROMs, but not with modems. Keep your metaphors light and effective.

Metaphors come in all shapes and sizes. This book should inspire you to seek new ways of representing your work, to think outside the constraints of HTML. Think of ways to make your visitors feel at home. Make the metaphor appropriate for your audience. Geologists might enjoy a virtual coal mine tour, but canaries won't.

The trick to presenting a successful metaphor on the Web is to couch it in HTML so that it loads quickly and yet doesn't look cheap. Key visual elements of your metaphor will have to be small enough to reinforce the metaphor over and over again.

Graphic designers are a largely untapped resource on the Web. They learn to use metaphor in school and

When Is a Metaphor Not a Metaphor?

When it's a simile. Simply replacing words with icons does not a metaphor make.

While international menu bars are very helpful to surfers from other countries, if your visitors can't speak English, they probably won't get much out of your site unless you also provide a translated version. Don't turn words into pictures and call it a site.

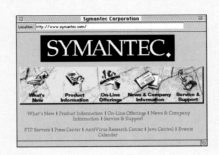

This is not to say you shouldn't have any symbols or icons on your site, or that you shouldn't be clever in presenting them. Icons play a supporting role in third-generation sites. Mixing metaphor and simile requires balance and restraint.

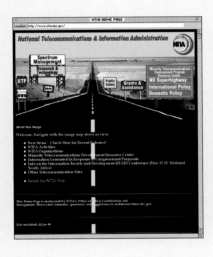

apply those lessons in making everything from business cards to TV commercials. Take advantage of them! Collaborate with a designer rather than trying to become one. Graphic designers who make sites should apply the visual lessons they've learned on paper to creating effective metaphors on the Web. Designers often check their visual skills at the door when entering the Web. Don't fall into the trap of making second-generation sites at first, just because they are easier to make. Start with third-generation design and the skillful use of metaphor.

Once you choose a metaphor, stick with it. It may sound easy, but once you get going, there will be tempta-

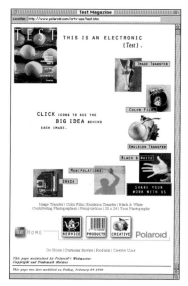

A

B

C

2.15 A-C Theme-based sites use consistent imagery and artwork.

tions. Keep it simple. A good metaphor helps select your audience. This proposal [2.14] for an entry was meant to be mysterious and inviting, setting up a metaphor for the entire site: outer space. (Compare this image to the previous space-town concept.)

Theme:
Interior Design for the Web

You don't need a metaphor to make a third-generation site. A consistent theme can work just as well. A theme can be visual or conceptual. Examples of themes: painterly, primitive, photographic, juvenile, art deco, typographic, futuristic, and so on. As with metaphor, themes can either enhance or get in the way [2.15 A-C].

A theme can be almost anything. The best are subtle and consistent. Think of storefronts. Retail stores differentiate themselves by presenting a thematic environment. Some – particularly toy stores – use metaphors (castles, playhouses, and more), but most use colors, textures, lighting, and graphics to uniquely identify their stores.

Commercial interior designers know about theme. They make a space functional and interesting, not cartoonish or repetitive. They must create both tangible and intangible value, pleasing the senses while serving the needs of the business.

Thematic sites are more difficult to create than you might think. There is a great temptation to throw in more of everything – sound, animation, fonts, graphics – leading to clutter and confusion. Using quality photography, for example, can make a difference on a theme-based site. Using the few colors available to site designers is a big challenge. Defining a subset of those colors to create an individual palette that expresses a particular identity is nearly impossible. A good thematic site is an exercise in subtlety and consistency.

Information-Based Sites

Many sites are not geared toward consumers. In the information realm, sites must satisfy impatient, directed visitors. These sites can't afford to put too much glitter in front of the information. Nevertheless, they can be compelling without using a lot of icons and banners.

Most information-based sites present endless pages of text and bulleted lists, with a predictable home page up front (NEWS | ABOUT US | CATALOG | FAQ | HELP). The best have a search engine enabling visitors to find things immediately, but if a customer doesn't know exactly what she wants, she is lost.

Information-based sites come in all shapes and sizes, but they rarely engage. The best way to overcome the information-overload approach is to establish a simple theme and keep opening doors in front of people. Put content, new information, and navigation on every page. Give them small opportunities to take unexpected turns or see new sections. Use a light theme or metaphor to make the experience worth coming back to.

Information-based sites must be balanced. They must pull in new people, while giving the regulars an easy

The Currency of the Web

A **hit** is any file downloaded. A hit can be a page of text, an in-line graphic, or a downloadable movie or sound file. Thus, if you have a page with ten pictures on it, a person coming to that page will generate 11 hits (if her browser can see images). Many people confuse hits with accesses or visitors, which makes 10,000 of them around noontime sound as though their site is packed with people (when it really isn't). Hits are the pennies of the Web.

An **access** is an entire page served. Accesses (also called *page hits*) are the smallest unit to track, because they can help you determine where people go in your site.

A **visitor** is the true one-dollar bill of the Web. Unfortunately, *unique visitors* are more difficult to define. That's why there's so much incentive to get visitors to register – people are anonymous as they view your site. For the most part, I simply make educated guesses about the number of unique visitors to my sites. Programs are now available to help webmasters track visitors going through their sites.

A **repeat visitor** is the ten-dollar bill of the Web. If a visitor bookmarks your site, it means she is willing to come back. In the mail-order business, such a person is called a *responder*.

If people order things on your site, they turn from visitors into **customers**, the ultimate goal. A customer is the highest level a visitor can attain. A good web site strives to turn a small percentage of random surfers into customers.

Webmasters & Webmistresses

A webmaster or webmistress is the person responsible for keeping the server running properly. Site designers are not webmasters any more than ship designers are first mates.

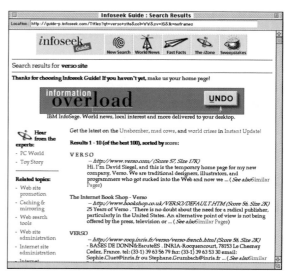

2.16 StockCenter entices people to see stock indexes and learn about their product while showing stock prices.

2.17 InfoSeek uses the left margin to give suggestions.

way to get exactly what they came for.

One example is the site I designed for StockCenter [**2.16**]. People go right to the information they want. From the left margin, they can choose from a number of possibilities.

InfoSeek [**2.17**], a popular search engine, uses tables to present the search results on the main area of the page, along with a selection of recommendations in the left margin. This added value to an information-based site keeps surfers coming back.

Information-based sites must offer both browse and search capabilities. Regular customers need a page they can bookmark, preferably listing the features of the site and providing the shortest path to any given page. There should be a search window, or at least a button to a search page, on every page in the site.

One way to present a lot of continually changing data is to use Netscape's frames feature. Frames can help, espe-

cially for presenting large sets of pages that users should compare. Information-based sites do not need frames, but they are candidates for frames. For now, a manufacturer who wants to present hundreds of products side by side might consider frames. I don't think frames are the only solution (at this writing, no web-wide search engine uses them), but designers of sites with large, frequently changing data sets should weigh the advantages and disadvantages of frames. Internet Explorer's *floating frames* might also help on sites like this. *(See "Frames and Framesets" in Chapter 4 for more information on frames.)*

Dynamic sites will be the norm in the information realm. Rather than bookmarking a static page, frequent users will fill out a form telling the site about their needs. The site will go to work for them, sending them e-mail messages when new items of interest arise, providing a custom, made-on-demand page just for them when they log in, and generally keeping their interests in mind as they cruise the site. A good dynamic site presents opportunities to learn new things and see new offerings while trying to meet 90 percent of the frequent surfer's needs on the first two pages.

Design makes an even bigger difference on information-based sites. Lessons from information design, interactive design, architecture, and user interface design will help third-generation site designers create new paradigms for navigating large data sets. While the rest of this book discusses more consumer-based models of design, many of the principles of third-generation site design apply to information-based sites as well.

Summary

People tend to surf with their shortest attention spans turned on. Think of the center of your site as the kitchen, where you're serving meals all day. Once visitors have been lured in by the aroma of good food, they start prowling around, opening cupboards, and raiding your cookie jar. A commitment to fresh daily content is often the best way to attract and keep a crowd. Invite the critics over for a taste. Keep handing out samples and don't present the bill until after the meal. Cook up a good site, and you'll always have a line of hungry customers waiting to get in your front door.

As Joseph Squier, author of The Place, states: "Independent of medium or tool or technique, there are timeless aspects of art that endure. Artists communicate."

Client/Server Computing

Servers are computers connected to the Internet around the clock, serving information. *Clients* are programs, like Netscape (a browser) and Eudora (a mail reader). When I use the word *client*, I always mean a *program* that resides on your computer as you use the Internet.

An Internet service provider (ISP) gives you access to the Internet. A server sits somewhere and sends files to everyone. You don't need to locate your site on the server of your service provider. Your site can be *hosted* on a server in Zurich, but your ISP should be a local company that gives you good access to the Internet for a good price.

The View Info Command

Netscape's browser has a little-used feature that gives you information about the pages you see.

While most people are used to the View Source command that shows the HTML of any file you see on the Web, Netscape Navigator will also give you quantitative statistics for any given image. This includes the size of each image, both when compressed (content length), and also in memory (decoded size). Add up all the numbers to see how large your page really is.

## CHAPTER 3

Preparing Images

COMPUTER IMAGES come in two fundamental types: *raster* and *vector*. Raster images, also called *bitmaps*, are made up of individual dots (pixels) arranged in a grid x pixels wide by y pixels high by z pixels deep (where z is known as *pixel depth* and determines the number of possible colors for each pixel). Raster images have fixed dimensions; their file size goes up with the size and resolution of the image. The screen image on your monitor is one large raster image, updated continuously.

Vector images are mathematical descriptions of an image (the formula for a circle is an example). This makes them resolution-independent; they can be scaled to any size and resolution for display on screens, printers, and so on. Their files are usually much smaller than those of comparable raster images. In traditional graphic design terminology, raster images represent *screen art,* while vector images represent *line art* (for example, photographs versus blueprints) [3.1 A-D].

Although vector formats like Post-Script are popular among print designers, they are just starting to appear on the Web. This chapter discusses raster formats GIF and JPEG – the most common formats on the Web. (In Chapter 12, I'll discuss Adobe's Portable Document Format (PDF) – a vector approach to designing on the Web.)

Several books attempt to document how browsers handle images. Yet most people who work at Netscape or Microsoft – in the browser divisions! – can't give you all the details covered here. This chapter presents my knowledge of how today's browsers display images; see the Book Site for additional details and updates.

Color Depth

The number of colors in an image determines the size of the image. One-bit images have only two states – on (white) and off (black). More bits per pixel means more colors [3.2]. However, more colors make larger image files, which means it takes more time to download them. Smaller is better.

The number of colors your system displays depends on the amount of video RAM installed. While professional designers usually have machines that can display 24-bit images, most consumer machines have *8-bit color,* which means they can display only 256 colors at a time. Web designers must, in general, make entire pages (all images combined) with fewer than 256 colors, to be seen properly by most surfers.

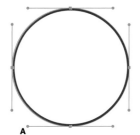
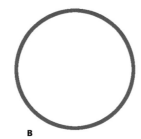
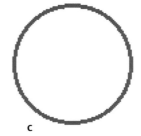
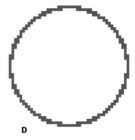

3.1 Vector images (A) are resolution-independent, while bitmaps (B-D) are tied to resolutions.

BIT DEPTH	EXPONENTS	NUMBER OF COLORS
1	2^1	2
2	2^2	4
3	2^3	8
4	2^4	16
5	2^5	32
6	2^6	64
7	2^7	128
8	2^8	256
16	2^{16}	16-BIT TRUE-COLOR
24	2^{24}	24-BIT TRUE-COLOR (8x8x8)
32	2^{32}	24-BIT TRUE-COLOR + 8-BIT ALPHA CHANNEL

3.2 Indexed images are 8 bits or fewer; true-color images have 24 bits or more.

The high end of the scale includes 32-bit images, which have an associated alpha channel. An *alpha channel* is typically used for transparency and overlays. *(Although neither of the formats covered in this chapter supports an 8-bit alpha channel, I will cover the subject in more detail in Chapter 14, "Beyond HTML.")*

It's not true that file size goes up dramatically as you increase the number of colors, because on the Web, no one ever sends an uncompressed image. The biggest factor affecting file size is compressibility, which I explain in more detail below.

Palettes

The two ways of storing color raster images are *indexed* and RGB. Images in RGB format – also known as full-color or true-color – use 8 bits (0 to 255) of Red, Green, and Blue values to form a 24-bit pixel (8+8+8=24). Images with 256 colors (or fewer) are called *indexed*. They have an associated *color palette*, called the *color lookup table,* or CLUT. The palette defines up to 256 colors, giving each one a number. The image then refers to each color by its position in the palette [**3.3 A-D**].

3.3 A-D Indexed images have palettes that determine the color range for the image.

45

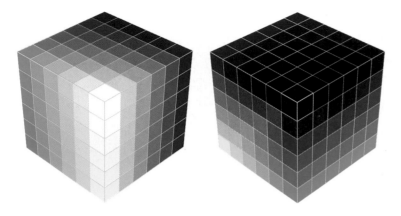

3.4 A, B The color cube. See this image on the Book Site.

The internal colors of the cube are the four evenly spaced colors between each corner, for a total of 216. This simple approach results in a *dithering palette*. Other palettes might have been more useful – this one has only four internal gray values, for example – but the color cube is easy to program. Most browsers now use Netscape's color cube.

On a monitor set for 8 bits, the browser automatically dithers the image using this palette. Setting your monitor to 256 colors will show you what your images will look like to surfers with low-end systems.

The Color Cube

The Netscape browser has its own palette, called *the color cube*, for displaying images on 256-color monitors on all platforms [**3.4 A, B**].

Netscape's six-sided color cube comprises 216 colors. Why not the full 256? Windows needs 20 colors for itself, other programs (and wallpaper) use another 20, and the balance – 216 colors – is available to the browser.

At the corners of the cube are all eight possible combinations of 255 and 0 (full on and full off) in RGB space [**3.5 A-C**].

> ### Pick from the Cube
>
> Load the color cube's palette into Photoshop's color picker. To create the palette, bring the color cube graphic into Photoshop, export the color table as "Color Cube Palette," and use the Load Swatches feature [3.6]. (See the Book Site to pick up the color cube graphic.)

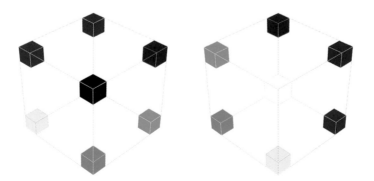

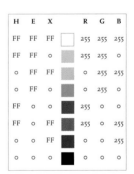

H	E	X		R	G	B
FF	FF	FF		255	255	255
FF	FF	0		255	255	0
0	FF	FF		0	255	255
0	FF	0		0	255	0
FF	0	0		255	0	0
FF	0	FF		255	0	255
0	0	FF		0	0	255
0	0	0		0	0	0

3.5 A-C The corners of the color cube.

The bottom line: Use these 216 colors in your images or they will be used for you.

Creating Images with the Color Cube

When using Painter or Photoshop to generate images, I try to use colors from the color cube. The general rule is to make sure large areas use colors from the cube, to prevent noticeable dithering.

As you work in layers, Photoshop or Painter will automatically anti-alias your image, creating lots of intermediate colors that aren't in the cube (see the next section, "Anti-Aliasing"). For now, use colors from the cube for large areas – until the browser companies change the rules again.

Mapping Images to the Color Cube

When you have no control over how an image is created, you'll have to convert it to the color cube's palette. To ensure consistency when displayed, convert images early in the process to keep yourself focused on the end result.

There are several different methods for pouring your images into the cube. A program like DeBabelizer offers the most choices. In Photoshop, use the Custom palette feature and load the color cube as the custom palette. (As of this writing, there is no way to save the color cube in Photoshop permanently. I keep copies of the cube in various places on my hard disk and load them as necessary. In DeBabelizer, you can either give it a name or use it as the super palette.)

The big choice here is *to dither or not to dither*. It's always best not to dither if possible. Dithering makes many

Dithering

Dithering is the process of using colors from the available palette to make up for colors not in the cube. Main colors are sprinkled throughout to simulate intermediate colors. If you need a color one-third of the way from color A to color B, use 33 percent pixels of color B sprinkled on top of color A. In practice, it works fairly well for photographic images, but not for most other types. Try to avoid dithering as much as possible; it makes your files much bigger.

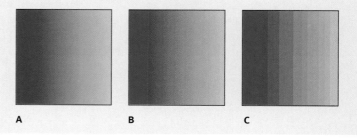

A   B   C

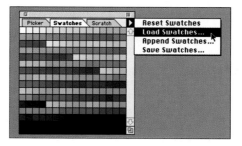

3.6 Loading the color cube into the picker.

Hex Values

In HTML, the <HEAD> tag requires hex values for specifying colors for background color, text color, and so on. Hex numbers are a way of specifying values from 0-15 with a single character (from 0-F). Use any two-digit combination (for red, green, and blue) of "HHH" – where H is in the set {00, 33, 66, 99, CC, FF}. A light blue is "#CCCCFF" and a middle orange is "#996600". As long as you use only these values, any combination will produce a color-cube color. If you're aiming for a broad audience, you should use only these combinations.

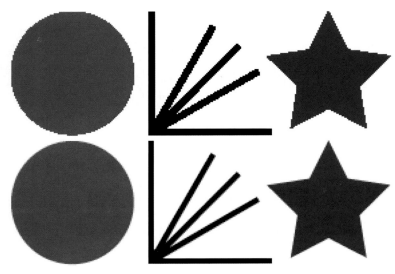

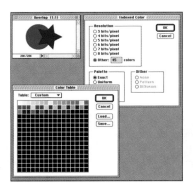

3.7 A-F Anti-aliasing helps prevent the jaggies.

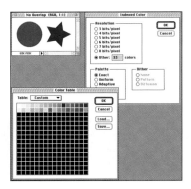

3.8 A, B Smooth curves or nearly 45° lines can result in lots of extra colors.

File Sizes on the Macintosh

To find out how big your file really is on the Macintosh, select the file in the Finder and use the Get Info command and look for the number in parentheses. This is the file size as it will be on your server. On Windows, the file size shown in the File Manager is the same as the size you'll see on the server.

photographic images look better but harder to compress, resulting in a larger file and a slower download.

Anti-Aliasing

Many books explain anti-aliasing in detail; a good book on color theory will add immensely to this discussion. In a nutshell, *anti-aliasing* is the process of adding intermediate colors to smooth out the jagged edges between areas of solid color [3.7 a-f].

Third-generation site designers strive to anti-alias all their images. Anti-aliasing adds more colors, increasing the size of the palette. Open Photoshop or Painter and make a large solid-color circle on a new layer. How many colors have you used? Chances are, over 200. The bigger the circle, the more colors you'll see. Because you want to have the smoothest edges possible, programs like Photoshop add lots of colors to the edges to blend them into the background. Overlapping even simple shapes adds extra intermediate colors to the palette **[3.8 A, B]**.

Anti-aliasing not only adds more colors, it makes images much less compressible as more intermediate colors are added. To reduce file size, you must anti-alias with the fewest number of colors possible, but no current programs do this automatically. You must anti-alias images by hand – a difficult but necessary process.

Occasionally, you can avoid anti-aliasing all together. Using rectilinear shapes relieves you of having to anti-alias anything, because there are no intermediate colors to smooth out the boundaries. A 45° line can be made either aliased or anti-aliased. An aliased 60° line can work, but it can also look jaggy. Any other angle or curve *must* be anti-aliased [3.9].

This is especially helpful if you have a patterned background, but in many cases reducing the noise or contrast of the background image works just as well.

Background Correction

A special case of anti-aliasing occurs when you use a foreground image over a given background in HTML. As you'll see later in this chapter, GIF images have only one color that you can designate as the transparent, so you must predetermine these transition colors beforehand. This means the images are anti-aliased into place. If you change the designated background color of an anti-aliased image, you'll get a *halo* around it. This is something to avoid in site design. For now, take the background into consideration every time you make an image and anti-alias it properly for that particular background [3.10 A, B].

Always keep the background on a separate layer in your image-creation software. Note that background correction is different for simple and complicated backgrounds.

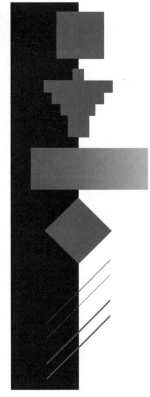

Keep It Simple

Good page design shouldn't rely on complex backgrounds – get rid of complicated backgrounds, and you solve the halo problem.

With simple backgrounds – using solid or nearly solid colors – make sure the edges blend into the background color. Your program does this automatically, as shown above. This works only for star fields and other almost-solid patterns.

Complicated backgrounds with large color transitions are another matter. To prevent halos, you must have either perfect registration between foreground and background *(see "Offsets and Alignment" in Chapter 4)* or have no anti-aliasing [3.11 A, B].

3.9 Some shapes need no anti-aliasing, others are borderline.

3.10 A, B Halos. One of the Seven Deadly Sins of the Web.

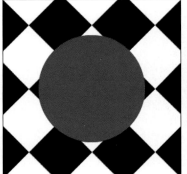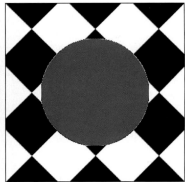

3.11 A, B Anti-aliasing against complicated backgrounds requires perfect registration, currently impossible across browsers.

The GIF Format

GIF (with a hard G) is the acronym for Graphics Interchange Format, the ubiquitous image format of the Web. The secret formula for GIF is owned and licensed by Unisys. It handles indexed images of up to 8 bits (256 colors).

GIF Compression

The GIF format uses a *compression algorithm* (recipe) called Lempel-Ziv-Welch, or LZW. This compression scheme is *lossless,* which means the resulting *de-*

compressed image looks exactly the same as the original. The average compression ratio for GIF images is 4:1. In general, use GIF compression for anything that isn't photographic. I use it for type, line-art, and even small photographs.

The LZW scheme uses pattern recognition techniques to achieve *run-length encoding.* The essence of the algorithm is to replace horizontal *runs* of same-colored pixels with a number indicating how long the sequence is **[3.12 A-D]**. Horizontal lines that are identical compress from line to line, for even more savings. Study the images and file sizes to get a feel for how GIF compression works **[3.13 A1-F1]**.

The compression scheme is quite powerful and can go beyond simple run-length encoding to compress complex images. A good implementation of the algorithm looks for repeated patterns of pixels as it creates the image file. It builds a table of the patterns found as it processes the file and replaces each repeated sequence with an index that refers to the original pixel sequence, now stored in the table.

In particular, this means any horizontal regularity will be compressed, even if it occurs on separate lines in the image. An exact circle stores in almost the same amount of space as its top half only, because the runs are identical on top and bottom halves. It doesn't have to be just a run of same-colored pixels; any sequence of colors that repeats will be compressed by LZW.

LZW compresses A5 and B3 down to almost the same size, for completely different reasons. Different implementations use slightly different approaches, but here is the basic idea. In A5, there

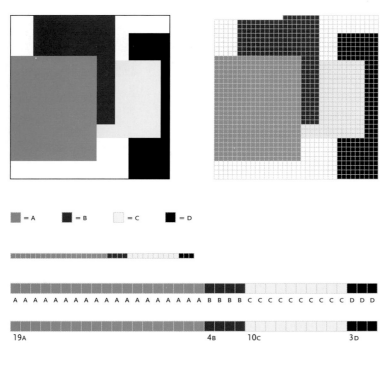

= A   = B   = C   = D

A A A A A A A A A A A A A A A A A A A B B B B C C C C C C C C C C D D D

19A   4B   10C   3D

19A 4B 10C 3D

3.12 A-D The original image (A) is divided into scan lines (B) and the pixel patterns analyzed. Any repeating pattern (C) is compressed by reducing it to a single unit and noting how many times it occurs in the line (D).

are two primary entries in the table: one for the black line and one for the white line. These patterns are then called alternately down the page: 2 black lines, 8 white lines, 2 black, 8 white, and so on. In B3, there is only one line to store. It has all the alternating black-and-white sequences for the entire line. This single line is then repeated 92 times by reference, not by actual pixel values. Similarly, the two full blends (E1, E2) compress to almost the same size for the same reasons as the two images explained above. Though the details are missing, you can look at the images in this illustration to determine more or less how LZW pattern recognition works.

When making GIF images, any recognizable regular feature will be compressed. Increasing the lengths of solid color runs will help make your files compressible.

GIF89a

GIF89a builds on the original (GIF87a) format with a few additional features, like *transparency*. Making GIFS would be straightforward, except that Photoshop's GIF-making process has had numerous problems. To remedy the situation for Photoshop 3.0.5 or higher, Adobe released the GIF89a Export plug-in [**3.14**]. Fractal Painter and DeBabelizer both make GIFS correctly.

To make a GIF in Photoshop, I usually index my image, then use the export plug-in. (Adobe's latest version of this filter is available at the Book Site.)

Always end your GIF file names with the suffix ".gif" – as in "sparky.gif".

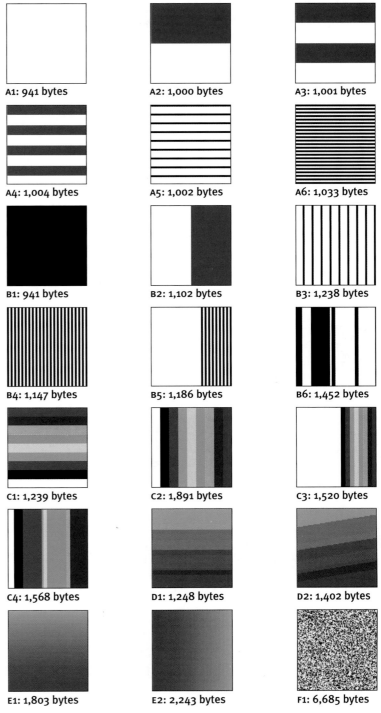

A1: 941 bytes

A2: 1,000 bytes

A3: 1,001 bytes

A4: 1,004 bytes

A5: 1,002 bytes

A6: 1,033 bytes

B1: 941 bytes

B2: 1,102 bytes

B3: 1,238 bytes

B4: 1,147 bytes

B5: 1,186 bytes

B6: 1,452 bytes

C1: 1,239 bytes

C2: 1,891 bytes

C3: 1,520 bytes

C4: 1,568 bytes

D1: 1,248 bytes

D2: 1,402 bytes

E1: 1,803 bytes

E2: 2,243 bytes

F1: 6,685 bytes

3.13 A1-F1 All images are 8-bit, 90 × 90 pixels (8,100 bytes). Longer horizontal runs result in better compression. Note GIF's ability to recognize patterns.

Interlacing

Normally, GIFs store pixels from the top of the image to the bottom. An *interlaced image* stores pixels out of linear order. Interlaced images arrive at your browser in evenly spaced blocks. Once the first block downloads, the browser repeats the data from that initial block, delivering a rough version of the final image so surfers get a preview of the image. Subsequent portions then complete the image in three more passes. This is a good example of a standard designed specifically for the on-line world.

To interlace an image, check the Interlaced checkbox on the software that does your GIF compression.

Transparency

In gif89a images, one color can be designated as transparent; a browser that supports gif89a will show all pixels of that particular color in the image as transparent, allowing the background to show through. This is a *chroma-key* operation; that is, you must choose a single color in your image that will become transparent. It will be replaced everywhere. Any pixels that are very close to this color – even indistinguishably close – will not become transparent [3.15].

Properly anti-aliased images with transparency are the basic building blocks of a third-generation site. They let designers visually break the bounds of rectangular images.

I don't use interlacing and transparency together. They have a history of causing problems with some browsers.

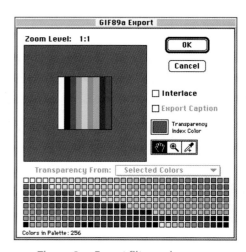

3.14 The GIF89a Export filter makes GIFs reliably.

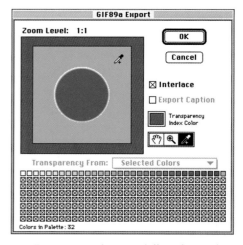

3.15 Transparency is essentially a chroma-key operation.

When to Interlace

An interlaced image is only slightly larger than a non-interlaced image. As a rule of thumb, use interlacing for any image larger than about 200 × 200 pixels.

Animation

The GIF format includes the ability to embed multiple GIF images into a single file for animation. Animated GIFs are easy to make. They even have different display options – for either continuous animation or a slide-show effect [3.16 A-L].

To create an animated GIF, make all the images PICT or BMP and run them through your animated-GIF-building program. The program will reduce colors to a common palette among all images, package them as GIFs, and tie the whole thing together as a single animated GIF. If you use GIFs instead of PICTS, make sure they all have the same color palette.

All animation programs specify which file types they'll accept. These programs change daily, so I won't catalog them here. *(A list of current favorites is on the Book Site.)*

Animated GIFs can take delays between individual frames in 1/100-second increments, as well as finite and infinite looping. GIF89a images are easier to make and more flexible than the old server-push CGI scripts. Once the image file downloads into the client's memory, it will continue to run, even if the connection gets interrupted or closed. You can use transparency in your images and specify how each image behaves as the next one loads [3.17].

There is *absolutely no compression* between animated GIF frames. If you have an image that is 2K, adding a second identical image makes it 4K. Ten in a row is 20K. This makes it less than ideal for real animated effects. Despite their ubiquity, the sooner we get away from GIF standards, the better.

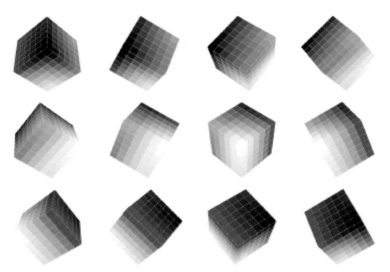

3.16 A-L Animated GIFs are easy to make and fun to use.

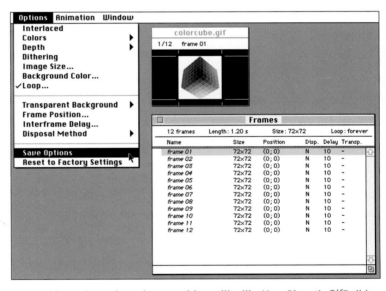

3.17 Making animated GIFs is easy with a utility like Yves Piguet's GifBuilder.

Poor-Man's Video

You can make a poor-man's video by converting QuickTime movies to a gif animation using GifBuilder or Smart Dubbing on the Macintosh.

The JPEG Format

JPEG (the common name for the raster image format defined by the Joint Photographic Experts Group) is the best way to compress photographic images. Because of the overhead involved, it doesn't work well for small images or line art. To reduce file size, JPEG separates the brightness information from the color hues. It essentially keeps a good copy of the black-and-white version of an image, to which your eyes are sensitive, and throws away most of the subtle color differences that you can't distinguish. Rather than doing it line by line, as GIF does, JPEG breaks the image into zones.

Compression

JPEG is a *lossy* process – information is always lost in the compression. Once compressed with JPEG, even using the highest quality settings, the image will not be the same as the original RGB version. It might look the same, because your eyes can't tell the difference, but the file is smaller. At higher compression ratios (lower quality settings), the image is noticeably different, whereas high-quality JPEGs are used as substitutes for the original. Use low-quality JPEGs on the Web, because they compress so well.

Compression ratios for JPEG range typically from 10:1 to 100:1, depending

A1 3-bit GIF, dither
2,985 bytes

A2 4-bit GIF, dither
3,728 bytes

A3 5-bit GIF, dither
4,624 bytes

A4 6-bit GIF, dither
5,486 bytes

B1 3-bit GIF, no dither
2,331 bytes

B2 4-bit GIF, no dither
3,181 bytes

B3 5-bit GIF, no dither
3,969 bytes

B4 6-bit GIF, no dither
4,964 bytes

C1 JPEG 25%
2,351 bytes

C2 JPEG 50%
3,267 bytes

C3 JPEG 75%
4,566 bytes

C4 JPEG 100%
15,817 bytes

3.18 A-F Images A-C are 92 × 132 pixels; D-F (facing page) are 166 × 238. JPEG files have several kilobytes of extra information, called *overhead*, that make them unsuitable for small pictures.

D1 3-bit GIF; dither; 7,446 bytes

E1 3-bit GIF; no dither; 5,097 bytes

F1 JPEG 25%; 4,264 bytes

D2 5-bit GIF; dither; 11,498 bytes

E2 5-bit GIF; no dither; 9,692 bytes

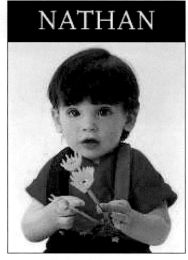

F2 JPEG 50%; 6,107 bytes

on the quality setting. The greater the compression, the smaller (and lossier) the file will be. In general, sharper images make larger files. Blurry pictures download quickly. Because of the overhead in the JPEG format, GIFs are a better choice for small pictures. I usually don't go to JPEG until my images are larger than about 100 × 100 pixels [**3.18 A-F**].

Always start with the lowest-quality JPEG setting you can, throwing away the most information and reducing file size as much as possible. If your program says: Worst, Okay, and Best, choose the Worst option. You'll be surprised at how acceptable low-quality JPEGs are.

When using JPEGs, your object isn't to reduce colors, it's to reduce file size. That's what the quality settings are for. Different software gives you different choices. Like Photoshop, many programs analyze each photograph and choose one of several methods before reducing, so you don't have to worry about the details. Set the quality level, look at the result, and decide to keep it or try again.

Perform a few experiments on your images to see what makes them compress better. Reducing the color palette alone usually won't help make the image more compressible. Unsharp Masking sharpens the image and makes the resulting JPEG file bigger; Gaussian blur makes it smaller. Blurring JPEGs is equivalent to reducing colors in GIFs.

Progressive Display

Like the interlaced GIF format, *progressive* JPEGs decode in successive passes, working in a grid to continually refine the quality of the image. Progressive JPEGs take more local computing power to decode. Creating progressive JPEG-encoded images is accomplished with various utility programs, including

DeBabelizer (see the list on the Book Site). As with interlaced GIFs, progressive JPEG files are slightly larger than non-progressives. Most major browsers can now see progressive JPEGs.

Reducing File Size

A common misconception is that you should reduce the number of colors to reduce the file size. While this often works, it is not a cause-and-effect relationship. Most of the concepts in this chapter apply to all image formats, but it is directed mostly at reducing GIFs, because I use GIFs more than 90 percent of the time. Smaller GIF files are always the goal.

Reducing the Palette

In general, palettes aren't very big (the biggest palette is only 800 bytes – less than 1K), so reducing the size of the actual palette doesn't have much effect.

When working with compressed images, don't think in terms of three dimensions (x by y by z). Think in terms of the compression scheme and what makes an image compressible.

When does reducing the number of colors help make the image more compressible? As it turns out, most of the time. The average image you want to put on a web page has some anti-aliasing on it, and that's where reducing colors can help. Because anti-aliasing introduces too many subtle color shades, reducing them will form many horizontal runs of more than one pixel [3.19 A, B].

The Golden Rule of File Size Reduction

Always start with the best image possible. Then reduce the size, colors, and quality of the image to below acceptable quality, then Undo. Reduce/Undo again and again, gradually raising the settings until you just break through to visual acceptability. Use this method any time you prepare images for the Web.

Adaptive Color Palettes

Although you can reduce colors several different ways, I normally use an *adaptive color palette* to let the computer help me reconstruct the image using fewer colors. Remember the circle with lots of colors? Reducing colors will make it more compressible. To understand exactly how the color-reduction process takes place, start with a normally anti-aliased image.

When you do color reduction using an adaptive color palette, Photoshop goes through an elaborate scheme to preserve the colors in your image. Behind the scenes, Photoshop builds a *histogram* of all the colors in the image rated by popularity. In practice, simple images [3.20] reduce well because Photoshop's *median cut* algorithm searches for areas of different color and does its best to preserve them (at the expense of intermediate colors). The histogram [3.21] helps the program determine how much weight to give certain colors in the resulting palette.

This histogram is not the RGB histogram you find in the user interface. It's a special color-popularity histogram Photoshop uses to help make an adaptive palette. While the adaptive palette machinery is quite complex, I want to show how you can influence the histogram to get a different palette than you get simply by asking for a reduced-color image.

How to Influence a Histogram

When the histogram method eliminates an important or favorite color, I don't have to increase colors. Instead, I can influence the process that makes

731 bytes   531 bytes

3.19 A, B Reducing colors helps increase the lengths of the runs, making the compressed image even more compressible.

3.20 Photoshop makes extra colors for good anti-aliasing.

3.21 Photoshop builds a histogram behind the scenes to help with adaptive-palette reduction. This histogram corresponds to figure 3.20 (not to scale).

8-Bit Images

Many people use 8-bit images on their web sites. I've never had to use a full 8-bit (256-color) image on any site I've created. Most of my images fall in the 15-35 color range, with 35 being quite a few colors. Even without dithering, you'd be surprised how small a palette you need.

3.22 A, B The original picture in RGB color (A), and after indexing to 32 colors (B).

3.23 A, B Selecting an area of the picture (A) influences the histogram. The resulting image has been influenced by the red pixels (B).

3.24 A, B By selecting more areas (A), you have more control over the colors that make it into the final palette (B).

the histogram to get a better palette. I will demonstrate this process using an image that dramatizes the situation. As an example, I'll show how to prepare a photo for making animated GIFs (since animated JPEGs don't exist). I start with an RGB image and reduce it to 32 colors [**3.22 A, B**].

After indexing with an adaptive color palette, Sabine's lips have lost their color. A quick look at the palette shows too many dark values for reproducing her hair, and too many light values for the background. The image is flat. I can try again with more colors, or I can try to influence the histogram.

This time I want the red pixels, which aren't very numerous, to have a place in the final palette. In Photoshop, it is easy to influence the histogram. It's a little-known secret, but Photoshop uses the current selection at the time of reducing the palette as the area from which to build the histogram. Reducing colors with no selection builds a histogram for the entire image. If I choose areas of relative importance, I can effectively block outside areas from inclusion in the histogram, skewing the resulting operation toward the colors I want. I draw a rectangle around Sabine's lips and index again [**3.23 A, B**].

Now the lips look great, but her forehead looks banded. After undoing, I Shift-select another area and try to bring back some of the tones in her forehead [**3.24 A, B**].

After a few tries, I find a combination that results in the optimum 5-bit palette for this image. It's a matter of taking detail from one area to put into another, but it doesn't take too much time and the results can be worth it (see "Eyeballing the Palette," below).

DeBabelizer's methods for reducing colors are much more powerful, have full color fidelity, and are much harder to learn. There are several methods of influencing histograms, for example, all of which involve non-intuitive steps for building up a specific palette, which can then be applied to the image. The next generation of DeBabelizer (2.0) promises to be much easier to use. The upside is that if you have 200 images to reduce, DeBabelizer will make them in minutes after you figure out how to do it once.

As you can see, there are tradeoffs. I might have added a few more colors, settling on a 34-color image, but then I would have had a 6-bit palette and the file size would go up more than necessary on a small picture like this. It comes out to 8K, which is pretty good for a GIF. This example dramatizes the general approach to getting the palette you want for a GIF; it does not imply that GIFS are the most appropriate way to compress photos like this.

Eyeballing the Palette

It's important to get used to looking at palettes, because if you see two colors that are very similar to each other, you're not done reducing yet.

No matter which program you use, the program can't determine which areas of your image are important. Only you can look at the palette and decide if it's the right one. A good rule of thumb is that prominent different colors should have three or four intermediate transition colors between them.

Adobe Photoshop Liabilities

Adobe Photoshop is an indispensable program for making images on the Web. But for web designers, it's less than ideal. Let me show you a problem. If you make a circle in which the most prominent color is a certain red (say, 205, 53, 21) and you reduce the colors using an adaptive color palette, Photoshop returns a palette in which that same color, which should be unchanged, has shifted to a very similar, but different, shade of red (in this case, 201, 51, 19). This occurs because Photoshop reduces colors from a 24-bit ($8 \times 8 \times 8$) color space to a 15-bit ($5 \times 5 \times 5$) color space before executing its Median Cut algorithm to find the best palette. After the reduction, the resulting 15-bit palette gets a few extra bits tacked on to show the final palette colors as RGB. Those extra bits cause the color shift you detect, and the color shift causes a dithered area when displayed on a browser with only 256 colors.

The only colors not affected are the eight at the corners of the color cube. Every other color will experience some shift after adaptive color reduction in Photoshop. If you are in a pinch, you can open the color table and type in the real values. While this works, it's tedious and no one should have to do it.

I hope to see a solution from Adobe, in the form of a true-color export plug-in (see the site: www.adobe.com). For now, I use DeBabelizer to do my final color reductions, because DeBabelizer does not shift colors. See the book site for late-breaking news on Photoshop and adaptive color palettes.

Finally, Photoshop doesn't let the user see the color palette while viewing the image. I've requested this feature over and over, but Adobe doesn't have time to do it. As an exercise in interactive product development, there are forms at the Book Site where you can give your feedback, which we will forward to various manufacturers.

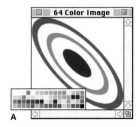

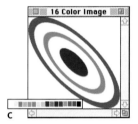

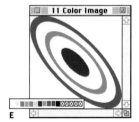

3.25 A-E For the Web, the 64-color image and the 32-color image look alike. The 16- and 13-color images are still acceptable, while the 11-color image shows problems.

Now I want to do a more practical experiment, showing how to dial in a palette for the absolute minimum number of colors necessary for the Web. I start with an RGB image of three rings and reduce it to 64 colors [3.25 A]. Because this is more than enough colors, I take it down to 32 and 16 colors [B, C]. The image is still acceptable. (For the purposes of this demonstration, I'm going from more colors to fewer, the opposite of the way I normally work.)

The 16-color image looks fine and gives me reason to believe I can do even better. I re-index the original to 13 and 11 colors [D, E].

Looking at the palettes for 13 and 11 colors, I can't help but wonder if I can squeeze this image to 11 colors with better color distribution. I go back to the RGB image and begin selecting areas to influence the histogram. I choose the top area as a baseline, to try to get more blues, but the red still dominates, so I include the bottom area to boost the green. Finally, the middle area turned a pink to a light blue and I had the palette I was looking for [3.26 A, B]. Without showing all these intermediate experiments, the final selection gave me a well-balanced palette in just three tries. The third image shows that 9 colors plus white is the theoretical limit for this image, as anything less shows unsightly artifacts of aliasing [C].

The Mac version of Photoshop adds the black, which isn't necessary. I can either strip it in DeBabelizer or forget about it. Because the palette for this image contains 16 colors, the black entry isn't taking up any extra room. The resulting file is 2,197 bytes.

This shows you can get away with

Equilibrium Software in Sausalito produces DeBabelizer, the Swiss Army Knife of the Web. DeBabelizer's amazing capabilities in opening and transforming graphics files are compromised only by its cumbersome user interface. While DeBabelizer has been out for the Macintosh for several years and has been an indispensable tool in building multimedia products like CD-ROMs, the company is now preparing an updated version that will work on both Macs and PCs.

DeBabelizer is much better than Photoshop at creating a common palette for several images, reducing colors, and working directly with palettes in general. It also has a very powerful scripting feature that lets you perform prescripted actions with a single command. Its web site has several free scripts for making web graphics (www.equilibrium.com).

Although DeBabelizer is very useful, I can't recommend buying the current (1.6x) version, because its learning curve is so steep. I expect DeBabelizer 2.0's improved user interface and web-specific features (like reading and writing animated GIFs) will make it one of the necessary "killer apps" for web authoring.

Fractal Design Painter

Fractal Design's Painter 4.0 is the third component of the web "killer app" trio. It is complementary to Photoshop, enabling you to experiment and enjoy making images. Painter is best for creative explorations and artistic expression, with tools that imitate real paint, canvas, and mixed media.

Unfortunately, you don't want to use Painter to index your images. The choices are limited, and the adaptive palette code suffers from the same problem as Photoshop does: Your exact colors will not survive the transition, even if they dominate the image.

As a creative tool, however, Painter has many excellent features for web authors. It makes image maps right inside the program. It has an *image hose* – one of my favorite features – that enables you to spray images around randomly, and a tiling feature for making scary (oops – I mean subtle) background images. The layers feature is as good as Photoshop's, and the interface is very intuitive for artists. I expect to see more great features that will make Painter a necessary creative tool for the Web.

only two intermediate colors if you choose them well, and influencing the histogram is the only mechanism we have for balancing palettes. Influencing histograms and eyeballing palettes usually results in the smallest file for optimum download times. This experiment does not mean you can use two intermediate colors for every image; it is simply to show that, with patience, you can reach the theoretical limit of reduction for any image. In the future, a PostScript description for this image combined with anti-aliasing on the client will reduce this image to around 100 bytes.

Image Inflation

You have worked to get your file sizes as small as possible. You now want a large background image that compresses well and makes your page look distinctive [3.27].

You reduce the colors in this huge image, compressing it to just 12K, so it loads like greased lightning. On your machine, it works beautifully. Yet certain visitors complain that your page causes their browser either to crash or to load incredibly slowly! What's happening? Your file has *image inflation* problems.

Your browser doesn't display GIF images. In fact, you've never *seen* a GIF image. Think of GIF as the freeze-dried state of an image, when it's packed up for shipping as small as it can be. When you see a web page, your browser downloads the GIFs and decodes them, reconstituting them to full strength ($x \times y \times z$) to display on your screen.

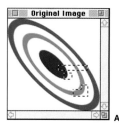

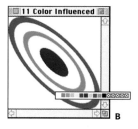

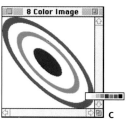

3.26 A-C The area selected (A) results in a well-balanced minimum palette of 11 colors (B) for a final size of 2,197 bytes. An 8-color palette (C) is simply not sufficient.

About Caching

Your browser program keeps web pages and images in memory so you don't have to wait to see things you've already downloaded. Your browser has two kinds of caches: a memory cache and a disk cache. The memory cache keeps all the images in a page in memory. Scrolling is fast because the whole page is in memory. It is the memory cache that gets overloaded by image inflation.

The disk cache keeps previously visited pages on disk so you don't have to wait when you hit the Back button. For surfers, this is good. For developers, this is a problem, because if you update your images and redisplay the page, you want it to read the new description of the image, not show you an older, cached version. Fortunately, most browsers come with a Check Documents preference setting to update images A) Every Time, or B) Once Per Session. Checking a document means to compare the date on the file with the date stored in the cache; if the file date is newer, it reads the image again. If the date is the same or older, it keeps the cached version as is.

Surfers should use Once Per Session to avoid frequent checking with sites that aren't likely to change that often. In this case, a cache size of 5-10 megabytes is fine. Developers must use the Every Time option to make sure their pages change as they make updates to local images. If your pages aren't changing, and they should, check this option and restart your browser. Unfortunately, developers who use this option must reduce the size of their disk cache to 1-2 megabytes to avoid sluggish performance as the entire cache is checked each time you reload a page.

3.27 A large non-tiling background is tempting to third-generation designers.

The decoded version can take up a lot of memory, much more than the GIF itself. How much memory? The answer: *It depends on the user's system.*

GIF images always inflate to the size of the image (in x and y) times 8 bits (1 byte) or more. (With Netscape on Macintosh, GIFs inflate to 8 bits, but PC GIFs inflate to the color depth of the client.) Thus, if you have a 500 × 500-pixel image that contains only 2 bits of color, it will usually inflate to 500 × 500 × 8-bit = 244 Kbytes, even if it compresses down to only 10K.

JPEG images are worse. They always inflate to fill the receiving system's color depth. If you can see millions of colors and you download that same 500 × 500 × 2-bit file, it will inflate to 500 × 500 × 24-bit = 750 Kbytes. Images that are 1200 × 1600 × 2-bits can compress to 18k, yet inflate to over 2 megabytes!

There is a solution, but for third-generation site designers, it's painful. The solution is to completely *avoid large-area images, no matter how small they compress.* Stay calm. The people who build browsers will find a way out of this. There are two possibilities. First, the browser makers can try to control GIF inflation, which is possible, but tricky. Second, the real solution is to get rid of this two-layer model and go to z-axis layering (see Chapter 14, "Beyond HTML").

A good rule of thumb is to keep the total image area on a page smaller than about 600 × 600 pixels, unless you know your surfers have more than 8 Mbytes of RAM.

Summary

A good image is a small image. Always strive for the minimum number of colors absolutely necessary for your image, following the real Golden Rule of file size reduction *(see Tip, this page).*

Page sizes tend to get smaller the more you work with images, trying different strategies and approaches. Image inflation is a problem for the third-generation site designer. Future browsers should give us features that alleviate these issues, but for now, be wary of using large-area images, no matter how small they compress.

I'll go through several real examples of file size reduction, anti-aliasing, setting type, and making GIFs and JPEGs in Part II of this book.

The Real Golden Rule of File Size Reduction

Reduce the size and complexity of your images, then lengthen the runs, hand edit, and influence the histogram if necessary before adding more colors. Switch to JPEG rather than dithering a GIF; compare file sizes before deciding on your format.

## CHAPTER 4

Laying out Pages

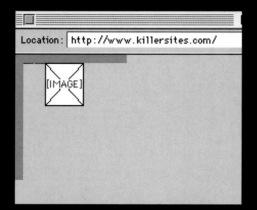

(A) `<IMG SRC="resources/dot_clear.gif"`
`HSPACE=10>`

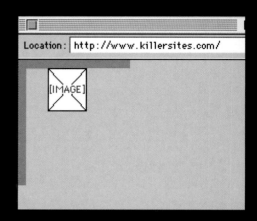

(B) `<IMG SRC="resources/dot_clear.gif"`
`WIDTH=21>`

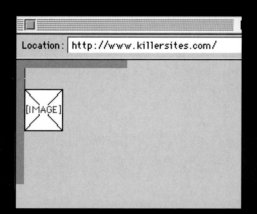

(C) `<IMG SRC="resources/dot_clear.gif"`
`VSPACE=10>`

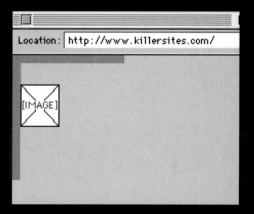

(D) `<IMG SRC="resources/dot_clear.gif"`
`HEIGHT=21>`

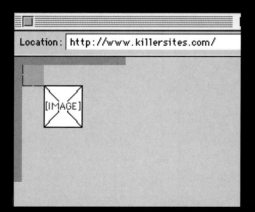

(E) `<IMG SRC="resources/dot_clear.gif"`
`VSPACE=10><BR><IMG SRC="resources/`
`dot_clear.gif" HSPACE=10>`

4.1 A-E I prefer HSPACE and VSPACE to WIDTH and HEIGHT. Here, the transparent pixel is enlarged and made blue, HSPACE or VSPACE is magenta, and the browser offsets are shown in dark gray.

BECAUSE OF THE current limits of HTML, a third-generation designer's central challenge is to have as much control as possible over the layout of elements on the page. In a page layout program like PageMaker, you place text and graphics where you want them. You balance visual elements with *white space* – the areas with no foreground elements – by grabbing elements and moving them. This is *direct manipulation.*

HTML does not give site designers a framework for direct two-dimensional manipulation. Site designers place elements on the page using two main tricks: the *single-pixel GIF trick* and the *invisible table trick.* The single-pixel GIF trick lets us push graphic elements around on the page, while the invisible table trick gives us columns, margins, gutters, and other approximations of traditional layout elements.

Each of these tricks is a *workaround* – it gives the site designer control, but not the right kind of control. We must manipulate white space to push text and images into place. I want to emphasize that this is not the way designers normally work. Designers rarely manipulate white space directly. They manipulate design elements in the foreground, balancing the white space created as they work.

Though this chapter is fundamentally about typography and page layout, the first half is devoted to explaining these two tricks in detail. *(The files you need are at the Book Site.)*

The Single-Pixel GIF Trick

This very useful tool can now be found on tens of thousands of web sites. By making a one pixel by one pixel transparent image, you can use the spacing and scaling attributes of HTML to move elements almost anywhere on your page. This trick makes it possible to make paragraph indents and other typographic effects.

To scale any image, include WIDTH=X and HEIGHT=Y arguments in the <IMG> tag. The single-pixel GIF will stretch to become x pixels wide and y pixels tall. Adjusting these parameters positions graphics and tables in single-pixel increments. You must specify both width and height to scale an image properly.

To space an image, include HSPACE=X or VSPACE=Y arguments in the <IMG> tag. If you use HSPACE=X, the browser will display x pixels of space on both sides of the single-pixel GIF, causing the effective width to be $2x+1$ pixels. In this way, you can position graphics and tables in two-pixel increments. You may specify either of these arguments independently.

This might seem complicated, but a few experiments will demystify the process **[4.1 A-E]**. Change the numbers, save the file, and reload the page. In practice, I usually use HSPACE or VSPACE, because they can be used independently. They are also safer to use – should the browser fail to render the transparency, only a single pixel will be colored.

In practice, I use HSPACE for paragraph indents and margins, and VSPACE for setting up a hierarchy of vertical white space in a document. I'll show examples after discussing the other tool in my bag of tricks: invisible tables.

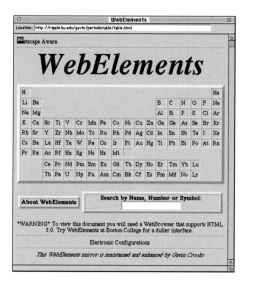

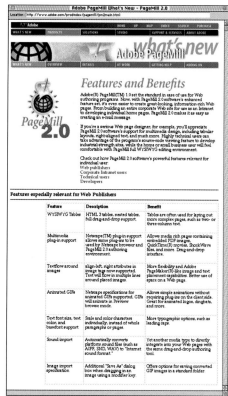

4.2 A, B Tables were intended for illustrations and, well, tabular material.

The Invisible Table Trick

Although tables weren't originally meant to hold columns of text, I use them to do page layout because there is nothing else available. I always turn table borders off using the `BORDER=0` argument to the table tag. Using table cells, I can approximate real typography using invisible cells for borders, gutters, etc.

Tables are tricky. There's no substitute for spending time working with them. In particular, Netscape and Microsoft browsers exhibit different behavior when displaying tables. The best way to read this chapter is with your computer in front of you, trying the exercises yourself.

Table Basics

The Framers of the Web had in mind a syntax for displaying tabular data [4.2 A, B]. Tables can be very difficult to build, so they made tables "smart": tables attempt to balance the contents, spreading columns judiciously across the page.

Many site designers leave their table borders turned on. Tables aren't forms. They present information, rather than ask for it. A good table presents information as cleanly as possible. Whether presenting straightforward text or information, always show a minimum of what Edward R. Tufte calls *chartjunk* — extra embellishments that take attention away from the data. Table borders are chartjunk [4.3 A, B]. *(Turn off the grid lines next time you print a spreadsheet, use bold for the headings and see whether you like that better.)*

68

HTML tables use an elaborate programming scheme to help solve layout problems automatically. Unfortunately, this scheme makes them difficult to control. My goal is to turn off as much of this intelligence as possible.

To translate a concept of Tufte's to the Web, table borders and separators present *non-data pixels.* Data pixels convey meaning; non-data pixels establish a framework for the data. The general rule is to reduce non-data pixels while maximizing data pixels.

Reduce non-data pixels. Always turn off your table borders!

There are many examples of tables on the Book Site. In this section, I will cover my top five third-generation table tricks.

Use absolute widths. Unconstrained tables try to create the best layout with whatever you put into them. As an experiment, try making a table that has five columns. Put images and text, in different sizes and amounts, into the tables. Overload some cells with lots of text or a huge image. Use the `<NOBR>` tag and watch what happens. Change the width of your browser window from wide open to very skinny.

In case you don't have your browser in front of you, the point is that table cells tend to be elastic. To constrain tables, set the widths of individual cells. Although I can set the width of a table, I usually specify the widths of each table cell and let the browser determine how wide to make the table.

I rarely set the *height* of a table or table cell. Like web pages, tables have

4.3 A, B Turning off borders reduces chartjunk.

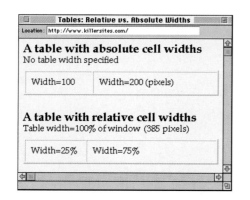
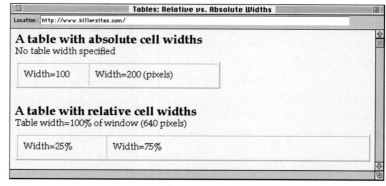

4.4 A, B Absolute widths keep columns from collapsing, while relative widths move with the browser window.

```
<TABLE BORDER="2">
 <TR>
  <TD WIDTH="100">
   Width=100
  </TD>
  <TD VALIGN=MIDDLE WIDTH="200">
   Width=200 (pixels)
  </TD>
 </TR>
</TABLE>
```

```
<TABLE BORDER="2">
 <TR>
  <TD WIDTH="25%">
   Width=25%
  </TD>
  <TD VALIGN=MIDDLE WIDTH="75%">
   Width=75%
  </TD>
 </TR>
</TABLE>
```

4.5 A, B HTML for absolute (LEFT) and relative (RIGHT) column widths.

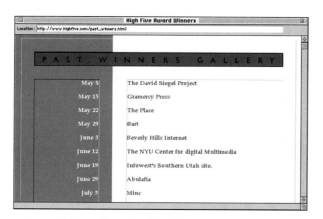
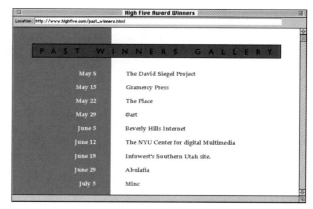

4.6 A, B Using cellspacing for white space assures a non-collapsible gutter. (Visit the page yourself and view the Document Source to see the HTML.)

infinite bottoms. You can specify the height, and you can use `<TD VALIGN= bottom>`, but then everything goes to the bottom. In general, tables grow and shrink to accommodate their contents.

To control the *width* of your table cells, use either relative or absolute widths **[4.4 A, B]**. To specify *relative cell widths,* use `<TD WIDTH=x%>`, where *x* is the percentage of the width of the table containing the cell. Relative cell widths give you flexible tables that re-flow when the window size changes. *Absolute cell widths* (use `<TD WIDTH= x>`) specify the width in pixels. This cell does not change size when the window does. Make the following table with both relative and absolute numbers **[4.5 A, B]**, then adjust the browser window width. *(You can see this on the Book Site, but it's more instructive to make your own.)*

Use CELLSPACING **and** CELLPADDING **to guarantee white space [4.6 A, B].** As far as the third-generation site designer is concerned, cellpadding and cellspacing are identical. *Cellpadding* describes the distance between the contents of a cell and its walls. *Cellspacing* describes the amount of space surrounding each cell. As implemented by Netscape, these tags apply to horizontal and vertical distances simultaneously. I often use cellspacing to create a *gutter,* where I want to separate two columns by a given amount. This is especially useful when designing forms *(See Chapter 8, "A Storefront").*

Use table cells to mortice images horizontally and vertically [4.7]. If you put two images next to each other, there

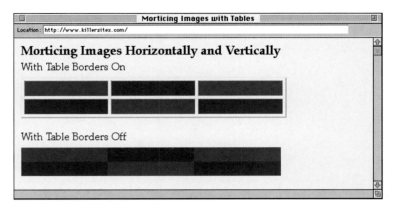

4.7 Table rows butt right on top of each other.

```
<TABLE BORDER="0" CELLPADDING="0"
CELLSPACING="0" WIDTH="450">
<TR>
 <TD><IMG SRC="resources/dot_red.gif"
  ALIGN=LEFT WIDTH="150" HEIGHT="50"
  BORDER="0"></TD>
 <TD><IMG SRC="resources/dot_blue.gif"
  ALIGN=LEFT WIDTH="150" HEIGHT="50"
  BORDER="0"></TD>
 <TD><IMG SRC="resources/dot_red.gif"
  ALIGN=LEFT WIDTH="150" HEIGHT="50"
  BORDER="0"></TD>
</TR>
<TR>
 <TD><IMG SRC="resources/dot_blue.gif"
  ALIGN=LEFT WIDTH="150" HEIGHT="50"
  BORDER="0"></TD>
 <TD><IMG SRC="resources/dot_red.gif"
  ALIGN=LEFT WIDTH="150" HEIGHT="50"
  BORDER="0"></TD>
 <TD><IMG SRC="resources/dot_blue.gif"
  ALIGN=LEFT WIDTH="150" HEIGHT="50"
  BORDER="0"></TD>
</TR>
</TABLE>
```

4.8 This code generates the table at the bottom of illustration 4.7.

will be a space between them. The only way to close this space is to put them in neighboring table cells and turn the borders off.

Now for the vertical mortice. Stacked tables always have a bit of white space between them. Rows in the same table do not. If you want images to mortice together, put them in neighboring cells and neighboring columns with borders turned off.

Use alignment to get flush-right text.

As any basic manual on HTML will show, alignment works for both text and images. I use alignment mostly to align things to the right edge of a table cell, when I'm going for a special typo-

graphic effect, like a gutter or a form. *(See various uses of alignment throughout the later chapters.)*

Although flush-right text is harder to read, it can be effective in certain situations. There are times when you may want to put some text in a margin or simply alternate alignment of paragraphs down the page. Experiment with flush-right text and see what you can create.

One note on justified text. Someday, a browser company will let designers use justified text on the Web. Thankfully, we've been spared this deadly sin, but I expect to see the day when I'll have to add it to the list. Don't be tempted! Steel yourself against poor word-spacing. Justified text works in novels and long-material publishing, but you must use it with finesse, and the Web is not the place. The resolution doesn't allow the fine adjustments you need to justify properly. The text of this book isn't justified, and I'm willing to bet it hasn't bothered you. Flush left is best.

Nest tables only when necessary [4.9].

I put tables inside of tables only if necessary. I use nested tables most often to make larger containers into which several tables fit. This is often a good alternative to frames (see below). They are difficult to debug, but they can help in complicated situations.

Master the fundamentals – invisible tables and the single-pixel GIF trick – and you're ready to create a dynamic third-generation site. The following sections demonstrate how to apply these tools to the typographic principles that drive a third-generation site.

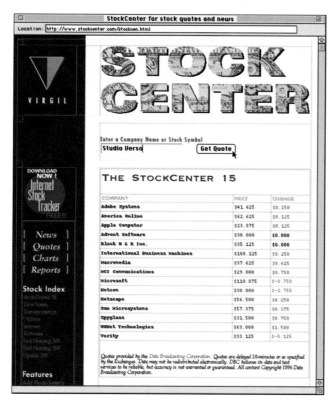

4.9 Use nested tables to divide your page into smaller areas (borders turned on for illustration).

Hard Returns

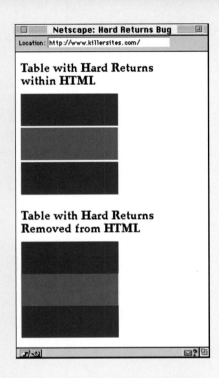

Be sure your HTML editor or text editor supports soft-wrapping (line breaks without returns). Although hard returns are not supposed to affect the execution of HTML code, Netscape Navigator has a lightly documented bug in the way it implements table cells. In this example, the rectangles stack right on top of each other. If you use a hard return before the </TD> tag, there is a gap. The only way to close the gap is to remove the carriage return.

```
<!-- Begin Bad Table -->
<table border=0 cellspacing=0
 cellpadding=0 width=150>
 <tr>
  <td>
   <IMG SRC="resources/dot_blue.gif"
    WIDTH="150" HEIGHT="50" BORDER="0">
  </td>
 </tr>
 <tr>
  <td>
   <IMG SRC="resources/dot_red.gif"
    WIDTH="150" HEIGHT="50" BORDER="0">
  </td>
 </tr>
 <tr valign=top>
  <td>
   <IMG SRC="resources/dot_blue.gif"
    WIDTH="150" HEIGHT="50" BORDER="0">
  </td>
 </tr>
</table>
<!-- End Bad Table -->


<!-- Begin Good Table -->
<TABLE BORDER=0 CELLSPACING=0
 CELLPADDING=0 WIDTH=150>
 <TR>
  <TD><IMG SRC="resources/dot_blue.gif"
   WIDTH="150" HEIGHT="50"
   BORDER="0"></TD>
 </TR>
 <TR>
  <TD><IMG SRC="resources/dot_red.gif"
   WIDTH="150" HEIGHT="50"
   BORDER="0"></TD>
 </TR>
 <TR VALIGN=LEFT>
  <TD><IMG SRC="resources/dot_blue.gif"
   WIDTH="150" HEIGHT="50"
   BORDER="0"></TD>
 </tr>
</table>
<!-- End Good Table -->
```

Vertical White Space

Good typography enforces a hierarchy of vertical white space throughout a document to convey meaning. On a third-generation site, systematic use of white space can vastly improve the presentation of text for easier reading and better comprehension.

Controlling Vertical White Space

Blank lines should not separate paragraphs. Magazines break paragraphs

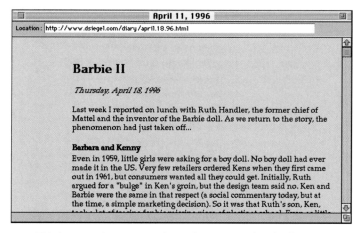

4.10 Third-generation typography makes sure each unit of vertical space is distinctive and functional.

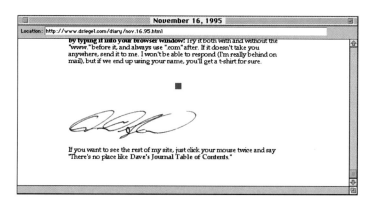

4.11 My journal uses a red square as a change of voice. No need for a horizontal rule.

into groups with subheads, novels use successive paragraphs with breaks only at chapters or subchapters. In both instances, as in this book, the white space tells you where one section ends and another begins.

I hardly ever use the `<P>` tag in a third-generation site. Between sections, I'll insert an appropriate amount of space using the single-pixel GIF, followed by a `<BR>` **[4.10]**. Each level in the hierarchy should be visually distinct from its neighbors. A vertical space of eight pixels and another of ten is difficult to distinguish, but the difference between zero and two is significant.

I use eight to ten pixels of vertical white space before a heading. I'll put more space before a larger heading than before a subhead.

One of the great things about hypertext is that major sections can be broken up into separate pages, so I limit my column length to what I consider readable in about a minute. Use sections and pages to break up your stories.

Careful vertical spacing is especially useful in the design of forms, which are too often just scattered white boxes with no grouping or hierarchy to help the user through the process *(See Chapter 8, "A Storefront")*.

Banish Horizontal Rules!

Third-generation sites don't use horizontal rules. They aren't necessary and they break the flow of the text. Look at well-designed books; they don't have horizontal rules. Well-designed sites don't either. Book designers sometimes use a nice little printer's mark, an ornament to separate sections of text without obstructing the reader's eye. On the Web, we can use new pages instead.

The only time I use an ornament is to depict a change of voice. That is, when I am done with a page and want to say something from a narrator's perspective or give copyright information [4.11].

Leading: Interline Spacing

Space between lines is called leading, because in the old days, when typographers set metal type by hand, they'd put a thin strip of lead between the lines.

There is no control over leading in today's HTML. For typographers who want leading, the single-pixel GIF trick comes to the rescue to give us the equivalent of poor-man's leading. By sprinkling thin vertical single-pixel GIFS into your HTML document every few words, and at the end of each paragraph, you will create leaded text, the way it was never meant to be [4.12].

In this example, the GIF's attribute VSPACE=8 inserts eight pixels of blank space above *and* below the image itself [4.13]. The lines literally fend each other off as they wrap down the page. At my studio, this is done by hand, painstakingly inserting <IMG VSPACE=8 SRC=resources/dot_clear.gif> every few words [4.14].

Note that this inline GIF method does not set line endings. These lines will be leaded regardless of the type size or line breaks. This text flows smoothly around objects and can even be put into relative-width tables. Furthermore, you can adjust leading using the "search and replace" feature of your word processor to change the numbers.

Subheads

Subheads (like the one above) should be closely associated with the paragraphs below. I put a little more space between a subhead and the first line of a paragraph than I would between successive lines within a paragraph. To get a little more space, use a single-pixel GIF with VSPACE=1 between the subhead and the first paragraph.

Whatever you do, don't leave a blank line between a subhead and its associated paragraph. This is another great reason to use indents on the paragraphs that follow: Everything will visually hang from the subhead, and a larger vertical space will denote a new section.

I often make subheads as GIFs. In that case, I leave just a little white space in the bottom of the image (a few pixels) so the text that follows won't be crammed right underneath the subhead.

The whole section – subhead and following paragraphs – should hang together as a single unit. Subheads, indents, margins, and narrow column measures (see below) are the hallmarks of third-generation typography.

Bullets

Bullets are everywhere. We see them in slide presentations, on forms, in how-to books, and now on web pages world-

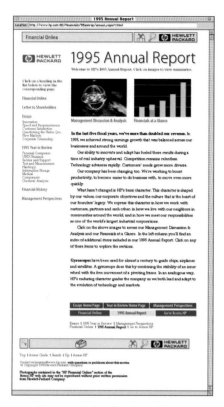

4.12 Poor-man's leading in action.

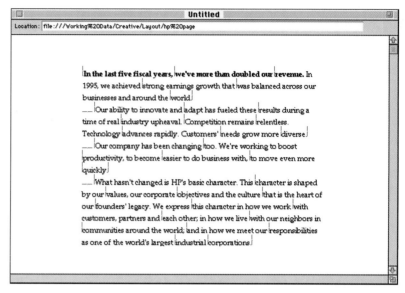

4.13 Here is an example of leaded text, excerpted from Hewlett-Packard's Financial Online site, that uses a blue single-pixel GIF, so you can see how the leading works. The magenta projections represent the space the VSPACE=8 attribute inserts. Changing the pixel to either white or clear makes it disappear. The code appears in 4.14 below.

4.14 HTML to simulate leaded text in illustration 4.13 above.

```
<IMG SRC="resources/dot_clear.gif" VSPACE=8><B>In the last five fiscal years,
<IMG SRC="resources/dot_clear.gif" VSPACE=8>we've more than doubled our
<IMG SRC="resources/dot_clear.gif" VSPACE=8>revenue.</B> In 1995, we achieved
<IMG SRC="resources/dot_clear.gif" VSPACE=8>strong earnings growth that
<IMG SRC="resources/dot_clear.gif" VSPACE=8>was balanced across our
<IMG SRC="resources/dot_clear.gif" VSPACE=8>businesses and around the
<IMG SRC="resources/dot_clear.gif" VSPACE=8>world.
<IMG SRC="resources/dot_clear.gif" VSPACE=8><BR>

<IMG SRC="resources/dot_clear.gif" HSPACE=8>
<IMG SRC="resources/dot_clear.gif" VSPACE=8>Our ability to innovate and
<IMG SRC="resources/dot_clear.gif" VSPACE=8>adapt has fueled these
<IMG SRC="resources/dot_clear.gif" VSPACE=8>results during a time of real
<IMG SRC="resources/dot_clear.gif" VSPACE=8>industry upheaval.
<IMG SRC="resources/dot_clear.gif" VSPACE=8>Competition remains
<IMG SRC="resources/dot_clear.gif" VSPACE=8>relentless. Technology
<IMG SRC="resources/dot_clear.gif" VSPACE=8>advances rapidly. Customers'
<IMG SRC="resources/dot_clear.gif" VSPACE=8>needs grow more
<IMG SRC="resources/dot_clear.gif" VSPACE=8>diverse.
<IMG SRC="resources/dot_clear.gif" VSPACE=8><BR>
```

wide. What are they doing? Like horizontal rules, bullets make up for unavailable space when putting a certain number of list elements on a page. Bullets come from the paper world, where pages end and people try to pack as much on one page as possible. In cyberspace, pixels are free – there's no page length to worry about.

Bullets are a last-resort approach to lists. They are ugly and do very little. Because they're identical, they convey no real information [4.15].

My rule on bullets is to design around them in all cases [4.16]. Information designers can use different colors or shapes of bullets to denote the status of a line item, but that's only for presenting search results and other tabular material. Status markers must be well thought out, not just red, green, and blue bullets.

About Scrolling

Scrolling is a traditional user interface no-no. The way it's done today, it should be. Scrolling is not inherently bad, however. Given better ways to scroll, surfers will scroll web pages as easily as they do word processor documents. As Alan Cooper points out in his excellent book *About Face: The Essentials of User-Interface Design*, scroll bars should have their arrows grouped together, not halfway across the screen from each other. Instead of the normal scrolling mechanism, I'd like to suggest a rocker plate (a two-dimensional variant of the rocker switch) located in the lower-right corner of the window. The plate would be on a virtual hinge right at the center, so it responds to

4.15 Bullets get in the way and convey no information.

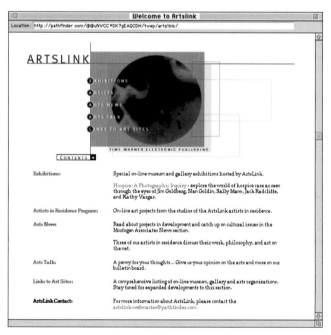

4.16 Designing around bullets: Use words rather than bullets.

4.17 Using a table to make a fixed-width left margin.

```
<TABLE>
 <TR>
   <!-- this cell establishes the margin -->
   <TD WIDTH=180><IMG SRC=resources/
   dot_clear.gif WIDTH=180></TD>
   <TD><!-- content goes in this cell --></TD>
 </TR>
</TABLE>
```

4.18 Creating a left margin with HTML.

keep loading and loading and loading. This is clearly too much material for one page. Find a way to break up long lists, whether you use a page with sub-entries (A-D, E-H, etc.) or one page for each letter, or frames. Don't put more than about 40 listings of anything on one page.

Horizontal White Space

Horizontal white space can make or break the established visual hierarchy on a page. Using invisible table cells and single-pixel GIFS, margins and indents can turn even the most mind-numbing wall-to-wall text into readable columns.

Spacing Between Letters

Type designers put narrow sidespaces on lowercase characters for a tight fit. Words should clump together, forming recognizable shapes. Don't add space between lowercase letters, unless you want to make them harder to read.

Caps, on the other hand, can be spaced out. Using Photoshop, you can make nice-looking words in all caps that download quickly. Pay attention to the spaces between words. If they start to look like the spaces between letters, your caps are too spread out. *(See Chapter 5, "Rendering Type.")*

Indentation

Use the single-pixel GIF trick to make indents for any paragraph that has a paragraph right above it. Paragraph indents are separators. When you see the first paragraph of a section indented,

small mouse movements. The more you drag it up, the faster it would scroll, and if you drag it to the center, scrolling stops. Users could start (or stop) autoscrolling by hitting the space bar, and speed up or slow down the scroll rate by moving the mouse over the plate. If the mouse left the plate, scrolling would stop. As companies give their browsers more capability, they will also have to give them more usability.

In practice, I don't mind scrolling a little. I mind scrolling a lot, but if the measure is narrow (see below) I find smooth scrolling fairly efficient. My general rule of thumb is to let people scroll no more than about six screens' worth before giving them a new page. Many alphabetic indexes on the Web present interminably long pages that as they do at the *New York Times,* you know they are too busy to bother with details like legibility and reader comfort. Indents are a signal. They don't signal the beginning of a new paragraph; they signal the transition between related paragraphs because nothing else does the job as well. I tend to use the smallest amount of space that is positively discernable and won't be skipped. There are times when, for style reasons, you might want a bigger indent, but they are rare.

Until HTML has a way to specify indents, the HTML to indent the beginning of a paragraph is:

```
<BR><IMG VSPACE=0 HSPACE=8
SRC="resources/dot_clear.gif">
```

Creating Margins

Web sites are different from traditional printed books in many ways, but not when it comes to margins. When presenting a column of text, a left margin aids the reader's eye in catching the beginning of the lines as it scans down the page.

Setting margins with the help of a table and a single-pixel GIF can easily and dramatically improve your site's typography.

To set a left margin, make a table with two columns, leave the left cell empty and place text in the second cell [4.17]. When the borders are turned off, the empty left cell acts as a margin. It's not a precise science, because tables weren't designed to be text containers for page layout. This section discusses how to make margins *(you'll find good*

examples of how wide to make them in the example chapters in Part II).

The best way to set the width of the margin cell is to designate the cell width in absolute numbers and add a single-pixel GIF to make sure it stays open [4.18].

This belt-and-suspenders approach to making margins is the best way I've found to keep things stable. It sounds redundant, but as browsers continue to change, it might turn out to save a lot of work later. Tables are difficult to nail down, so use any means necessary to get them to behave.

I wouldn't normally center a column of text. I like to make sure I have a good relationship between a column of text and its left margin. In general, the left margin should be *at least* one-fifth the width of a column of text, and preferably one-fourth.

One thing you can do is add two columns on the left: one absolute (the minimum) and a relative-width cell that stretches to increase the margin in case your surfers have wider windows. In fact, you can extend this concept to add another relative cell on the right, to get a hybrid margin scheme that works exceptionally well. The four-column approach [4.19 A-C] gives you a column of text that looks good under normal circumstances, compresses if the window is really narrow, yet won't extend if the window is made too wide. It takes a few more lines of HTML *(pick it up at the Book Site),* but once you get it working you can use it over and over [4.20].

To set a right margin, simply add a column to the right of the text. *Not!* It won't matter at all if you have a col-

4.19 A-C This four-column table uses one hard and one soft column to make a left margin. When viewed normally (A), it keeps the given column width, but if made narrow, it will shrink the column appropriately (B) and if the window is opened wide (C), it won't follow the window edge. See Chapter 10 for a three-column alternative.

A

B

C

4.20 HTML for a four-column table.

```
<table width=100% border=1 cellpadding=0 cellspacing=0>

   <tr>
      <!-- ABSOLUTE BLANK CELL -->
      <td width=60><IMG SRC="resources/dot_clear.gif"
      ALIGN=TOP BORDER="0" HSPACE="30"></td>

      <!-- RELATIVE BLANK CELL -->
      <td width=10%>

      <!-- BEGIN TEXT CELL -->
      <td width=390><font size=+1>
      <center><font color=#9999ff><B>Center this!</B>
      </font></center>
      <IMG vspace=1 SRC="resources/dot_clear.gif"><BR>
      Your text here</td>
   </tr>
</table>
```

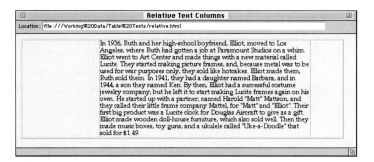

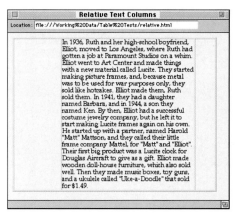

4.21 A, B Relative text columns help guarantee a right margin. The proportions shown are 25%, 65%, and 10% of the overall page width. This preserves both margins under all circumstances.

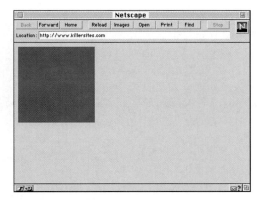

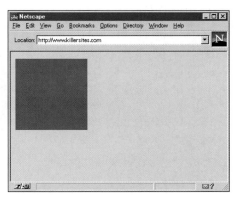

4.23 A, B Virtually all browsers have different offsets on different platforms. All Netscape browsers have different offsets.

```
<HTML><HEAD></HEAD>
<BODY BGCOLOR="#ccccff">
<IMG SRC="square.gif">
</BODY>
</HTML>
```

4.22 A good way to see whether your browser has automatic offsets.

Margins and Offsets

Offsets are not margins, and LEFT-MARGIN does not give you a true margin. A true margin is a visual concept, not a rigid mathematical one. Margins can have things in them. Quote marks and initial capital letters should be allowed to *hang* in the margin a bit, for true visual alignment. When offsets can be set to zero, always set them to zero and use table cells for margins.

umn to the right of a fixed-size text column. There's no way to ensure a right column, unless you make your text column relative.

Relative text columns can work in certain situations, especially if you don't mind them being narrow. The big problem occurs when people open their browser windows wide – you don't want a column of text that exceeds about 12 words *(see "Line Length" below)*. If you find yourself using a relative column width to guarantee a right margin, you might want to start with cell widths as 25%, 65%, and 10% of the overall page width, respectively **[4.21 A, B]**.

I haven't shown every possible way to make margins, but these examples should prove that there is more than one way to make a good web page.

Line Length

Many people who use computers are accustomed to long lines of text and one-inch margins. But good typography is easy on the reader, not a challenge. Long lines of text make it harder for the eye to get back to the left margin and pick up the next line. Ideally, each paragraph should have 10-12 words on a line for normal reading, but that's beyond a designer's control, because you don't know the web surfer's font sizes.

Macintosh designers, set your fonts a bit larger than normal (16 for text, 14 for monospace) to approximate average font sizes on Windows machines.

The best way to adjust line length is to set your fonts to a normal size and judge for yourself. I often use cells that are 380 pixels wide. A table cell of 200 would be narrow, and anything over 450 is too wide for easy reading.

Narrow column measures are not as bad on the Web as they are on paper. Scrolling isn't inherently bad, but too much scrolling can get tiresome.

Offsets and Alignment

Way back in 1995, I wanted to make my foreground images align perfectly with my background images. I tried, but they kept moving around when people visited my pages with different browsers. This is the dreaded *browser offset* problem.

To see my dilemma on your screen, make the following HTML file **[4.22]**, putting a square image in the upper left corner. (Alternatively, visit the Book Site to see a live demonstration page that shows you exactly what your offset is.)

The square won't be exactly in the upper left corner. It will be offset from the blue background by a certain number of pixels, both vertically and horizontally. The number of pixels depends on your browser **[4.23 A, B]**.

The bottom line: Misalignment of the foreground and background is virtually guaranteed.

Microsoft's Internet Explorer team was the first to recognize a need for precise alignment. They created two tag attributes: LEFTMARGIN and TOP-MARGIN. They aren't set to zero by default (for backward compatibility), but they go where no tags have gone before: to the edges of the browser win-

82

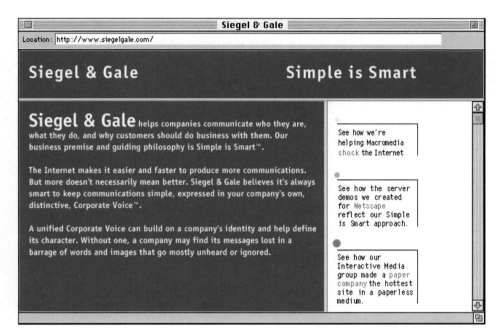

4.24 Frames let you use multiple windows for different purposes. A typical site has a title frame, a directory frame, and a target frame.

dow. In the future, all third-generation sites will take advantage of this tiny but important feature.

Frames and Framesets

Frames are a power feature of Netscape Navigator 2.0 that takes the Web to a new level. Frames let you display several URLs on one page and arrange them the way you want. Unfortunately, power tools can kill.

Frames are a *meta-document format* – they display multiple HTML documents simultaneously [4.24]. They are not HTML. To make a frame, you describe a frameset document, which contains a number of frames – windows containing HTML documents. You can specify the relative and absolute sizes of the windows. You can also include some default HTML in case the surfer arrives with a browser that can't

Frame Magic

If you make a frame-based page, use it for indexed material. Always make it a "dead end" area of your site, not the home page. Never put links inside your target frame, unless those links use special target names (or JavaScripts). The following "Magic Target Names" will help keep you out of trouble:

TARGET="_top" blows away all frames and takes you to the intended URL in a clean browser window.

TARGET="_blank" opens a clean new browser window that appears in front of the previous one.

TARGET="_self" makes the link load in its own window.

TARGET="_parent" makes the link load in the full body of the window, even if it is being viewed through some other frame. Using this tag blows away any frames through which people might be seeing your pages.

4.25 Frames can't solve all your problems. Flattening your site doesn't make it more accessible, only more inscrutable.

4.26 Frame-based sites can present navigation problems. Note that in this example, there are no fewer than five primary clickable zones.

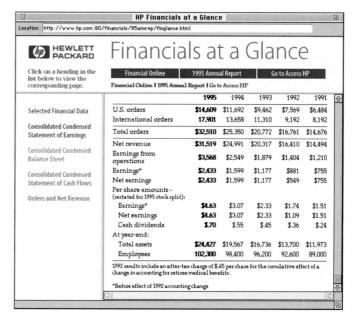

4.27 Frames can be useful when you want to compare several items.

see frames. You can name windows and use them as targets for hotlinks – when a visitor clicks on a hotlink, the resulting URL displays in another frame.

Visually, frames – like table borders – are barriers. They serve to separate, rather than associate. The reason frames are ugly is that you can't turn them to zero. Being able to color frame borders is nice; being able to set them to zero is necessary before anyone will make a good-looking frames page.

Frames can't solve all your problems. They invite several pages to load, which slows down surfing. Site designers often use them to compensate for bad design or lack of an overall concept. As implemented, frames are also ugly, because you can't turn off the borders or change the borders' color. *(Fortunately, Internet Explorer allows frame borders to be turned off; I expect Netscape to follow suit.)*

There are three main reasons people use frames: for hierarchies, for fun, and for indexes into flat databases. But only one of these is a good enough reason to justify using them. A hotlist is a bad use of frames. A good use of frames would be to present an index for a directory *(see Chapter 9, "A Hotlist," for a discussion of directories versus hotlists)*.

Frames for fun. Frames are often just another techno-feature people use to make their pages "cool." Bad design magnified.

Frames for hierarchies. Many people use frames to present hierarchies. In general, I never put frames on the

---

I n the most drastic changes to the juvenile justice system since the founding of the first family court a century ago, almost all 50 states have overhauled their laws in the past two years, allowing more youths to be tried as adults and scrapping longtime protections like the confidentiality of juvenile court proceedings.

The major thrust of the new laws is to get more juveniles into the adult criminal justice system, where they presumably will serve longer sentences under more punitive conditions.

Proponents of the changes say that getting tough with teen-agers is the only way to stop the epidemic of juvenile crime. Over the past decade, for example, arrest rates for homicides committed by 14- to 17-year-olds have more than tripled.

And the number of teen-agers is projected to increase by 20 percent over the next decade, setting off a new surge in crime, many criminologists believe.

"The thinking behind the juvenile court, that everything be done in the best interest of the child, is from a bygone era," said Patricia L. West, director of the Virginia Department of Juvenile Justice, which was created by the state Legislature in April.

While the original juvenile court, established in Chicago in 1899, was intended to

Deadly Sin Number One

Blank Line Typography

In second-generation typography, site designers use a blank line to add space between paragraphs. In third-generation typography, site designers use indents.

Of indents, the great typographer Jan Tschichold said, "So far, no device more economical or even equally good has been found to designate a group of sentences. There has been no shortage of attempts, though, to replace an old habit with a new one."

When you use blank lines as paragraph separators, the meaning of a blank line goes away. It turns into punctuation. In third-generation typography, indents separate paragraphs, and the right amount of vertical white space – maybe a blank line, maybe a bit more – separates sections, clumping paragraphs into logical groups for better reading.

front page of a site [4.25, 4.26]. In other words, I don't make frame-based sites, and I don't usually like it when I get to one. This is my personal opinion. I think the concept of frames is good, but that it is very deep water – user interfacewise – and they haven't been executed well enough to use. Many sites that were frame-based have taken their frames down.

A good example of the navigation problems presented by frames is the Back button. Originally, hitting the Back button took you to the last page visited before you came to the frame. That is completely inconsistent with normal Back button behavior. Then Netscape changed it to reverse back along the clickstream. This has its own problems, especially if you've been clicking back and forth among several choices in an index.

Frames for indexes. I use frames as indexes into larger, flat data spaces that would otherwise be awkward in HTML, because it would take too many pages. Suppose you have a yo-yo catalog that offers 200 different kinds of yo-yos. Putting up a regular HTML index, even if you group them carefully, still means having to go through a lot of pages to browse the yo-yos. In these situations, use frames as windows into flat databases *(see Chapter 8, "A Storefront")*.

The yo-yo catalog is a good example of a flat database, where you have many items with similar-sized descriptions. (If each item broke down into many descriptive entries, that would be an even more difficult problem, possibly beyond the ability of frames to present well.) Frames are especially

good for catalog pages, so you can flip back and forth between items to compare them.

In these cases, I make my frames page a destination, or a *dead end*. On the yo-yo site, the catalog page would use frames, where visitors can click on the index frame, see things in the target frame, and that's it. When the visitors are done, they either hit the Back button or use a link that has the `TARGET="_top"` command to lose the frames and take you to back to a standard HTML document. Careful use of frames in this way will make your database extendable and make it easy to compare items in the target window. Try to keep the list of links in the index window uncluttered and hierarchical (use vertical white space!) without growing too big [4.27].

This section isn't meant to address the larger issues of database presentation on the Web. It simply discusses a legitimate way to use frames for indexes. There are other good strategies for presenting database information in HTML, but they are beyond the scope of this book.

Frames that present hierarchies are fundamentally different from frames that present indexes. Because the user interface is the same, users will continue to be confused by frames.

One solution would be to make a set of buttons for navigating each individual frame and let the browser's Back button take you back to the page you saw before entering the frame document.

The problem is that you end up with a lot of navigation "chrome" on the screen. To get around this problem, browser manufacturers could keep the frame navigation bar hidden until the user's mouse was near the top of the frame, then the bar automatically lowers into position until either clicked on or the mouse moves away.

Summary

The differentiating factor between second-generation and third-generation typography is the degree of control site designers have over the positioning of elements. In second-generation typography, you had to use a blank line to space down, and horizontal spacing was impossible. Many people used horizontal rules to get more vertical space. Third-generation site designers carefully arrange everything on the page in single-pixel increments, from the size of the typefaces to the width of our margins. They reduce non-data pixels and present data pixels with utmost care. Until something better comes along, we use the single-pixel GIF trick and invisible tables. Frames can help present large flat databases, like catalogs, but should not be allowed to take over a site.

Reference

Read *The Form of the Book* by Jan Tschichold (Hartley and Marks Publishers, 1991). Pronounced "Yan Chick-old," he was one of the most influential typographic designers of this century. It is easily one of the most important books on typography and typographic principles ever written. This invaluable resource contains a trove of typographic tips.

Floating Frames

A new feature of Microsoft's Internet Explorer, floating frames are more useful than Netscape's original concept of frames.

A floating frame puts a window into any HTML page, in the same manner as you would put a table. It lets you insert another page of HTML into any regular page on your site. Because floating frames weren't available at the time this book went to press, see the Book Site for more information about this promising new way to extend our HTML documents into the multi-URL dimension.

The best way to render type isn't always to make a huge web page of type images, text on the ubiquitous existing you, isn't able to download and play. For now, to control what my visitors see, I render type GIF images. This section how to do it with

Rendering Type

The Balkanization of the Web: Overview

Location: http://www.dsiegel.com/balkanization/intro.html

THE BALKANIZATION OF THE WEB
by David Siegel

> Just as water, gas, and electricity are brought into our houses from far off to satisfy our needs in response to a minimal effort, so we shall be supplied with visual or audiory images, which will appear and disappear at a simple movement of the hand, hardly more than a sign.
>
> —Paul Valery, Aesthetics.

THIS ESSAY IS ABOUT HTML and the underpinnings of the Web. It is about foundations. The web is not a single structure. Because the Web has now "crossed the chasm," from its technical roots to the colorful world of consumers, it can't be extended by any single group or any single philosophy. Marshall McLuhan envisioned a "Global Village," sort of a big tent that included everyone. I claim the tent has already established three main rings: Information, Exchange, and Entertainment. Each needs its own appropriate infrastructure, built on a common foundation. (A quick detour

5.1 How not to do it: poorly rendered type.

VERSO 1:1   BICUBIC REDUCTION

VERSO 48PT VERSO

VERSO 36PT VERSO

VERSO 24PT VERSO

VERSO 18PT VERSO

VERSO 12PT VERSO

VERSO 9PT VERSO

VERSD 7PT VERSO

5.2 Especially at smaller sizes, reduce large type images in Photoshop to fit rather than set it directly to size; the final result will be smoother. Make sure you use bicubic interpolation for this operation.

Preserving Character Shapes

If you use Adobe Type Manager (ATM) to render your Type 1 fonts, make sure to open the ATM control panel and choose "Preserve Character Shapes." If you don't, the descenders of your characters may be cut off.

TYPE PLAYS AN IMPORTANT ROLE on almost any web page. You see it in images, text fonts, display type, and the ubiquitous ASCII art. Soon, you'll be able to embed real fonts into your pages. For now, render your type as GIF images [5.1]. This section shows how to do it.

In general, good designers are picky about typefaces and styles, so they add type to their web sites by rendering type images in Photoshop and including those graphics with the <IMG> tag in HTML. Always use GIFs for type images. The JPEG format makes type look blurry.

Reduce Type in Photoshop

The best way to render type is to make it very large and then let Photoshop reduce it. If you want to render type below about 20-point, make it large first and reduce it [5.2]. Above 20 points, most type will render well enough without this step.

High-quality fonts contain *hints* to help render the characters consistently and appropriately on screen at small sizes. Photoshop doesn't use these hints. Render a line of small m's in Photoshop – they won't all look the same. As the technology improves, rendering will improve. For now, to create type smaller than 20 points, first generate the type at around 80 or 140 points, then scale it down to the target size [5.3].

Photoshop offers no numerical control in the Image>Effects>Scale command. You can work around this by creating a layer in Photoshop containing type in the target size as a

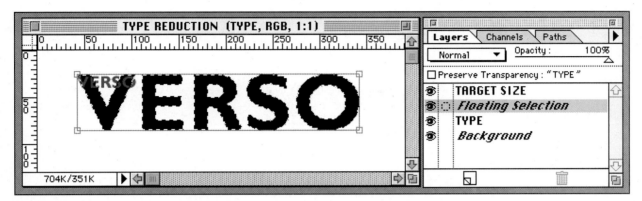

5.3 Scale your type down to the target size in Photoshop.

guide, then scaling the larger type down on its own layer to match. When the layers match, hide the guide layer.

Do It Last

If you've ever watched a good carpenter work, you'll see she leaves all her nails sticking out a bit until the piece is finished. When everything is just right, she takes a minute to "set" all the nails at once. Why? Because it's a lot easier to pull nails before you set them. The same applies to web sites, especially if they have lots of type.

Rendering type as GIFs is tedious work. Because changes usually come at the last minute, I wait for final copy before making final type images.

Do It All at Once

Whenever possible, generate all the type images for an entire site from a single master file. This way, all sizes, colors, weights, and intermediate colors will be consistent.

1. Reduce (index) the colors of the master file to the least acceptable number.

2. Select and cut each individual type element closely, leaving no extra space around the edges.

3. Paste each element into a new file, noting the image dimensions.

4. Export GIFs from the new files using an exact palette, assigning meaningful file names.

5. Enter the dimensions and pathnames of the gifs into your <IMG> tags.

For large projects, sometimes I modify step 2 and use a standard fixed-size rectangle for all the elements. This makes step 5 easier, because all the images will have the same dimensions. Otherwise, if the images vary in size, make a list noting the names and pixel dimensions of the GIF files as you save them; you'll need these when coding the HTML.

For Large Jobs, Keep a Record

Photoshop doesn't retain the text you type as you work. I like to keep all my text in a word processor. I grab what I

91

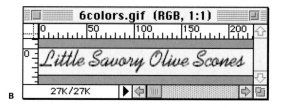

5.4 One image reduced to 5 (A), 6 (B), 7 (C), and 8 (D) colors. Follow the Golden Rule to get the smallest file: Start out too low and work up to the minimum acceptable set of colors.

need from this file and paste it into Photoshop's Type tool dialog box. I can spell check and concentrate on getting the words right. I can save old versions and choose fonts faster than in Photoshop. I can also note the steps for rendering a job's type right along with the text. Having a record like this makes the inevitable revisions a snap.

Some designers make all their type in Illustrator (or FreeHand), create large outlines, then copy and paste the outlines into Photoshop for reduction. This method involves an extra step, because making large type directly in Photoshop and pasting it in from outlines is equivalent. If you want to set type on a curve or apply some other special effect to the outlines, however, you must usually transfer it from a program like Illustrator.

Reduce Colors, Increase Runs

Type looks best without jaggies, but anti-aliasing introduces many intermediate colors along the edges *(see "Anti-Aliasing" in Chapter 3)*. Intermediate colors reduce the compressibility of the image and occupy valuable space in the color palette. Always try to keep the number of transition colors to a minimum while preserving the smoothing effect of anti-aliasing.

You almost never need more than six intermediate colors when setting type on a flat background.

If you are setting type on a solid background, you usually need only four intermediate colors. If you count the two main colors, this means you can always

Height and Width Tags

Always use HEIGHT and WIDTH tags for all images. This improves page loading speed, because the text can flow into final position before the images arrive. Some HTML editor tools, like BBEdit for the Mac, put the dimensions in for you automatically.

reduce type to between 2 and 3 bits deep [**5.4 A-D**].

Occasionally, you can do without anti-aliasing entirely. If you have a large area of type and need to get the file sizes down, or if you're going for a hard-edged look, try setting type without anti-aliasing.

The Poor-Man's Bold

"What to do when bold is too dark and regular is too light?" Using Adobe Multiple Master fonts, you can interpolate the stem weight to make the font you need. Alternatively, you can use this trick to get an intermediate weight: Render the characters you want. Then copy and paste this image right back on top of itself. Photoshop's transparency feature will darken the intermediate colors slightly. You can adjust the transparency of the copied layer to change the weight of the letters.

Invest in Good-Quality Fonts

How many web pages have large banners rendered as GIFs in Times Roman? Try something else! But as font prices have gone down, so has quality. Buy only fonts made for the graphic design market, not those that come packaged on a CD-ROM of 2,000 fonts. Cheap fonts are inferior and will make your pages look uneven. Some fonts I use:

Sans Serif: Avenir, Rotis, Univers, Gill Sans, Myriad, Stone Sans, Futura, Syntax, Frutiger, OCR-B, Copperplate.

Serif: Sabon, Galliard, Bauer Bodoni, Walbaum, Stone, Melior, Serifa.

Scripts: Künstler, Snell Roundhand, Isadora, Mistral.

I also like Adobe's Tekton and Graphite, and AGFA's Eagle-feather, but then, I designed them. All these fonts are well made, and will render correctly. Multiple Master fonts like Myriad are particularly handy, giving you unlimited weights and widths. There are hundreds of other good fonts to choose from – and thousands of bad ones.

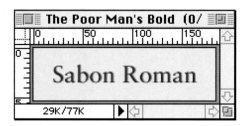

A

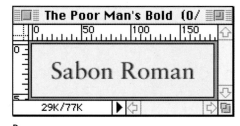

B

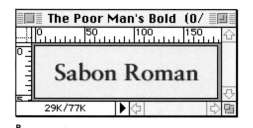

C

D

5.5 The regular weight (A), copied and shifted right one pixel (B), 50% transparency applied to the copy (C), and at 25% transparency (D).

Keep Type in Layers

Always keep type on a separate layer in Photoshop. Since Photoshop anti-aliases layers automatically, you'll be able to change type and background colors at any time. If you set type into the background, you will lose this flexibility.

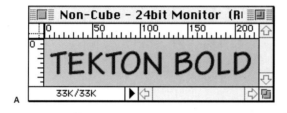

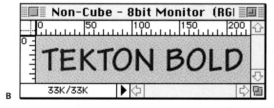

5.6 This is how predithered type will appear on monitors set to thousands of colors (A) and 256 colors (B).

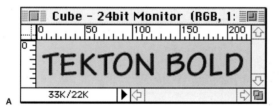

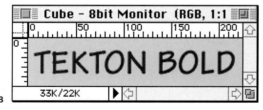

5.7 This type is optimized for both high (A) and low-end displays (B).

For even more weight, copy the type and paste it again, shifted over or down one pixel (but not both) **[5.5 A-D]**. This often helps when a regular is too light and a bold is too heavy or unavailable. Never go more than one pixel in either direction.

Dither on the Client

Properly reduced type gets its main colors from the color cube, is anti-aliased, and is reduced to the fewest number of intermediate colors necessary. However, you don't need to index every color in your type image to the color cube. If all your main areas of color come from the color cube, but the intermediate shades are too subtle, they will dither when displayed in only 256 colors **[5.6 A, B]**. That's okay! Let them dither.

If you let the client (in this case, the browser program) do the dithering (which it does automatically to colors outside the cube), visitors who can see more than 256 colors will benefit, and the low-end visitors won't know the difference **[5.7 A, B]**. The file size doesn't change.

Hand Retouching

Sometimes you have to use the Pencil tool to fix type after you've reduced colors. When you can't reduce the number of colors any further, a few artifacts remain in the image. I zoom in and look for uneven areas of color, like sawteeth in the vertical edges, and fix them by hand **[5.8]**. I fix, fill, and round up stray pixels.

I sometimes get caught up in anti-

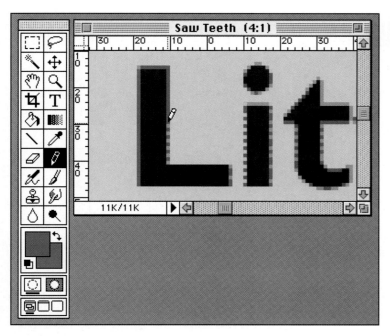

5.8 Eliminate saw teeth before shipping.

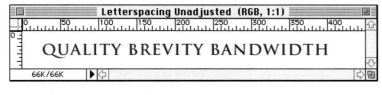

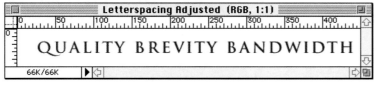

5.9 Letterspacing, before (ABOVE) and after (BELOW).

Interpolation

Photoshop has three settings for interpolation: linear, bicubic, and nearest-neighbor.

The first two are for anti-aliased images, while nearest-neighbor is for hard images with no intermediate colors needed to soften transitions.

You can select one of these methods in the Preferences dialog box, but Photoshop comes from the factory with bicubic turned on.

Experiment with all three methods when you're having difficulties reducing graphics. For most purposes, bicubic is the best method.

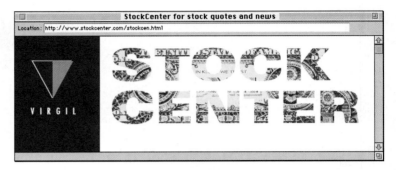

Shadows

If you're making one shadow for many shapes on several layers in your document, you can create it on one layer automatically. View the desired foreground layers only (hiding the background layer), then merge the layers into a new layer that contains the separate elements on it, which you can then darken.

Keep in mind that shadows aren't just black; they actually *darken the tonal value* of the surfaces they fall on.

5.10 Without the drop shadow, type fades into the background (ABOVE). Adding a black drop shadow (BELOW) emphasizes the type.

aliasing a curve by hand. Be prepared to put in long hours once you start fiddling with curves. It's also tempting to want to fix letter stems with intermediate colors at their edges, but don't do it. If you clean too much, you'll change the weight of your letters for the worse.

Develop your eye. Experiment until you can recognize when hand retouching is worth your time.

Fine Points of Spacing

Fine typography has always included hand spacing of capital letters and special character pairs. Words set in caps should generally be *letterspaced* – loose, so each letter appears distinctly in its own whitespace. Words set in upper- and lowercase should be spaced tightly, so whole words appear as units. Good

fonts provide many built-in *kerning pairs* to make certain letter combinations look good together automatically in software like PageMaker. Photoshop, however, can't take advantage of this built-in intelligence. You have to make fine spacing adjustments by hand [**5.9 A, B**].

An especially good introduction to a broad range of typographic design issues is *Stop Stealing Sheep*, by Erik Spiekermann and E. M. Ginger (Hayden, 1993). See the Book Site for a list of good books on typography, and pointers to online bookstores that carry them.

Drop Shadows

Drop shadows are misunderstood and overused. The most common reasons to use drop shadows are to help differentiate the type against the background, to give a "cool" 3-D effect, and to "jazz up the page a bit." The first is the most important.

The best drop shadows help enhance edges. When the type and background contain similar colors, a drop shadow gives a hard edge to bring out the character shapes [5.10 A, B]. Most paper magazine covers use this trick. In these situations, you don't need much shadow.

Drop shadows are occasionally useful as true shadows for 3-D effects, but these instances should be rare. Second-generation sites often sport headlines floating three inches off the background and flying extruded logos. Third-generation sites don't rely on 3-D lettering to make a splash.

To make a drop shadow, I copy the object into its own layer by dragging it onto the New Layer icon. By reducing the brightness and contrast, I turn the new layer very dark. Then I place it underneath the object layer, moving it until the shadow appears one pixel down. After hiding the marquee, I use the arrow keys to move the shadow layer left and right, to see which is better. If necessary, I go down two pixels, then perhaps three, but rarely more.

Once you've made a shadow choice, be careful to give the same look to all shadows on the same page. If one shadow falls down and to the left, all of the shadows should fall down and to the left – but don't bother trying to match the drop shadows built into the Mac and Windows operating systems. If you are trying to achieve the effect of multiple light sources, you should probably rethink the design – drop shadows rarely work effectively in such situations.

Drop shadows can be any color that works, or simply a darker tint of the background art, but you'll still need anti-aliased edges. Test in 256-color display mode before shipping.

Initial Caps

Initial caps mark a first paragraph as special, attracting reader attention (studies show people more often read the text that follows). Initial caps do not need to be huge, neither should they be made with too few colors – they need to look great. Invest in some good display typefaces or special initial-caps fonts and make elegant first paragraphs.

The two types of initial caps are bounded [5.11] and unbounded [5.12]. An unbounded initial cap has a transparent background. *Bounded caps* sit in boxes, with or without borders. Bounded caps should always be inset (dropped, as in *drop cap*) in the paragraph, with the text aligned to the top. Add extra space around the box so the text doesn't crowd it. Display faces work best.

Unbounded initial caps can be inset, standing, or hanging out in the margin, (probably in a different table cell). Cut the right edge very close to the character. A "J" makes a good unbounded cap, an "F" doesn't, because it will be too far away from its neighboring characters. Unbounded, same-color drop caps are a subtle way to start new pages. You don't know how large a visitor's fonts are, so if your drop cap

5.11 Initial Caps can make a page look sophisticated.

5.12 An unbounded initial cap standing on the baseline.

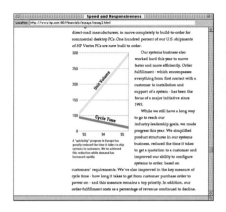

5.13 Captions under images look sharp and don't get lost.

5.14 Small caps can be effective if used sparingly.

offsets three lines of text on your screen, there could be a gap on someone else's screen. Add some white space at the bottom so text lines aren't jammed up against the bottom of your character as they wrap around.

A good rule of thumb: no more than one initial cap per page.

Captions

Add captions to your photos and illustrations. There's no need to struggle with HTML to do captions well. A small caption below each image in an article adds very little to the size of the file, guarantees the right relationship of caption and image, and frees you from having to worry about it later. The downside is that you won't be able to make changes to the text easily, but captions are always tied to images, so they're not hard to get right the first time.

Make sure to bring captions right underneath (or next to) your images. Too much white space causes them to float away. Add just a few pixels between an illustration and its caption.

Make them bold or use a contrasting color, but avoid italics, since they don't look as good at small sizes on computer screens **[5.13]**. Don't worry about adding extra colors to your image; just make sure they compress well by eliminating extra intermediate colors.

Small Caps

True small caps are the mark of an advanced typographer. Beginning a new chapter (or web magazine article) with a few words in small caps draws attention, inviting the reader to pick up the line and continue reading. Use them when you want a formal voice: titles, names, stationery, invitations (Web invitations with secret URLs are even more fun than printed ones), important documents, and more.

Small caps are usually just a little taller than a lowercase x (the *x-height*), and they are often slightly wider than regular caps. There are four ways to put them into your web pages.

In your HTML, use a *size difference* (`<FONT SIZE=-1>`) to make small caps directly in the text **[5.14]**. It won't

look perfect, because the initial characters will be too dark, but it will load
quickly. It's a nice touch on a page that
already has a lot of images, or where
you want a fast, formal look.

You can also *manufacture small caps*
in a GIF image. If you don't have a font
with small caps, you can make your
own. Don't just reduce the size of the
caps. Reduced caps will be lighter than
their associated real caps and the line
will look uneven [5.15]. Many desktop-
publishing programs simply reduce
the caps by about 75%; you can always
tell, because they are too light.

Instead, use a font where you have
a slightly heavier version available –
usually a demi-bold or a book weight –
and add the regular caps to the slightly
bolder caps set in a smaller size for a
poor-man's small caps [5.16].

The best way to get small caps is to
buy a set. Type designers go out of their
way to make small caps work well with
regular caps. I often use the small caps
of a beautiful typeface called Sabon
(designed by Jan Tschichold). Eagle-
feather's small caps are also quite
distinctive [5.17 A, B].

Summary

Choose your fonts with care, anti-alias
them well, make them compressible
yet smooth, and stick with the GIF format until something better takes over.
Your type will still be fuzzy, but it's the
best we can do until screens have
higher resolutions.

Very soon, browsers will be able to
see fonts embedded in an HTML document. See the Book Site for details on
this promising new development.

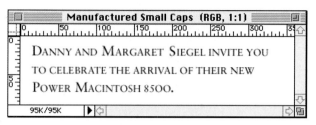

5.15 Manufactured small caps look uneven.

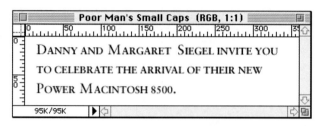

5.16 Use a slightly heavier weight to get a "poor-man's small caps."

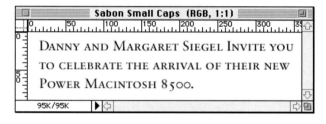

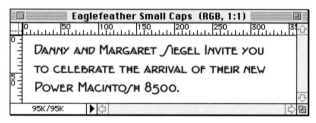

5.17 Both Sabon's and Eaglefeather's small caps are designed to work well with the caps.

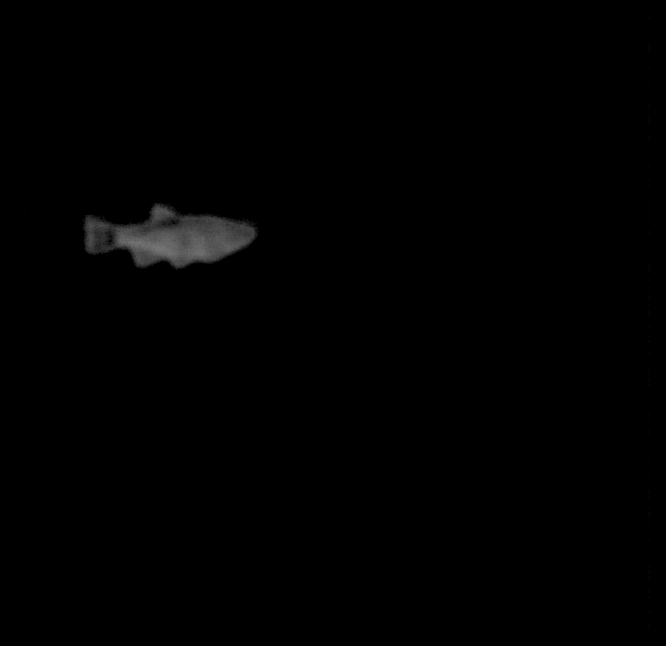

Part II

A Page Makeover

Browser offsets

Anti-aliasing

Tiling backgrounds

Page structure

Control of vertical space

Sharon Stargazer's Home Page

Location: http://www.killersites.com/

SHARON STARGAZER

Hey! What are you doing looking at your computer? You should be out looking at the stars. This month, look for Mars near the horizon just after sunset. It's the big red one!

News Flash

I am having an astronomy party! Come as your favorite constellation! Read my **digital invitation** to see if you're invited! (hint: if you're in the Milky Way, you're invited.)

About Me

Everything you ever wanted to know about me and my life looking at the stars. You'll find some of my favorite **people** here, too. You'll also see work by other researchers, including Dan Mills, Stacy Rosenblatt, Tatjana Keller, Rebecca Shulman, and Richard Powers. Check them out!

Space: The Final Frontier

Some day I will find my own Comet and name it **Comet Stargazer**. Until then, you can read some of my papers on interstellar gravity waves.

Space Poetry

Images of space come in several flavors. I have a large collection of **space poetry** that grows every day. Submit your own poem for my collection!

I hope you'll come back for more space goodies soon!

Ciao,

Sharon Stargazer

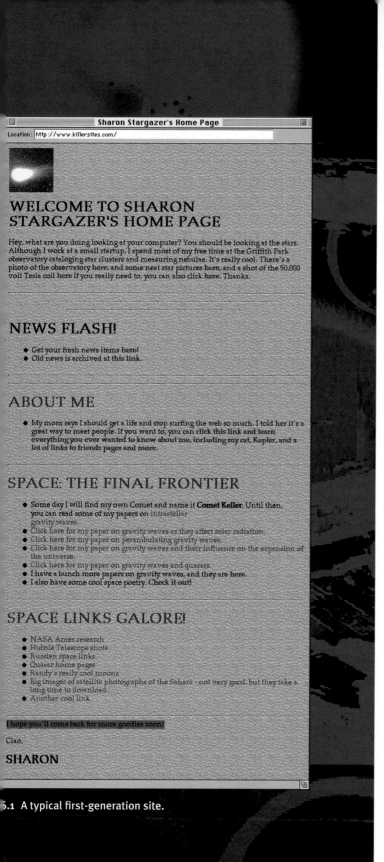

The following text is inside the browser window image:

Sharon Stargazer's Home Page

Location: http://www.killersites.com/

WELCOME TO SHARON STARGAZER'S HOME PAGE

Hey, what are you doing looking at your computer? You should be looking at the stars. Although I work at a small startup, I spend most of my free time at the Griffith Park observatory cataloging star clusters and measuring nebulae. It's really cool. There's a photo of the observatory here, and some neat star pictures here, and a shot of the 50,000 volt Tesla coil here If you really need to, you can also click here. Thanks.

NEWS FLASH!

- Get your fresh news items here!
- Old news is archived at this link.

ABOUT ME

- My mom says I should get a life and stop surfing the web so much. I told her it's a great way to meet people. If you want to, you can click this link and learn everything you ever wanted to know about me, including my cat, Kepler, and a lot of links to friends pages and more.

SPACE: THE FINAL FRONTIER

- Some day I will find my own Comet and name it **Comet Keller**. Until then, you can read some of my papers on intrastellar gravity waves.
- Click here for my paper on gravity waves as they affect solar radiation.
- Click here for my paper on perambulating gravity waves.
- Click here for my paper on gravity waves and their influence on the expansion of the universe.
- Click here for my paper on gravity waves and quasars.
- I have a bunch more papers on gravity waves, and they are here.
- I also have some cool space poetry. Check it out!

SPACE LINKS GALORE!

- NASA Ames research
- Hubble Telescope shots
- Russian space links
- Quasar home pages
- Randy's really cool moons
- Big images of satellite photographs of the Sahara - not very good, but they take a long time to download.
- Another cool link

I hope you'll come back for more goodies soon!

Ciao,

SHARON

End of browser window image content.

6.1 A typical first-generation site.

GREAT SITES are built one page at a time. To illustrate several methods and principles presented in previous chapters, I'll go through a typical web page makeover from start to finish. This should give you a starting point for doing projects in a more precise, layout-oriented way. Rather than making an entire site (front door, entry, etc.), I'll make a simple, elegant personal home page.

The purpose of this chapter is to present third-generation working methods, bringing many of the concepts from earlier chapters into a real-world example. Follow along and see how much control you can get over the page.

For most first-generation home pages, a makeover is like shooting fish in a barrel. Almost anything you do will improve the look [6.1].

This scroll-down page is a "table of contents" with very little content. It shows neither Sharon's enthusiasm for astronomy nor much of her personality. Black type is hard to read on a gray background, and the textured background makes things worse. There's precious little information on what to expect behind the text links, and the colors aren't intuitive. The edge-to-edge typography gets worse as you open the window, and the horizontal rules add insult to injury. Furthermore, the list of links takes your attention away from what she has to offer. Sharon is ready for a third-generation page.

Strategy

Rather than edit the existing HTML,

I'll start with a fresh "sheet of paper" and build it up from scratch. I want to use a background image that combines stars for theme and white as a background for text. I'll get there in steps, starting with a dark blue bar down the left side and modifying it later. Then I'll put everything into a table and set up a simple layout with no bullets, rules, or HTML "junk." Finally, I'll discuss some possible additions.

The Redesign

First I'll make a background image. Then I'll position a foreground image on top of the background and add the text. Once it's in good shape, I'll add a few finishing touches. As an encore, I'll get myself out of a mess caused by inconsistent browser offsets.

A Clean, Tiling Background

Most tiling background images add texture to a page. Many backgrounds try to create a 3-D effect, which interferes with the text, causing it to float above the page. But background images can also give a page *structure*. In this case, a blue bar down the left side provides a strong contrast with the white area, setting it apart from the noisy clutter of the desktop. I start by making a very wide, short image that tiles (repeats) vertically in the browser window.

In Photoshop, I open a new file, 25 pixels high by 1200 wide. Why 25 pixels high? It only needs to be one pixel tall to tile, but if you try it with a 1 × 1200 file, you'll see that it takes far too long for the browser to replicate

this file over and over. Instead, it "rolls down" very slowly. It works, but it puts too much demand on the client computer. In my experiments, I've found that 25-pixel-high images download and unroll faster than other heights, though the difference between 25 and, say, 20 pixels is small. More than 25 makes for too long a download, and GIF inflation can become a problem on large background images (*see "Image Inflation" in Chapter 3*).

The width of 1200 prevents the background from tiling horizontally on large monitors. If you make it, say, 600 pixels wide, it might look fine on your machine, but on a larger monitor, a second blue column will appear to the right of the text. I can make this image large, yet keep the file size small, because solid areas compress well **[6.2]**. For the sake of maximum contrast and compression, I would never make the right side anything but white.

On a new layer, I make a rectangle 120 pixels wide and fill it with blue. This color should come from the color cube. I choose an RGB value of 0, 0, 51, which in hex is simply the darkest blue you can get: "#000033" *(if this isn't clear, please read "The Color Cube," in Chapter 3, before continuing).*

I export the file as a GIF, using Adobe's GIF89a plug-in *(see "The GIF Format" in Chapter 3 for details, or get the latest version at the Book Site).* For now, I use the default settings that come with the filter: no transparency, no interlacing. Even though it is quite wide, this 1-bit image compresses down to a mere 374 bytes.

Now for the HTML. I type the

Layer Management

Always leave the background layer of a Photoshop document a single color. Everything else goes into separate layers for easy anti-aliasing and flexibility.

Many tools anti-alias by default, which can either be beneficial or horrific. For instance, ellipses should be anti-aliased, while rectangles should not.

In Photoshop, I like to use the HSB rather than the RGB slider, because it's easier to make colors that go together.

I make sure I'm in RGB mode, because CMYK isn't for display screens, and I always use pixels, rather than inches, as my standard unit of measurement.

6.2 The blue area on the left tiles down to become the vertical bar. Make the file 1200 pixels wide overall, so that it doesn't tile again to the right.

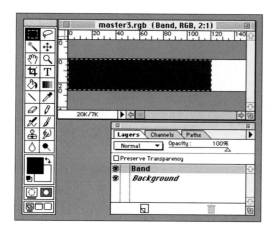

6.3 The tiling background as it looks in the browser.

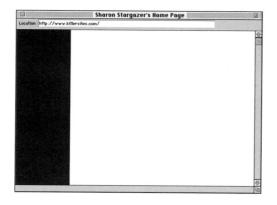

following code into a new file, open it with Netscape, and – voilà! **[6.3]**

```
<HTML>
<HEAD><TITLE>
Sharon's Home Page
</TITLE></HEAD>
<BODY BGCOLOR="#FFFFFF"
 BACKGROUND="spine.gif">
</BODY></HTML>
```

A Third-Generation Banner

I'd like to put a red circle in the foreground, centered on the border between blue and white. This breaks the plane of the blue bar, causing it to stand out above all other elements. Visually, it will become the "frontmost" image, drawing the eye like a lit match. I am going to put Sharon's name over it, so you know right away whose page it is. (To me, this is better than `<H1>`, but that's just my opinion.) I'll start with a circle 80 pixels in diameter, two-thirds the width of the blue band. This should give me a balanced look – not too scrawny, yet not overpowering. I open a new Photoshop document, 120 × 120 pixels – a bit larger than the circle. On a new layer, I draw a red circle using the ellipse tool, which is anti-aliased by default. Anti-aliasing makes the edges of the circle look smooth **[6.4 A, B]**.

I export the circle as a GIF, using the GIF89a Export plug-in's eyedropper to designate pure white as the transparent color. I view this GIF at various positions, using the image's HSPACE and VSPACE arguments to space them over, rather than bothering with extra single-pixel GIFs **[6.5, 6.6]**.

What's going on? Because GIF supports only one level of transparen-

6.4 A, B A circle, aliased (LEFT) and anti-aliased (RIGHT).

6.7 This image contains many colors to make the edge look smooth.

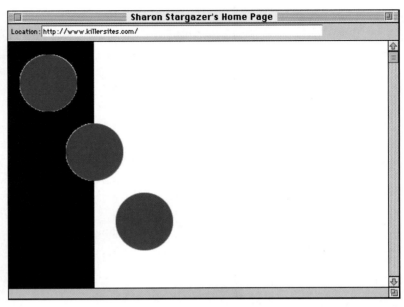

6.6 The use of anti-aliased foreground images requires precise alignment over backgrounds with major color changes.

cy, all the near-white pixels (which are actually shades of pink) make the shape look good against white, but not against blue. I anti-aliased the circle against a background of solid white, but half the background is blue **[6.7]**. I'm in trouble.

To anti-alias the GIF properly, I add a new layer, draw a blue rectangle, and position the circle against it **[6.8]**.

Note: These anti-aliasing problems wouldn't happen if we had 256 levels (8 bits) of transparency, but with GIFs, we can designate only one color (1 level) as transparent.

```
<HTML>
<HEAD><TITLE>Sharon Stargazer's Home Page</TITLE></HEAD>
<!-- Page Parameters -->
<BODY BGCOLOR="#FFFFFF" BACKGROUND="spine.gif">

<!-- Begin Red Circle Placement -->
<IMG VSPACE=15 HSPACE=20 WIDTH=80 HEIGHT=80
  SRC="redcircle.gif"><BR>
<IMG VSPACE=15 HSPACE=80 WIDTH=80 HEIGHT=80
  SRC="redcircle.gif"><BR>
<IMG VSPACE=15 HSPACE=140 WIDTH=80 HEIGHT=80
  SRC="redcircle.gif">
<!-- End Red Circle Placement -->

</BODY></HTML>
```

6.5 Note the use of HSPACE to control the horizontal position of the circle.

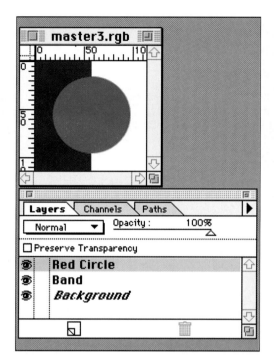

6.8 Create a layer for each image, positioning the circle precisely.

6.9 Flatten the image, then select the blue area with the magic wand. Delete it.

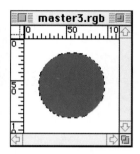

6.10 Select everything *but* the circle. Invert the selection.

6.11 Place copied selection into a new file.

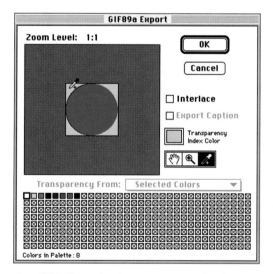

6.12 With Photoshop's GIF89a export plug-in, you can designate a single color as transparent.

I flatten the image. Now I want to get rid of the large blue and white areas, so I can take the anti-aliased circle over to my other file. This is a three-step process. First, I select the blue area using the magic wand *with no anti-aliasing* and a tolerance of zero [6.9].

Second, I add the white area to the selection by Shift-clicking the magic wand on the white area [6.10]. I invert the selection, giving me a circle that contains the entire anti-aliased image.

Third, I simply copy the circle and paste it into a new file, which will be just big enough to accommodate the copied image [6.11] – no sense shipping extra invisible bits.

I reduce this image to eight colors using an adaptive color palette

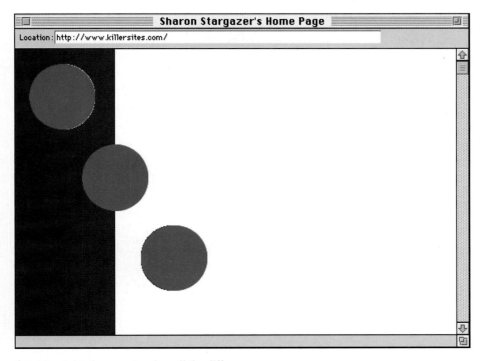

6.13 The right placement makes all the difference.

(see "Reducing File Size" in Chapter 3). This gives me just enough shades of red to make the anti-aliasing work. Then I export the image as a GIF, designating pure white to be transparent **[6.12]**.

I replace the existing circle image with the new one (using the same file name to avoid the hassle of changing the HTML) to see how it looks **[6.13]**.

Unfortunately, anti-aliasing a foreground image is not always this simple. In fact, just a few pages from here, things get more complicated. Now, however, I want to add Sharon's name in front of the circle. I return to the Photoshop file and expand the canvas size by a few hundred pixels on the right side to make room.

To complement the clean look of the page, I experiment with a few sans-serif typefaces, with the name both in upper- and lowercase. Gill Sans bold caps with six units of spacing is one of my favorites **[6.14]**. Sans-serifs are usually a good choice, because many serifed fonts have features that become quite blurry when anti-aliased.

The Text

Now for the table work. (In many of the illustrations that follow, I've made the transparent single-pixel GIFs blue with magenta spacers and turned the table borders on, so you can see the construction.)

Look carefully at the code for this table **[6.15]**. You'll see how I use verti-

6.14 Sans-serif type-faces generally read better on screen.

cal space to move text down in small increments, replacing bullets with good typography. If you build a page like this, you can vary all the numbers for vertical space in the HTML file and watch the page change accordingly. Set up a hierarchy of white space, with text close to subheads and sections separated by an amount of space that sets the

sections apart *(see "Vertical White Space" in Chapter 4)*.

Finally, I make a GIF with Sharon's name in a script typeface called Shelley (see "Hand Retouching" in Chapter 5) and add it to the page. This is a nice touch that doesn't take long to make. Another possibility would have been to scan Sharon's actual signature, but

6.15 The table for this page is straightforward. The left margin is 135 pixels wide (see next page for image, 6.16).

```
<HTML>
<HEAD><TITLE>Sharon Stargazer's Home Page</TITLE></HEAD>
<!-- Page Parameters -->
<BODY BGCOLOR="#FFFFFF" TEXT="#666666" LINK="#CC0000"
 ALINK="#FF3300" VLINK="#330099" BACKGROUND="images/
 spine.gif">

<IMG SRC="resources/dot_clear.gif" ALIGN=TOP VSPACE=15
 BORDER="0"><BR>
<IMG SRC="resources/dot_clear.gif" ALIGN=TOP HSPACE=35
 HEIGHT=0 BORDER="0">
<IMG SRC="./images/header.gif" ALIGN=top WIDTH="361"
 HEIGHT="86" BORDER="0" VSPACE="5"><BR>
<IMG VSPACE=5 SRC="resources/dot_clear.gif">

<!-- Begin the table -->
<TABLE BORDER=0 CELLPADDING=0 CELLSPACING=0 WIDTH=485>
 <TR>
 <!-- A "blank" cell with a single-pixel gif as filler -->
 <TD WIDTH=135><IMG HEIGHT=0 WIDTH=135 SRC="resources/
 dot_clear.gif"></TD>
 <TD WIDTH=350>Hey! What are you doing looking at your
 computer? You should be out looking at the stars.
 This month, look for Mars near the horizon just after
 sunset. It's the big red one!
```

```
<BR><IMG VSPACE=8 SRC="resources/dot_clear.gif"><BR>
<B>News Flash</B>
<BR><IMG VSPACE=1 SRC="resources/dot_clear.gif"><BR>

I am having an astronomy party! Come as your favorite
constellation! Read my <A HREF="me/invite.html">digital
invitation</A> to see if you're invited! (Hint: if you're
in the Milky Way, you're invited.)

<BR><IMG VSPACE=8 SRC="resources/dot_clear.gif"><BR>
<B><A HREF="me/index.html">About Me</A></B>
<BR><IMG VSPACE=1 SRC="resources/dot_clear.gif"><BR>

Everything you ever wanted to know about me and my life look-
ing at the stars. You'll find some of my favorite <B>
<A HREF="me/people.html">people</A></B> here, too. You'll
also see work by other researchers, <A HREF="me/
mills.html">Dan Mills</A>, <A HREF="rosenblatt/
index.html">Stacy Rosenblatt</A>, <A HREF="keller/
index.html">Tatjana Keller</At>, <A HREF="shulman/
index.html">Rebecca Shulman</A>, and <A HREF="powers/
index.html">Richard Powers</A>. Check them out!

<BR><IMG VSPACE=8 SRC="resources/dot_clear.gif"><BR>
<B><A HREF="space/index.html">Space: The Final Frontier
</A></B>
<BR><IMG VSPACE=1 SRC="resources/dot_clear.gif"><BR>

Some day I will find my own comet and name it <B>Comet
Stargazer</B>. Until then, you can read some of my papers on
<A HREF="waves/index.html">interstellar gravity waves.</A>

<BR><IMG VSPACE=8 SRC="resources/dot_clear.gif"><BR>
<B><A HREF="poems/index.html">Space Poetry</A></B>
<BR><IMG VSPACE=1 SRC="resources/dot_clear.gif"><BR>

Images of space come in several flavors. I have a large
collection of <A HREF="poems/index.html">space poetry</A>
that grows every day. Submit your own poem for my collection!

<BR><IMG VSPACE=10 SRC="resources/dot_clear.gif"><BR>
I hope you'll come back for more space goodies soon!
<P>
Ciao,
<BR><IMG VSPACE=2 SRC="resources/dot_clear.gif"><BR>

<IMG SRC="./images/signature.gif" ALIGN=TOP WIDTH="213"
HEIGHT="38" BORDER="0">

</TD>
</TR>
</TABLE>
</BODY></HTML>
```

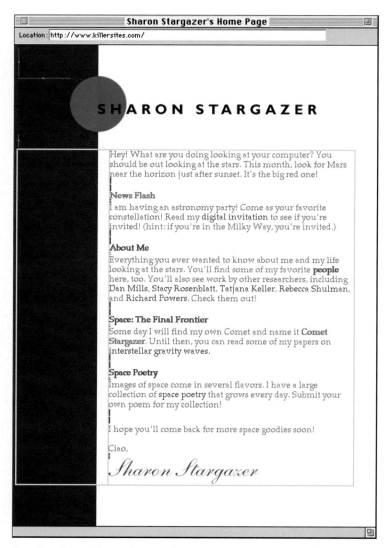

6.16 Now it's really coming together!

Sharon, alas, does not actually exist.

Pushing the Envelope

Now that I've built a page, I'm ready to make it better. I like the look I've established, but it's not very astronomical. I go to NASA's site for inspiration and find a familiar, impressive shot of the earth [**6.17**].

NASA's reproduction guidelines say I can use this image for Sharon's page (as a taxpayer, I've already paid for it). I want to substitute the earth for the red circle, and then make the blue band represent space with the help of a few stars.

Here's a tricky part: getting the earth separated from its background so I can anti-alias it properly. When "cutting" an image out of a photograph like this, I use the marquee tool rather than the magic wand. The magic wand rarely works well for this kind of operation, because there are usually too many subtle and irregular color gradations in a photograph.

I feather the circular selection by one pixel [**6.18**], cut, paste into a new

6.17 Many copyright-free images are available at US Government sites like NASA. But make sure you read their guidelines first.

file, and reduce the earth to the size of the red circle: 80 pixels square [**6.19**].

I bring the earth into my master (RGB) Photoshop document. The red circle on its own layer tells me where to position the earth on a new layer. I hide the red circle, save the file, and re-index the image. Because I feathered the earth image, it will automatically pick up the dark blue anti-aliasing on the left and the white anti-aliasing on the right [**6.20**]. Bring the type back, and – whoops! [**6.21**]

Now the type doesn't work. It needs a new color. Here's a neat trick: I make a new layer by dragging the current layer onto the "new layer" icon, which duplicates the layer quickly. In this new layer, I select the image only. Then I choose a nice ochre from the color cube *(conveniently stored in my color picker; see "The Color Cube" in Chapter 3 for details)* and fill the selection. The type changes color. I turn off the black layer and look at it [**6.22**].

Can you see the problem? There isn't enough contrast with the background. I tried some other colors, but the real solution is to add a drop shadow to set the name off from the background. When I do a drop shadow on type, I often cast the shadow down and to the left, because that makes the leading edges, stems and feet of the characters stand out strongly against the shadows [**6.23**].

With the earth and type looking good, I flatten the layers and cut and paste it into a new file. Unlike the red circle I did earlier, this time I can't safely pick white as my transparent color when exporting the GIF. Why? Chances are, at least a few pixels in the

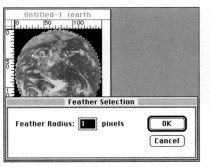

6.18 Feather selection for a soft edge.

6.19 Replacement for the circle.

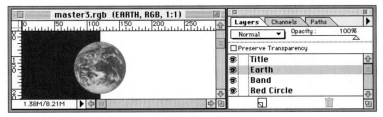

6.20 The earth goes on its own layer.

6.21 The type is placed over the earth.

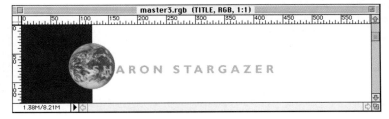

6.22 The ochre text is better than bold, but...

6.23 A drop shadow helps make the text more legible.

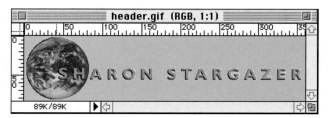

6.24 Bright green is the chroma-key color for this image. Note the halos around the earth and type.

6.25 The top image in final form.

clouds will be white – like the background – especially after I reduce the number of colors in the image to lengthen the runs and improve compression *(see "Reducing File Size" in Chapter 3)*. If I designate white as the color to make transparent, the clouds could get "holes" in them. Instead, I have to choose a chroma-key color that will become transparent. A chroma-key color is one that doesn't occur anywhere in the image *(see "The GIF Format" in Chapter 3)*. I use the magic wand (tolerance=0, anti-aliasing off) to select both the blue and white background areas and replace them with bright green **[6.24]**. This is the chroma-key color. If there are no free spots left in the palette for a chroma-key, it's unfortunate – you have to add one, making your palette a little larger.

I make the GIF as always, choosing green rather than white as the transparent color, save the image again, reload in the browser window, and voilà – the green is gone, and the earth shines brightly **[6.25]**.

The Finishing Touch

To complete the original idea, I make a star pattern in the blue background area. This turns out to be pretty difficult. Stars aren't white. They're all different colors. If the pattern of stars is too regular, or if your background strip is too short, repetition will be obvious. Too tall and it will take a long time to load. Getting a reasonable pattern only 25 pixels high is easier if you have the right tool for the job.

With tiling backgrounds, you must watch the edges closely to get a smooth

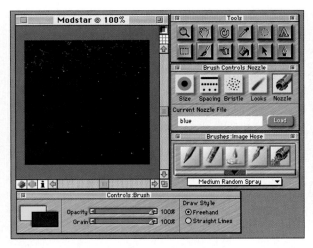

6.26 Painter's tiling and Image Hose features lay the ground for my star field. It's a powerful tool: don't get carried away!

6.28 The earth moved! Different browsers currently have different offsets: This is the same page viewed with Internet Explorer 2.0.

6.27 The final page, ready to go – almost.

Anti-Aliased Layers

To select everything on a layer in Photoshop while preserving transparency and anti-aliased edges, simply select all, then *wiggle* the arrow keys back and forth (one pixel left, one pixel right). This will select everything, ready to fill.

Caution: On the Mac, Command-Option-T doesn't do the same thing! It leaves the anti-aliasing behind. Use the "wiggle method" instead.

A different but equally good Mac method is to click the Preserve Transparency box, then simply Option-delete the entire layer to fill. See which method you prefer.

Deadly Sin Number Two

Horizontal Rules

Horizontal rules are a weak substitute for proper hierarchy and organization of vertical space on web pages.

There are millions of horizontal rules on the Web, doing nothing but taking up space and breaking the natural flow of pages. Horizontal rules are not spacers; they are barriers.

The only time they are useful is in very crowded newspaper front pages, where space is so tight that the proper amount of white space is too "expensive." Newspapers need to resort to these kinds of compromises; web pages don't.

transition. Fortunately, Fractal Design Painter has a tiling feature that helps do it automatically. Using the "image hose," loaded with little stars and with tiling turned on, I get a good start on the star field [6.26].

Painter does most of the work; making it perfect takes some manual editing. Of course, now that I've done it, you can just take mine right off the book site and use or modify it rather than start from scratch.

Look at the final page and compare it to the original gray site [6.27]. *(You can probably tell from the fact that the chapter doesn't end here that the story isn't over.)*

Background Registration

Now for the fun part: a cross-platform browser check [6.28].

This is a big disappointment. All of my careful image placement and background correction turn to garbage unless I can register the background and foreground images precisely, at least in the horizontal direction. Most browsers currently have different offsets, both horizontally and vertically *(see "Offsets" in Chapter 4)*. That completely trashes my work. There are two solutions:

1. Don't anti-alias foreground images that appear over major color transitions.

Because of browser offsets, you really can't put an anti-aliased image over a background that has two or more prominent areas of color. If you put the earth entirely over the dark blue star pattern, or make the star pattern wider, you can get away with anti-

6.29 Sharon might like this, but it's not for me.

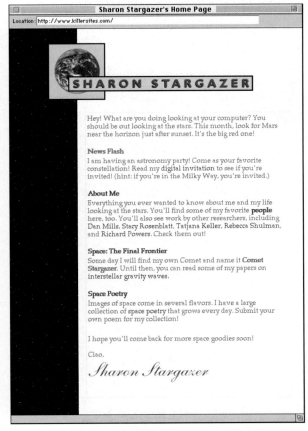

6.30 No anti-aliasing means no offset problems.

aliasing only to the dark blue color, because the stars are too small to cause noticeable anti-aliasing problems. In fact, Sharon herself might be quite pleased with this version **[6.29]**.

Personally, I resist these kinds of pages, unless they are mostly thematic and don't have much text. Yes, it looks "cool," but it is hard to read. The only reason it works at all is that the dark blue dominates, the bright pixels are few, and the vertical hierarchy pulls its weight. If you don't have much text on your home page, this could be your solution. I prefer dark text on a light background.

My solution is to make the top banner into an image that doesn't anti-alias **[6.30]** *(See "Anti-Aliasing" in Chapter 3 for details)*.

This banner can move all over the place and it won't matter. As long as the width of the empty margin cell is enough to compensate for all browser offsets, it will be fine.

Notice I have resisted the urge to make a big fat rectangle and fill it. Big rectangular banners are an easy way to make sites, but not to engage your audience. After some trial and error with the color cube, I find some colors that work together. The bordered

117

6.31 A, B Internet Explorer was the first browser to give us zero offsets. Here is the final page, with transparent GIFs and borders visible (LEFT), and as seen through Internet Explorer (RIGHT).

banner approach is a success. It's not as nice as the original, but it works.

ternet Explorer, the page finally renders as it should **[6.31 A, B]**.

2. Set offsets to zero for third- and fourth-generation browsers and wait for people to get them.

Internet Explorer 2.0 gives me the ability to set the offsets to zero. Netscape Navigator 3.0 does not. Internet Explorer 2.0 can read two important tags: LEFTMARGIN and TOPMARGIN, which I set to zero immediately, rearranging some of the HTML. Viewed through In-

```
<BODY LEFTMARGIN="0"
TOPMARGIN="0" BGCOLOR="#FFFFFF"
TEXT="#666666" LINK="#CC0000"
ALINK="#FF3300" VLINK="#330099"
BACKGROUND="images/spine.gif">
```

I'd like to design every page I make with no offsets (true typographic margins are not the same as browser-window offsets), but Netscape won't let me. Because of this, I must throw in the towel and use a solution that doesn't rely on perfect registration between background and foreground.

Netscape Navigator 4 should have many new features for layout control; I expect setting offsets to zero will be among them.

The lesson: If a foreground image has any anti-aliasing on the edges, it must register perfectly unless the background is a solid color. Images that don't have anti-aliasing don't need registration. Background registration is practically impossible until more surfers can see zero offsets.

Summary

Believe it or not, this entire page weighs less than 13K. This is not a full site, but it *is* a third-generation home page. Notice how little HTML there is. Most of the work is in Photoshop, struggling with anti-aliasing and transparency issues. The page is easy to update and keep alive, the graphics look great, and surfers will love it.

To aid navigation throughout, add a small version of the earth to all the pages of the site and link it back to the front page.

Application

It is a good idea to add current content to a page like this. To keep going, I might put "the astronomy site of the week" or the "astronomy fact of the week" at the top of the page, to draw people to the site regularly. If enough people come to this page to see the current information, undoubtedly many will also cruise the rest of the site. Any other urgent news items should go right at the top of the page, below the title.

If I really wanted to impress people, I'd make an animated GIF of the world spinning behind Sharon's name *(see "The GIF Format" in Chapter 3)*. Then I could use a downscaled version around the site as a navigation device. If they click on the little spinning globe, they will go back to the front page.

To go *all* the way, I'd include an animated background GIF on the front page that very subtly makes the stars twinkle. There's only one problem with that plan: At the time I write this, no browser can see animated background GIFs. Maybe, for the sake of surfers in general, it's just as well.

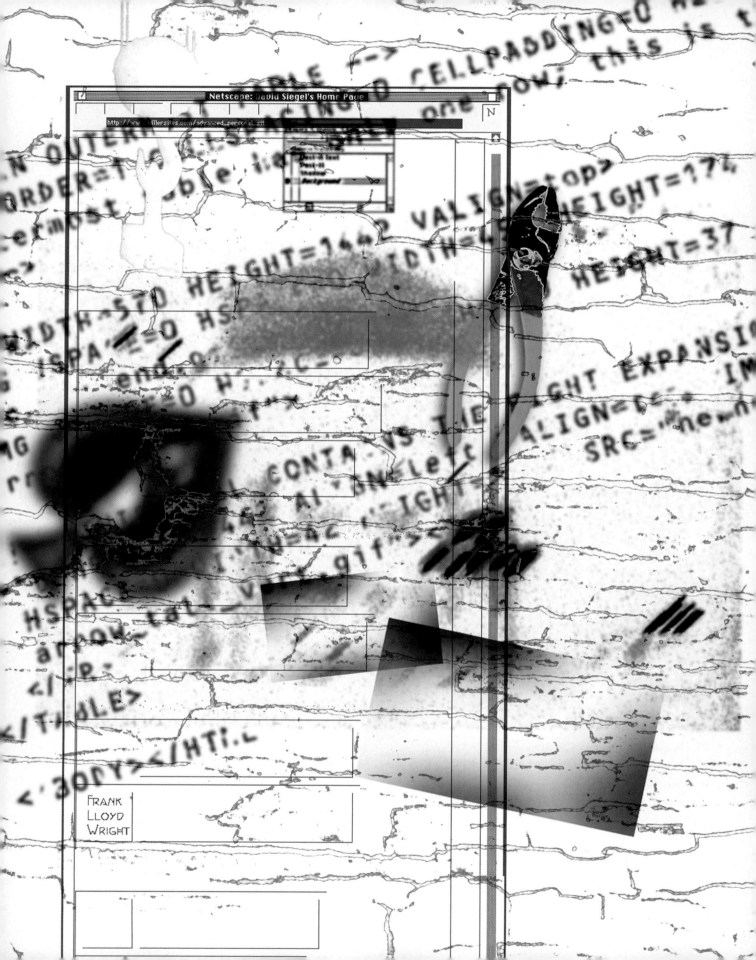

Netscape: David Siegel's Home Page

http://www.killersites.com/advanced_personal_sit...

FRANK
LLOYD
WRIGHT

How to split

Nesting tabl

Creating a si

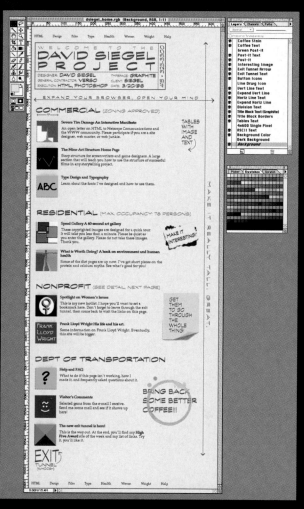

7.1 Make your mistakes in Photoshop, not HTML. Creating a layer for each element keeps things flexible.

THIS CHAPTER explains how I made the core page of my personal site and added a nice entrance. I have always had a strong interest in architecture, and I've designed a number of type-faces based on the distinctive hand-writing of architects. I wanted a blue-print metaphor – to give the feeling of looking at a plan for my site.

The plan has the title block on top, telling visitors what's going on as soon as the page starts to load. There are four main sections: professional, personal, non-profit, and various pages about my site (leading to my list of links). Once a page has more than about six choices, use a hierarchical grouping to prevent showing a long vertical list of equally weighted links. I use the opportunity to bring out the metaphor by labeling these sections with catchy phrases and dropping a surprise graphic into each area. Break-ing the page into areas this way makes scrolling an adventure.

Strategy

The page should play more with the "sheet of paper" metaphor as the visi-tor scrolls down. The two intersecting arrows that span the height and width of the page reinforce a sense of space and boundedness – just like paper. They illustrate the main trick of this chapter: splitting the arrows into two separate GIFs and mortising them back together with a table.

I could make a huge background image with these arrows, but a back-ground GIF with the blue elements would inflate too much for many surfers' systems *(see "The GIF Format" in Chapter 5).* I also wanted a set of text links to appear at the top of the page, for those who have been there before and want to go right to a particular page.

Photoshop

At my studio, we prototype everything in Photoshop, so we can make all the design decisions before any HTML work begins. Each item always goes on its own layer – I use many more layers than elements, because several layers are experiments **[7.1]**. For example, I tried the "Make it really tall" graphic turned bottom-to-top (as an architect would do it), but I think it reads better top-to-bottom (as the page scrolls).

The Blueprint Metaphor

I want to use a light blue background – the color of a faded blueprint **[7.2]**. By changing the color of the background layer in Photoshop, I get a feel for how this will play on the Web (remember that colors tend to appear darker on PCs than on Macs).

Because the metaphor depends on it, I would like to use the light blue color, even though it's not in the color cube. What will visitors with 8-bit displays see? A quick test in Netscape and Internet Explorer with 256 colors shows they will see white. If they saw a dark cross-hatching pattern, that would be bad. I finally decide on `bgcolor="#EDEDFF"`.

I make the title block and all the hand lettering using my Graphite typeface, which is an Adobe Multiple-

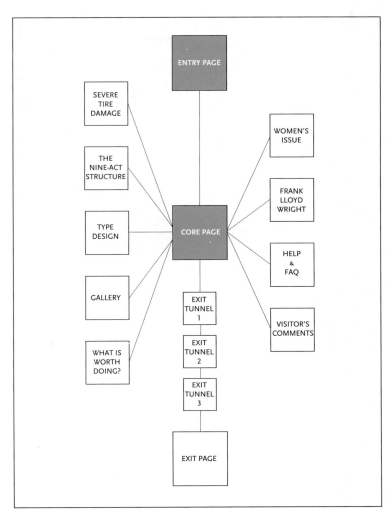

Simplified site plan.

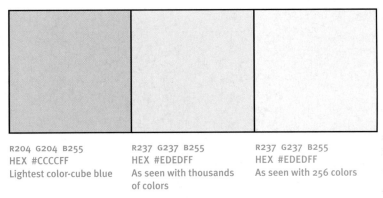

R204 G204 B255
HEX #CCCCFF
Lightest color-cube blue

R237 G237 B255
HEX #EDEDFF
As seen with thousands of colors

R237 G237 B255
HEX #EDEDFF
As seen with 256 colors

7.2 Compare the colors: The lightest color-cube blue is too dark, while the non-color-cube blue performs acceptably on all systems.

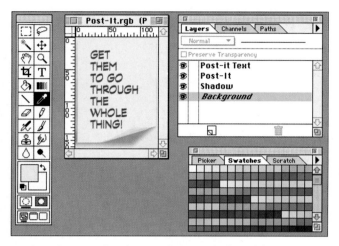

7.3 I use layers and paths to make a convincing sticky note.

7.5 Measure twice, cut once: With complicated table work, I like to tape a marked-up image to my monitor.

7.4 Scans great, with half the caffeine of doing it by hand.

Master typeface. With ATM's Font Creator, I make special wide and narrow versions of Graphite. For example, the section dividers are the real workhorses of the page, so I make them with an extra-bold, extra-wide version of Graphite. For the color, I choose a dark blue ("#000033") from the color cube. Who needs black text on every page? Because type is made of so much white space, light-colored text doesn't work very well – darker is better.

Special Effects

I make my own yellow sticky note in Photoshop, along with a realistic coffee stain. I use three layers to make the sticky note. The yellow layer with the type wasn't difficult, but the shadow was.

The best way to make a shadow like this is to use Photoshop's *paths* feature. Get your shadow path just right, then fill the path using a feather of four pixels. I keep adjusting the path shape until the real shadow appears [7.3].

The coffee stain was straightforward. I used a coffee cup to stain a piece of paper, scanned the paper (is this cheating?), and adjusted the color, transparency and contrast [7.4].

Finally, I make the buttons for each section, pointing to the branches of my site. I decide on a 74 × 74-pixel square, with a one-pixel bevel that raises them just off the page. (One pixel of beveling is about all I can stand – knee-jerk beveling has reached epidemic proportions on the Web.) Bevels are essentially a shadow effect. I want the shadows to go down and to the left also. Note that the one-pixel bevel edges of the buttons are lightened and darkened, rather than painted over, for a good shading effect [7.8 c].

Reduce Colors, Lengthen Runs

I'm ready to make the elements that will compose the page. The first thing I do is print out the Photoshop page and draw boxes on it with a ruler to decide where the table cells will be [7.5]. I have split the horizontal arrow, so the cross-over point is part of the vertical arrow image.

Now that I know the individual images needed, I make the GIFs in two passes. I can index all the images made out of blue and white together, for a consistent look. Then I can go back and index the others. First, I hide all the layers containing any colors other than blue [7.6]. I flatten this entire page and use adaptive color reduction with no dithering.

Remember that anti-aliasing one solid color to another takes only four or five intermediate colors *(see "Anti-Aliasing" in Chapter 3)*. I reduce this image to a 3-bit palette (8 colors) — white, blue, and six intermediates [7.7 A]. That's plenty. I export the GIFs without interlacing, because in this situation it's not worth the (admittedly small) price [7.7 B]. Why didn't I reduce to a custom palette – the Netscape 216? Because the dark blue color already comes from the color cube, but I don't want to restrict the intermediate colors to the color cube *(see "Dither on the Client" in Chapter 5)*. I want the intermediate colors to look best on systems with more than 256 colors.

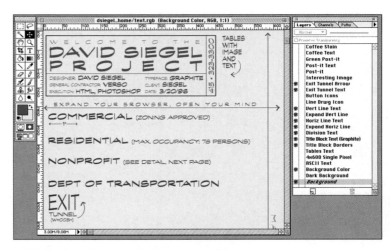

7.6 Anti-alias all same-color images together.

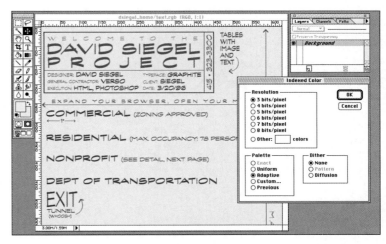

7.7 A Three bits is all you need for anti-aliased type with a solid background *(see "Anti-Aliasing" in Chapter 3)*.

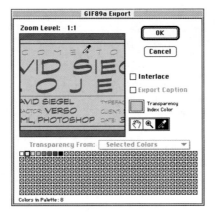

7.7 B When exporting, I designate the light blue background to be the transparent color.

7.8 A, B, C Start with a small number of colors and work up when indexing to an adaptive color palette.

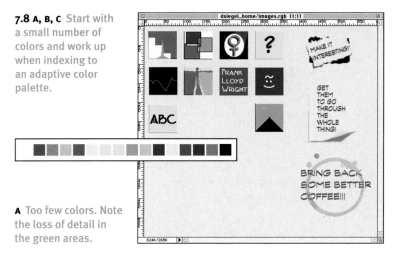

A Too few colors. Note the loss of detail in the green areas.

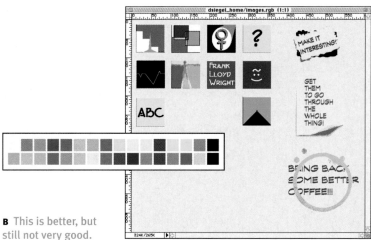

B This is better, but still not very good.

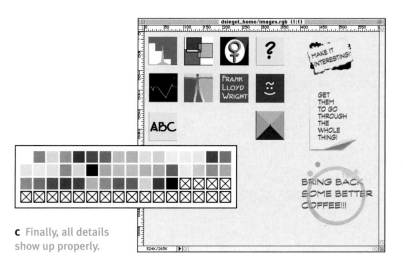

C Finally, all details show up properly.

They end up as 8-color (3-bit) GIFs.

Now for the rest of the images. I can index these images together or separately, but doing them together is faster and really doesn't hurt. Remember, palettes are small things; compressibility is what counts. I hide all the blue-type layers and reveal the rest [**7.8 A, B, C**]. The same adaptive-palette approach works here, but I'll need more colors. As always, I start with a low number (16 is good) and work up to find the lowest acceptable number (44 colors). The fewer the colors, the longer the runs, the more compressible the images will be.

In the sticky note, there are some jaggies along the yellow-gray border. I want the shadow to look good, but I don't want to add more colors. I'll occasionally settle for a few jaggies if I can't get a file small enough [**7.9 A, B, C**].

HTML

I've already sketched the tables by hand; now all I have to do is create them in HTML. This kind of work is easy if you take a systematic approach, commenting your code carefully so you don't get lost, making sure everything works as you take each step.

Nested Tables

I take an "outside in" approach to constructing nested tables. Once I get the outer table set up, the rest of the job looks easier [**7.10, 7.11**].

Getting the arrow to line up perfectly isn't very difficult, because I cut the image up and now I'm just putting it back together. Note the ALIGN=left

7.9 A, B, C Experiment with various bit depths to find one that's just right.

The Zen of Drop Shadows

Drop shadows are generally misunderstood and overused. They are helpful for lifting things slightly off the page, as in the sticky note above, but their enduring place in the designer's palette is as a means of enhancing edges. Dark type on a light background generally needs no such enhancement.

Drop shadows help distinguish foreground from background when there's not much contrast between them. Most drop shadows fall down and to the right, including those of the Mac and Windows operating systems. With type in particular, however, the left side of a character is more important, because the eye seeks these leading edges as it scans a line from left to right.

For this reason, I often drop shadows down and to the left. Each situation has a best solution – have a good reason for your choice. And once you choose, be consistent!

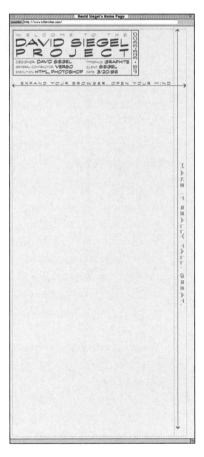

7.10 Start a complicated page by nailing its outside tables into place *(see HTML on the following page).*

127

7.11 Comments will help keep the code organized as the page expands. Always use HEIGHT and WIDTH tags for your images.

```
<!-- PAGE PARAMETERS -->
<HTML><HEAD><TITLE>David Siegel's Home Page</TITLE></HEAD>
<BODY BGCOLOR="#EDEDFF" TEXT="#000055" LINK="#CC0000"
ALINK="#FF3300" VLINK="#005522">

<!-- BEGIN OUTERMOST TABLE -->
<TABLE BORDER=1 CELLSPACING=0 CELLPADDING=0 HEIGHT=1442>
<!-- Outermost table has only one row; this is the left
  side -->
  <TR>
  <TD WIDTH=570 HEIGHT=1442 VALIGN=top>
  <IMG VSPACE=0 HSPACE=0 WIDTH=455 HEIGHT=174 SRC="newhome/
    back_legend.gif">
  <IMG VSPACE=0 HSPACE=0 WIDTH=570 HEIGHT=37 SRC="newhome/
    arrow_horiz.gif">

  <!-- THIS CELL CONTAINS THE RIGHT EXPANSION ARROW -->
  <TD ALIGN=left VALIGN=top><IMG VSPACE=0
    HSPACE=0 WIDTH=42 HEIGHT=1418 SRC="newhome/
    arrow_tall_vert.gif"></TD>
  </TR>
</TABLE>

</BODY></HTML>
```

for the tall arrow. That mortices the two images. Without it, there would be a crack, giving away my trick.

The Inner Tables

As the page takes shape, I plug in the cell contents one at a time. Once I splice the arrows back together, I can see the light at the end of the table. Right after that comes the "Commercial Section" image. For the body of each section, I make several two-cell tables for each featured area of the site [7.12].

I plug these in, repeat for the other sections, and the page takes shape [7.13].

I add the four right-margin elements at the ends of my inner tables. The modular table approach lets me adjust each right margin to fit its image individually. These little tables make it easy to copy and paste as individual units when I want to add new items to my page *(you can view the source HTML at the Book Site)* [7.14].

That's all there is to it. I add some text links at top and bottom, and I'm ready for visitors.

This page is not as flexible as I'd like, of course. As I add new features, the right-hand vertical arrow must be remade (In fact, I have lengthened that darn arrow seven or eight times now). The page looks great, and people keep coming, so it must be worth the trouble.

Finally, the text links at top and bottom are separated by single-pixel GIFs to achieve horizontal white space. Notice I do not use vertical separator bars! They are as bad as horizontal rules. In the past, these separators had a function. They separated entries like this when displayed on a search engine. If a search engine picks up my page and displays the top line or two, the entry will be something like "HTML DESIGN FILM TYPE HEALTH WOMEN WRIGHT HELP". If I use vertical separators, it will be "HTML | DESIGN | FILM | TYPE | HEALTH | WOMEN | WRIGHT | HELP".

I admit the second one is better, but there's a way around the problem. In the next chapter, I'll show how to add special code to your page that only the search engines can see. You can put whatever you want there without affecting the design of the page.

A Business-Card Welcome

The main page is a good anchor, but it's pretty big for a destination URL. I'd like to put out a welcome mat to give people a feel for what they are about to encounter. My personal site has a complex entryway, but for this chapter I'll suggest a simple, elegant approach that can work for any personal site: a business card, scanned (or made from scratch in Photoshop), all by itself on a page [**7.15**]. Click the card to enter.

The exit from my site, linked from the bottom of the core page, leads surfers back into the currents of the Web with a list of links. (Chapter 11 discusses the particulars of my exit tunnel.)

Summary

This entire page weighs under 60K. I know it must be worth the wait, since

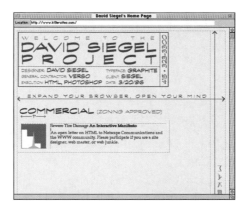

7.12 This basic unit of code plugs into the page's main table.

7.13 Note the use of CELLPADDING and the single-pixel GIF to control white space.

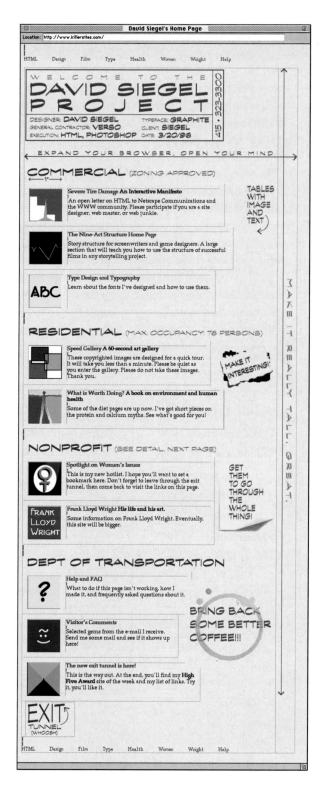

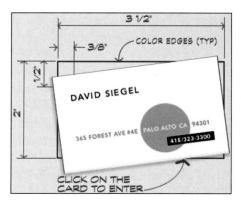

7.15 A nicely designed business card can make a good entry to your site.

I get so much positive mail from people who see it. The blueprint metaphor takes you out of the Web and into a different, yet familiar world. I achieved it by splitting images and locking them into tables. The page loads quickly yet feels expansive. Splitting images can help get around the limitations of tables when mixing text and image.

Notice I don't have a "NEWS" section. Because the table takes some seconds to load, I usually put in some items of interest right at the top of the page, so people have something to read as it loads. Although I haven't shown it, this is an effective way to tell people what's new while they are waiting and you have their attention. As the saying goes: "Content is king!"

7.14 Now that I'm pleased with the way the site looks, I can turn off my borders and upload the files to my server.

Application

One of Matthew Butterick's designs for his on-line 'zine, *Dex,* is a great application of the main technique explained in this chapter: how to cut a large image up to make a killer home page [7.16]. Matthew gives the scrolling visitor a visual treat by creating the illusion of a seamless display of playing cards. Visit the site and you'll see how effective it is.

7.16 Table borders turned on: *Dex* magic secrets – revealed at last!

Deadly Sin
Number Three

Background Images That Interfere

Backgrounds on the Web have reached epidemic proportions. Wallpaper is nice, but reading the handwriting on the wall can cause damage to the retina.

People use background images because they add a "theme" to the page, or because they "fill up all that unused space." It's the kitchen-sink school of page design, which often escalates to homicidal (not killer) site design. Backgrounds do more damage to web pages than almost anything else.

Thoughtless designers get carried away, the pixels fly, and surfers get hurt. The only good background is a solid or nearly solid color: gift-wrap makes bad stationery.

## CHAPTER 8

A Storefront

What you'll learn in this chapter:

Making templates

Client-side image maps

GIF versus JPEG

Frames

Influencing a histogram

Forms

8.1 Familiar materials, endless possibilities.

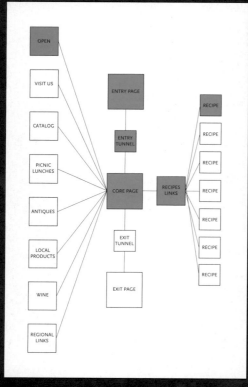

Site Diagram

JIMTOWN STORE is a mom-and-pop country store in California's scenic Alexander Valley. Great food, local products, wine-country color, and an interesting history make it a cultural and epicurean landmark. The Web offers Jimtown Store a way to position itself squarely on the itinerary of visitors to Sonoma County, and a chance to build a mailing list for its growing catalog business. It gives the owners, John Werner and Carrie Brown, a way to get going on the Web, gauge demand, and spread awareness among out-of-towners.

In addition to illustrating the development of a third-generation site, this chapter also shows how I work with clients (in this chapter, the word "client" refers to the store owners, not the browser). After my first meeting with John and Carrie, I take away a pile of photos, brochures, napkin scribbles, and ideas.

Strategy

Jimtown Store has already built a strong visual identity in its landmark gas station storefront and homemade look, extending to its products, packaging, and print materials. I'll bring these assets to the Web, using scanned photographs, brochures, and maps as starting points. This strategy is appropriate and within reach of most small businesses, most of which have a sizeable investment in paper brochures and flyers **[8.1]**.

Modem-Friendly Design

Optimizing printed material for use on

8.2 The Jimtown color palette.

8.3 The painting captures the homey charm of Jimtown better than any glossy photo.

the Web is challenging enough technically, but the more important challenge is conceptual – integrating the images into a cohesive metaphor. In second-generation site design, images are often merely decorative, or at best, illustrative. In third-generation design, images become structural elements of a site. Because these images are so important, I have to make sure they don't tax visitors' systems too much. I will spend a lot of time making a few key images look great, rather than including too many.

I will also use Netscape's frames feature to make an expandable page of recipes. Though I rarely use frames – mostly because they are ugly and make navigation too complicated – they can be quite helpful if you expect to make

a large, growing database of something, like products or recipes.

Jimtown Store's single most distinctive asset is the store itself, painted in sunny yellow with green trim. These colors occur throughout Jimtown's print materials and are a natural choice for the site's color palette. The red and blue of the store's interior make nice accents **[8.2]**.

The Metaphor

My first idea for an entrance tunnel was to have a place where all the Jims on the Web could register and form a kind of "Jim Club." It would have been good for the Jims, but not for business. Instead I decide to make something that places Jimtown on the map.

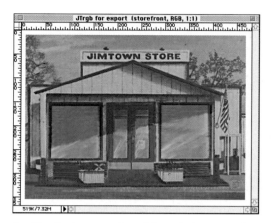

8.4 The final RGB version of the painting. Note the enlarged entry area.

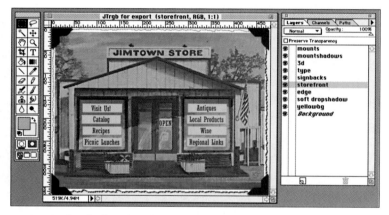

8.5 I make the signboards using rectangles and adding shadows.

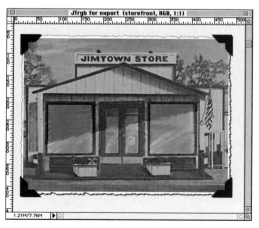

8.6 The edge and photo mounts call for a light background like yellow.

I play with a lot of metaphors by doodling on paper. Then I notice the old-fashioned deckle-edge cards inset with photo mounts in their brochure, and that gives me an idea: simply present the store through a series of postcards – some of maps, others of the store. The postcard size and ratio of 4:3 happen to work well for browser windows.

Phase 1: Photoshop

This site will need a lot of work in Photoshop. I must make three postcards that look great together and download quickly. The photos and cards I'm given are less than ideal – especially the existing colors, which I must map to the color cube, emphasizing the Jimtown palette.

Building the Anchor Image

Several of the store images were photographic, but one was a folk-art painting on a board [8.3]. I chose the painting over the photographs because I had to change it significantly to make it work in the postcard format, and it's a lot easier to edit a painting than a photograph. Substantially changing photographs is just too hard.

The store windows actually have hanging yellow signboards, which the owners move around to emphasize various specials and delicacies. This gives me an idea for a navigation scheme: I'll make clickable signs in the windows.

After extended surgery in Photoshop – enlarging the entryway, doors, and windows to make room for the signs, towing the truck and replacing

136

it with porch material, and generally touching up – the store is ready for business [8.4].

In the windows, I draw simple rectangular signboards and fill them with a yellow from the color cube. I set the text in a typeface called Rockwell Condensed, using a red from the Jimtown palette [8.5].

I trim the storefront image in a 4:3 ratio to approximately 470 pixels horizontally, so that with a few pixels of border treatment it will fit snugly in a browser's default window width. This will be my postcard size. On a new layer in Photoshop, I draw a deckle edge by hand and reproduce it for the other three sides. This looks a bit flat, so on new layers I make a drop shadow for the card and some old-fashioned photo mounts in the dark blue accent color I picked out earlier. While I'm thinking color, I pour the Jimtown palette's yellow into the background [8.6].

When rendering type, I stick with color-cube colors for both back- and foreground colors *(see "Dither on the Client" in Chapter 5)*.

Reducing the File Size

The painterly gradations of this image will surely suffer in translation to the color cube. This makes for a good image-compression exercise. If I can't find an acceptable balance between image size and quality, I might have to go back to the drawing board for this image, and possibly for the metaphor as well. That's why I carry this image to completion before working on the rest of the site.

When indexing images and export-

FREE SPEECH ONLINE

BLUE RIBBON CAMPAIGN

Deadly Sin Number Four

The Slow Load

Conversations among friends can survive long silent pauses, but few Web pages can afford to take long to load.

A good rule of thumb is that most pages in a site should be under 30K, a few can be 30-50K, and perhaps one or two can weigh in at 70K. Pages larger than that should either belong to 800-pound gorillas or be put on a diet.

If you want to force your visitors to go out to lunch while your page loads, fill it full of 8-bit dithered GIFs in the foreground, and don't forget an enormous high-quality JPEG in the background.

Spread out heavier loads by reusing elements cleverly; once loaded, they are cached and therefore load again almost instantly.

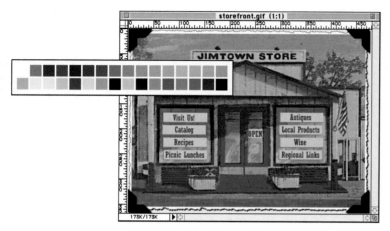

8.7 Without dithering, this image looks patchy.

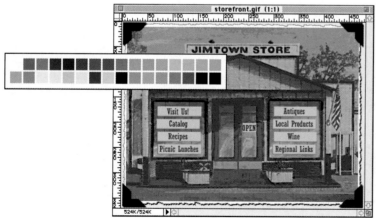

8.8 A, B Photoshop uses any area selected before indexing to build the histogram (ABOVE), thus influencing the resulting palette and image (BELOW).

ing GIFs, I always save a backup copy of the file to protect me from myself. You can't imagine how much time I have lost after inadvertently overwriting my layered RGB Photoshop files with indexed images. (I have a theory that when you die and go to heaven, the workstation they give you has all the files you ever lost on its hard disk.)

I index the image to a 5-bit adaptive palette with no dithering and export a GIF as a trial **[8.7]**.

Two problems: The image quality is poor, and the file is a fat 50K. With this few colors, dithering would improve the quality, but it would also shorten the runs. A larger palette would do the same. Both dithering and larger palettes make files less compressible as GIFs. What I need is a *better* palette — one that will cause less important areas like the sky to clump into even longer runs but will preserve the look of more important areas like the storefront. I can get it by *influencing the histogram (see "Reducing File Size" in Chapter 3)*.

To influence the histogram, I revert to RGB mode and Shift-select the areas heavy in the key colors: yellow and green, red and dark blue. I select the deckle edge and image mounts, too, because it's important that they have accurate color. I re-index (5-bit, adaptive, no dither) and export as another GIF **[8.8 A, B]**.

Rats. This has shaved only 4K from the first attempt, and the image quality is only marginally better. The image isn't compressing very well because the runs are still too short. Further palette reduction (to, say, 25 colors) will ruin its painterly quality.

Images like this are good candidates

for the JPEG compression scheme. I revert to my last-saved RGB copy and save
as a JPEG image, choosing low image
quality (high compression) **[8.9]**.

This yields a more dramatic savings
over GIF: The image is now 33K. Most
of the image looks great – far better
than the GIF versions. The only downside is that the type has become blurry
and looks bad. Hard edges and type are
the first casualties of JPEG compression
(see "The JPEG Format" in Chapter 3).

Which image to use? It's a judgment call, but I'm leaning toward the
JPEG, because the 33K file size is awful-
ly appealing. If the blurriness of the
type is objectionable to the client, I can
probably save again with improved
quality (sacrificing some compression)
and still come out better overall than
the 46K GIF. It would be nice to combine the best of both methods, but
there really is no way to do that without
z-axis layering *(see "Tomorrow's Web
Sites" in Chapter 14)*. Now that I am
confident this core image will work,
I'll turn to the postcard images for the
entryway.

Where Is Jimtown?

The entryway is a simple sequence of
two postcard-maps that places the store
geographically, builds anticipation, and
brands the Jimtown name, logo, and
location on the way in. If nothing else,
surfers will remember the name and
location of Jimtown after visiting this
site **[8.10]**.

Making the US Map

I return to my master Photoshop docu-

8.9 A low-quality JPEG yields substantial file size reduction.

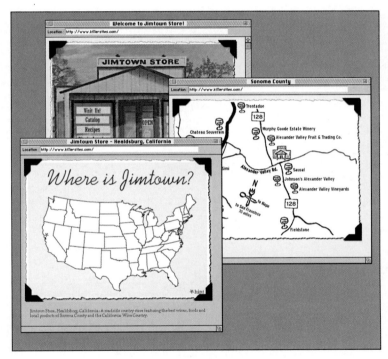

8.10 Image map links will take people from each hot spot to the next postcard.

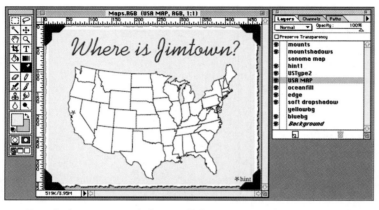

8.11 Note the layers I use to help myself choose among alternate possibilities.

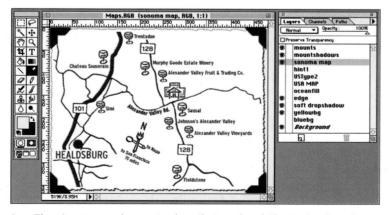

8.12 A good splash screen must weigh in under 25K. At 19K, this image is a keeper.

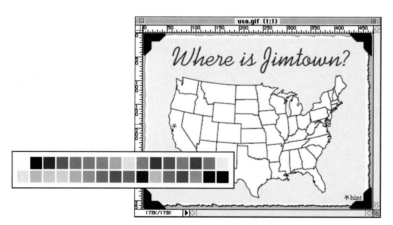

8.13 There's not enough room to show Jimtown in relation to San Francisco.

ment and hide all layers except the postcard edge treatment, the photo mounts, and the page background. I find a stock EPS image of the US and paste it into a new layer as pixels from Illustrator. I duplicate this on yet another layer, erase the state lines, and fill the country outline with white. This makes a backing for the map on a separate layer, which lets me select and color the state lines freely. I tint the lines with the blue used in the image mounts **[8.11]**.

The type is Kaufmann Script, a popular face reminiscent of the hand-lettered signs in the store. I want to establish green-on-yellow as fore- and background colors for the type on the card. For the page background itself I choose a light color-cube blue, because yellow here wouldn't provide enough contrast with the mostly yellow card. Adding a big hint on the map in red spoils the "Where is Jimtown?" game but draws people into the site.

Indexed to a 5-bit adaptive palette with no dithering, this full-screen image reduces to a lean 19K **[8.12]**. With interlacing (worth a few extra kilobytes for large images like this), the page goes to 23K. An animated GIF with a little delay before the red hint comes on would be a nice touch, but it would make the page too large for an entry. Even cutting it into several areas would push it past 20K. Smaller is better. I leave it as is.

Making the Sonoma Map

The second map begins life as a photocopy of a brochure. I scan it, then reconstruct each element manually, redoing the type, introducing wine-glass icons from yet another Jimtown brochure, and building a compass rose from fork and spoon. I make sure people are oriented by referring to San Francisco, because there's no room to show it on this map. The storefront logo, in red like the hint on the preceding page, foreshadows the next page and beckons them on through the entry tunnel [8.13]. This entire page comes in under 20K.

The Final Mock-Up

Now that these three images are working, it's time to flesh out the core page. I modify some copy from the Jimtown brochure and render a heading in green Kaufmann Script below the card area – all in Photoshop. This serves as a model for the section headers. I lift a mailbox from a photo of the storefront and place it, free-floating, at the foot of the page [8.14].

To prepare all this for my client meeting, I even use aliased type and mock up the browser window in Photoshop, making all three full pages look like I made them in HTML. Because several layers still have some elements I decided not to use, I can show John the process by which I made my decisions.

Phase 2: HTML

Because tables can be difficult to work with, it pays to set up one good template that reflects a grid structure appropriate to all or many of the pages you're creating. This way, once you've made a few pages, you've made the

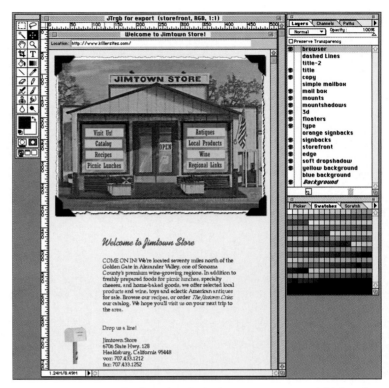

8.14 Mocking up sites in Photoshop is the best way to present initial work to a client.

rest. Careful planning, consistency, and clean execution will save the day – maybe even a few.

The postcards are 480 pixels wide, so this will be the absolute width of my layout. I divide 480 into 9 parts: 2 units for a left margin, 6 for a central text area, and 1 for a right margin. This translates to table columns of 107, 320, and 53 pixels, respectively. This division of a 9-unit grid is one of the formulas advocated by the great typographer Jan Tschichold, though he had books with facing pages in mind. Keeping the left and center columns in absolute pixel measurements is integral to the structure of the page. The right column really isn't there, because

141

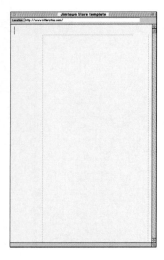

```
<HTML>
<HEAD>
<TITLE>Jimtown Store template</TITLE>
</HEAD>

<!-- Page Parameters -->
<BODY BGCOLOR="#FFFFCC" TEXT="#003300" LINK="#990000"
 VLINK="#000033" ALINK="#FFFFCC">

<!-- Vertical Spacer -->
<IMG HEIGHT=24 WIDTH=1 SRC="../resources/dot_clear.gif">

<!-- Begin Table -->
<TABLE WIDTH=480 BORDER=0 CELLPADDING=0 CELLSPACING=0>

  <TR>

  <!-- Left blank cell -->
  <TD WIDTH=107><IMG HSPACE=53 resources/
   dot_clear.gif></TD>

  <!-- Begin cell with images and text -->
  <TD WIDTH=320></TD>
  <!-- End cell with images and text -->

  <!-- Right Blank Cell -->
  <TD WIDTH=53><IMG HSPACE=26 resources/
   dot_clear.gif></TD>
  </TR>
</TABLE>
<!-- End Table -->
<BR>

<!-- Vertical Spacer -->
<IMG HEIGHT=48 WIDTH=1 SRC="../resources/dot_clear.gif">

</BODY>
</HTML>
```

8.15 A, B The basic HTML template for the Jimtown site (ABOVE), and as it appears in the browser window (TOP LEFT).

there's no convenient way to tell a browser window how wide to open *(see "Horizontal White Space" in Chapter 4)*. I add it anyway – it will put a scroll bar at the bottom of the window of anyone seeing my pages in too narrow a window for pleasurable reading.

The Template

The HTML for this table is straightforward. Set simply in a page, it becomes the basic template for this site **[8.15]**.

All my table measurements are absolute (pixels, rather than percentages). I want the text to have a fixed relationship to the images; both are part of the composition.

The header of the template reflects the Jimtown palette:

```
<BODY BGCOLOR="#FFFFCC"
TEXT="#003300" LINK="#990000"
VLINK="#000033"
ALINK="#FFFFCC">
```

The text is dark green, the links are dark red, and visited links are the same dark blue as the photo mounts. Red is always a good link color, and visited links should be discernible but not jump off the page the way unvisited links should. The active link color is the yellow of the background – it provides visual feedback without introducing another color.

The Core Page

I begin with the core page, because this will have the most complex layout and navigation features **[8.16]**.

The template table was built around the width of the postcard – 480 pixels

8.16 The core page.

```
<HTML>
<HEAD><TITLE>Welcome to Jimtown Store!</TITLE></HEAD>

<!--Page Parameters-->
<BODY BGCOLOR="#FFFFCC" TEXT="#003300" LINK="#990000" VLINK="#000033"
 ALINK="#FFFFCC">

<IMG SRC="storefront.jpg" ALT="Image of Jimtown Store, with links to other
 points in the site" WIDTH="480" HEIGHT="368" BORDER="0">
<BR>

<!--Spacer-->
<IMG HEIGHT=24 WIDTH=1 SRC="../resources/dot_clear.gif">

<!--Begin text table-->
<TABLE WIDTH=480 BORDER=1 CELLPADDING=0 CELLSPACING=0>

  <tr>
    <!--Blank Cell-->
    <TD WIDTH=107></TD>

    <!--Text Cell-->
    <TD WIDTH=320><IMG SRC="welcome.gif" ALT="Welcome to Jimtown Store!"
     WIDTH="320" HEIGHT="28" BORDER="0">
    <BR>
    <BR>
    <A HREF="open.html"><font size=-1>COME ON IN</font></A>! We're located
seventy miles north of the Golden Gate in Alexander Valley, one of Sonoma
County's premium wine-growing regions. In addition to freshly prepared foods
for <A HREF="picnic.html">picnic lunches</A>, specialty cheeses, and home-
baked goods, we offer selected <A HREF="local.html">local products</A> and
<A HREF="wine.html">wine</A>, toys and eclectic American
<A HREF="antiques.html">antiques</A> for sale. Browse our
<A HREF="recipes.html">recipes</A>, or order <A HREF="catalog.html">
<i>The Jimtown Crier</i></A>, our catalog. We hope you'll
<A HREF="visit.html">visit us</A> on your next trip to the
<A HREF="regional.html">area</A>.<BR><BR> </TD>

    <!--Blank Cell-->
    <TD WIDTH=53></TD>
  </tr>

  <tr>
    <!--Mailbox Image-->
    <TD WIDTH=107 VALIGN=TOP ALIGN=CENTER >
    <A HREF="mailto:jw@jimtown.com"><IMG SRC="mailbox.gif" ALT="mailbox
     icon" WIDTH="54" HEIGHT="87" BORDER="0"></A></TD>

    <TD WIDTH=320><A HREF="mailto:jw@jimtown.com">Drop us a line!</A>
    <BR><BR>
    Jimtown Store
    <BR>
```

```
    <FONT SIZE=-1>6706 State Hwy. 128<BR>
    Healdsburg, California 95448<BR>
    vox: 707.433.1212<BR>
    fax: 707.433.1252</FONT><BR></TD>

    <!--Blank Cell-->
    <TD WIDTH=53></TD>
  </TR>
</TABLE>
<!--End text table-->

<BR>
<IMG HEIGHT=24 WIDTH=1 SRC="../resources/dot_clear.gif">
</BODY>
</HTML>
```

8.17 The 2:6:1 ratio is embodied in the <TD> parameters of this table.

– so I don't need to build the card into the table. It sits in the upper left-hand corner of the page, and the 3-column table falls neatly below it [8.17].

Placing the mailbox is a matter of specifying a new row, centering the image in the margin cell, and aligning it to the top.

I want some space between the text and the company contact information. This is where most designers would add a horizontal rule, but with great effort I manage to resist the urge. Instead, I simply add some white space before beginning the next table row. There are many different ways to make vertical white space. Rather than using a single-pixel GIF, in this case I add two <BR> tags and an invisible character, , to the cell, which spaces down two lines both in Netscape and Internet Explorer.

I asked John and Carrie for a paragraph that has each of the nine areas of the site worked into it, so each key word becomes a text link to an inner page. This serves as a verbal introduc-

tion and a backup in case visitors don't get the clickable window signs, or their browsers don't yet support *client-side image maps*.

Building a Client-Side Image Map

This simple site does not need complicated navigation. The storefront serves as the central map. This image has nine hot zones, each a bit larger than the associated signs on the painting [8.18]. An image with clickable areas like this is called an image map.

A thorough discussion of image maps is beyond the scope of this book. The most important thing is to make *client-side image maps*. A client-side image map puts the so-called *map file* into the HTML of the page, so the visitor's browser (the client) knows which file to get as soon as the surfer clicks her mouse. In contrast, old-style *server-side image maps* depend on a trip to the server to make sense of the surfer's click. This makes them slow, and they can't be tested or demonstrated

145

```
<!-- image map -->
<IMG SRC="storefront.jpg" ALT="Image of Jimtown Store, with links to other
points in the site" WIDTH="480" HEIGHT="368" BORDER="0" USEMAP="#storemap"
ISMAP>

<!-- Begin client-side image map -->
<MAP NAME="storemap">
<AREA SHAPE=rect COORDS="298,241,384,262" HREF="regional.html">
<AREA SHAPE=rect COORDS="300,217,386,237" HREF="wine.html">
<AREA SHAPE=rect COORDS="298,192,385,211" HREF="local.html">
<AREA SHAPE=rect COORDS="300,167,386,187" HREF="antiques.html">
<AREA SHAPE=rect COORDS="181,156,278,292" HREF="open.html">
<AREA SHAPE=rect COORDS="71,242,157,263" HREF="picnic.html">
<AREA SHAPE=rect COORDS="70,217,157,238" HREF="recipes.html">
<AREA SHAPE=rect COORDS="69,193,154,213" HREF="catalog.html">
<AREA SHAPE=rect COORDS="70,168,157,188" HREF="visit.html">
</MAP>
<!--End client-side image map-->
```

8.19 The client-side image map is part of the core page.

8.18 Make your hot zones oversized to accommodate inaccurate pointing.

off-line. I build back-up links into the core page's text until all surfers can use client-side image maps.

In the HTML for the core page's image map **[8.19]**, the first element replaces the main image reference, while the second goes at the end of the file, before the </HTML> tag.

In general, you must use a special program to make an image map file. Unfortunately, many of these programs generate only the old server-side image map files. You may need an additional translation program or to translate the old style by hand to conform to the newer client-side syntax. Compare the example above to any server-side image map and you'll see the difference. *(The Book Site features pointers to free or shareware tools for making image maps.)*

Most image map tools assume you're using GIFs as your map images, so they will read only GIFs. In this case, the storefront image is a JPEG. Here's a trick: I save a copy as a GIF, open it with an image map program, make the map, then throw away the GIF. The browser doesn't care what kind of image I use for the image map.

With the core page finished, I lay out the site by copying the template many times and giving the files the names I used in the map file.

The Interior Pages

All the images for the interior pages are 320 × 240 pixels, to match the width of the text column in the larger dimension, and to preserve the aspect ratio of the postcards [8.20]. I can include either landscape or portrait images in this format. By sticking with consistent dimensions, I make site construction and maintenance easier.

Home-Style Navigation

For most of the pages in the site, I don't need random access navigation. Random access means you can get to any page from any other. It's necessary on the core page, but too imposing for the interior pages. Instead, I encourage frequent return trips to the core page. These round trips aren't tedious, because the core page will stay in the browser's memory. This is called caching (pronounced "cashing"); cached images reload very quickly.

The little red Jimtown icon at the foot of the interior pages makes a perfect homing beacon [8.21]. Anything else would be too complex. How does a visitor get back to the entrance – the "Where is Jimtown?" card? She can either go Back in her browser's

8.21 The Jimtown logo makes a perfect homing device.

8.20 A model interior page for the Jimtown site.

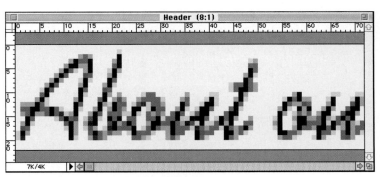

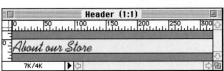

8.22 I need seven colors to render the type: green, yellow, and five intermediate shades (ABOVE). All my headers are 320 pixels wide (BELOW).

147

```
<HTML>
<HEAD>
<TITLE>Jimtown Store Catalog</TITLE>
</HEAD>

<!-- Page Parameters -->
<BODY BGCOLOR="#FFFFCC" TEXT="#003300" LINK="#990000" VLINK="#000033"
ALINK="#FFFFCC">

<!-- Vertical Spacer -->
<IMG HEIGHT=24 WIDTH=1 SRC="dot_clear.gif">

<!-- Begin Form -->
<FORM METHOD="POST" ACTION="http://foo.bar.com/cgi-bin/scripts/form">

<!-- Begin Table -->
<TABLE BORDER=1 CELLSPACING=6 CELLPADDING=0 WIDTH=480>

   <!-- 1st Row -->
   <TR>
      <TD WIDTH=107> </TD>
      <!-- Descriptive Text -->
      <TD WIDTH=320><IMG SRC="catalog.gif" ALT="Order our Catalog" WIDTH="320"
       HEIGHT="28" BORDER="0"><BR><BR><font size=-1>HERE AT THE STORE</font>
       we'd like to make it easy for you to get more info or actually buy
       things from our catalog, <i>The Jimtown Crier</i>. Leave us some of
       your vitals and we'll mail you a copy.<br>
      <IMG HEIGHT=24 WIDTH=1 SRC="dot_clear.gif"><br></TD>
      <TD WIDTH=53> </TD>
   </TR>

   <!-- 2nd Row -->
   <TR>
      <TD align=right>Name:</TD>
      <TD><input type="text" name="namefield" size="24" value=""></TD>
   </TR>

   <!-- 3rd Row -->
   <TR>
      <TD align=right>Address:</TD>
      <TD><input type="text" name="addressfield1" size="32"></TD>
   </TR>

   <!-- 4th Row -->
   <TR>
      <TD align=right>Address:</TD>
      <TD><input type="text" name="addressfield2" size="32"></TD>
   </TR>
```

```
   <!-- 5th Row -->
   <TR>
     <TD align=right>City:</TD>
     <TD><input type="text" name="cityfield" size="24">
          State: <input type="text" name="statefield"
     size="4"></TD>
   </TR>

   <!-- 6th Row -->
   <TR>
     <TD align=right>Zip Code:</TD>
     <TD><input type="text" name="zipfield" size="12"></TD>
   </TR>

   <!-- 7th Row -->
   <TR>
     <TD align=right>Phone:</TD>
     <TD><input type="text" name="phonefield" size="16"></TD>
   </TR>

   <!-- 8th Row -->
   <TR>
     <TD align=right>Fax:</TD>
     <TD><input type="text" name="faxfield" size="16"></TD>
   </TR>

   <!-- 9th Row -->
   <TR>
     <TD align=right>Email:</TD>
     <TD><input type="text" name="emailfield" size="24"></TD>
   </TR>

   <!-- 10th Row -->
   <TR>
     <TD> </TD>
     <TD><IMG HEIGHT=15 WIDTH=1 SRC="dot_clear.gif"><BR>
     <INPUT TYPE=image border=0 SRC="submit.gif" VALUE="Send"></TD>
   </TR>

</table></form><BR>

<A HREF="core.html" NAME="Jimtown Storefront">
<IMG SRC="home.gif" ALT="Return to the Jimtown Storefront" WIDTH="74"
 HEIGHT="60" VSPACE=18 HSPACE=100 BORDER="0"></A><br>
<IMG HEIGHT=48 WIDTH=1 SRC="dot_clear.gif">

</BODY>
</HTML>
```

8.23 Always start with another form and modify it.

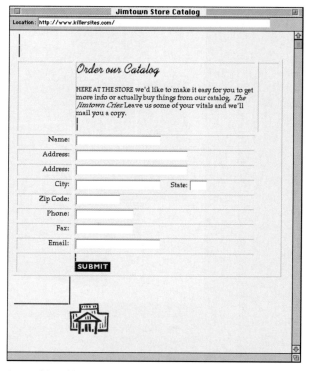

8.24 This table uses C E L L S P A C I N G = 6 for white space control.

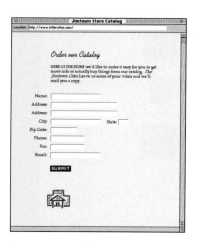
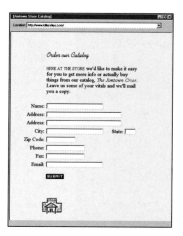

8.25 A, B Macs (LEFT) and PCs (RIGHT) render form elements differently.

Go menu, or enter the URL. I am much more interested in people bookmarking the home page than getting back to the entrance.

I look for opportunities in the text to link intrasite pages. Intrasite links refer to another part of the store. Anything that links outside the site goes into the *Regional Links* exit page, so people won't leave the site prematurely.

Making Headlines

The best way to make the type for a site like this is to know every single headline beforehand. I get consistent results by putting all the type together on a single page, reducing the colors, and making the GIF images from that master page. *(For details on these procedures, see Chapter 5, "Rendering Type.")*

The headline GIFs are all 24-point Kaufmann Script. It's big enough that I can type it without having to reduce from a larger size. I tried the regular and the bold, but I wanted something in between. After typing all the headlines, I select the entire image, hold the Option key down, and hit the down arrow once. This makes a copy of the entire image, shifted down one pixel, giving the type a slightly bolder look.

This curvy script demands more colors than a sans-serif to render properly. After a few experiments, I end up reducing to seven colors **[8.22 A, B]**.

Once the image is indexed, I set a fixed-size rectangle marquee and try to enclose each block of type in the same way: no pixels of yellow to the left, and one or two at most on top. I paste each cut image into a new file and re-index.

I try to be consistent. All of my header GIFS are 320 pixels wide, regardless of the length of the text. The reason is mostly convenience, so I can mix and match the headers without having to type in new dimensions every time.

Of course, clients *always* need more headlines after making the initial site. Things change, especially on the Web. To make additional headlines, I type them into the large headline RGB page and re-index, then cut the new headlines out and export GIFS.

The Order Form

Most forms on the Web are ugly – it's as if the functional requirements of a form somehow make even conscientious designers give up. Because different browsers render user input fields very differently, layout can indeed be a challenge. By laying out forms in tables, however, and being aware of the cross-platform differences, you can design forms well **[8.23]**.

Don't be afraid of form elements. You can place them as you would anything else. This table follows the same proportions as the other pages: 2:6:1. Instead of white space in the first column, however, I right-align the form field headers. This alignment scheme reinforces the site's left margin line.

Forms Look Different on Different Machines

Forms are one thing that really change from browser to browser, platform to platform. In particular, the widths of the user input fields can vary widely. If you specify too wide a user input field, your table might break. Generally speaking, PC browser user input fields are wider than Macintosh ones. Because I design on a Mac, I usually end up shortening my fields considerably after viewing them on a PC. Too short is better than too long.

Mac designers – make sure to look at your forms on Windows machines and vice versa!

I use cellspacing to get the elements to keep a little distance from one another, as you can see with the borders turned on **[8.24]**.

Instead of accepting the ugly generic Submit buttons browsers put up by default, I make my own, usually in a dark color with text knocked out **[8.25 A, B]**. Unfortunately, I have yet to figure out how to substitute a GIF for the Reset button. If my form were long enough to require one, I'd have to settle for the standard-issue buttons.

What happens when people submit a form? Forms send user input data to a program running on a Web server. This needn't be intimidating. Sometimes these programs are complicated, but in this case, the program simply e-mails the feedback to John Werner's Internet account.

The form won't work until a program is set up and running on your server to accept form input. It's beyond the scope of this book to explain how to write these programs, but I want to make the point that they are fairly easy to set up. Many more technical books explain the procedures in detail. Your service provider will either help you get one set up or find someone who can.

151

```
<HTML>
<HEAD><TITLE>Recipes</TITLE></HEAD>

<FRAMESET ROWS=90,*>
        <FRAME SRC="top_frame.html">
        <FRAMESET COLS=140,*>
                <FRAME SRC="left_frame.html">
                <FRAME NAME="right"
                 SRC="right_frame_01.html">
        </FRAMESET>
</FRAMESET>
</HTML>
```

8.26 Frames are useful in limited situations, like a list of recipes that form a dead end in your site.

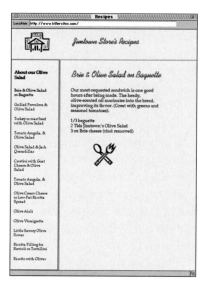

8.27 To see recipe files on their own, hold down on the *link* and choose New Window With This Link.

Personally, I don't know how to write these things. There are people in my studio who do, and I gratefully keep them supplied with fresh pizza to keep my forms working.

The Recipe Page: Frames

My goal is to make the recipes a substantive feature of the site, drawing people from other food and Sonoma sites to the growing list of refined country-style recipes provided by the Jimtown staff. I don't normally use Netscape's frames feature, but in dead-end situations like this, function wins over form. It won't be incredibly beautiful, but the recipes will be easy to see and print on demand. The basic approach is to list the titles in the left frame, which will drive the display of recipes on the right. *(See "Frames and Framesets" in Chapter 4 for details.)*

Remember: Frames are not really

152

HTML. They let you see HTML documents through them. Framesets specify the default dimensions of frames, or windows, that point to HTML documents [8.26].

The frame dimensions relate to the margins I've used throughout the site. I choose the left side as the links frame and the right side as the target frame. Any links you click in the links frame appear in the target frame. It's a simple matter of setting up the html in the links file so the links point to the target file. Use the <BASE TARGET="right"> tag in the left file to link to the file on the right.

I follow the golden rule of frames *and make sure there are no through-frame links*. That is, I make sure that all the html files in the target frame have absolutely no links in them.

Each recipe goes in its own file. To accommodate the frames, the recipe files must have a smaller left margin than the other pages [8.27, 8.28].

I link the home icon to the core page. The syntax of this button is important, because it dismisses the frames [8.29].

The best thing about this frame-based approach is that it's easy to add more recipes, attracting food enthusiasts from all over the Web. It's also a benefit to surfers, who don't have to keep going in and out of recipes to get around. It's much easier to peruse a dozen recipes through frames than with straight HTML. Used this way, frames can be a good design choice.

The Entry Blurbs

To set up the entry page, I add a few

```
<HTML>
<HEAD>

<TITLE>Menu</TITLE>

</HEAD>

<!-- Page Parameters -->
<BODY BGCOLOR="#FFFFCC" TEXT="#003300"
 LINK="#990000" VLINK="#000033"
 ALINK="#FFFFCC">

<TABLE BORDER=0 CELLPADDING="0"
 CELLSPACING="0" WIDTH="320">

   <TR>
     <TD WIDTH="20" ROWSPAN="3" nowrap></TD>
     <TD><IMG SRC="../jimtown/head_brie.gif"
     ALT="About our Store" ALIGN=TOP
     WIDTH="267" HEIGHT="28" BORDER="0"
     VSPACE="20"></TD>
   </TR>

   <TR>
     <TD Width="267">Our most-requested
     sandwich is one good hours after being
     made. The heady, olive-scented oil
     marinates into the bread, improving its
     flavor. (Great with greens and seasonal
     tomatoes).<BR><BR>
     1/3 baguette<BR>
     2 Tbls Jimtown's Olive Salad<BR>
     3 oz Brie cheese (rind removed)</TD>
   </TR>

   <TR>
     <TD><IMG SRC="../jimtown
     spoonfork_2.gif" ALT="About our Store"
     ALIGN=TOP WIDTH="70" HEIGHT="72"
     BORDER="0" HSPACE="60"
     VSPACE="20"><BR></TD>
   </TR>

</TABLE>

</BODY>
</HTML>
```

8.28 A typical recipe.

Search Engines

A new site needs all the help it can get. Search engines send out *spider programs* that crawl the Web, gathering key words from sites and putting them into huge databases. I like to load a site like this with keywords that will improve its chances of appearing in a database search. In addition to a good description in the `<TITLE>` tag, which registers on most search engines, there are two general approaches, both of which can help publicize your site (most search engines ignore any words you put in comments).

The visible way is to put a succinct sentence at the bottom of your entry page that sums up your business. This is a good idea, unless it really goes against the intended effect of the front page, which may be trying to be more mysterious. When in doubt, I leave a little description like this on the front page for all who happen to come by.

The invisible way uses hidden tags to tell search engines exactly what the page is about. This is great for visual sites that don't want to put a lot of words in HTML on the front page. One invisible way is to put key words in the ALT tag of an image. Some search engines ignore these, others don't. The more reliable way is to use "meta" tags.

The code for appropriate Jimtown *description*, *keywords*, and *distribution* meta tags is below. Fill in the descriptions for your sites, put the tags at the top of your first page, and check the search engines occasionally to see if they've picked you up. It's always a good idea to put these tags into your pages.

```
<META NAME="DESCRIPTION" CONTENT="A well-bread
crossroads emporium featuring the finest in
Sonoma cuisine. Local wines, homemade special-
ties, cheese, picnic lunches, fresh roasted
coffee, Napa fruit, fresh baked goods, an-
tiques, Wine Country tour information, and the
best olive salad in Healdsburg, Alexander Val-
ley or Sonoma County.">

<META NAME="KEYWORDS" CONTENT="Healdsburg Napa
Alexander Valley Sonoma tours food wine country
vineyard champagne espresso emporium delicates-
sen lunch dinner picnic fruit bread cheese an-
tiques olive salad sandwich">

<META NAME="DISTRIBUTION" CONTENT="global">
```

things to the front page that help people and search engines know where they are. At the bottom of the front page, I add a short text blurb **[8.30]**.

The entry blurb also tells search engines quite a bit about the site, as does the `<TITLE>` tag at the top of the page. I add three special "meta" tags for the search engines to pick up: `description`, `keywords`, and `distribution` (*see sidebar, left*).

Summary

Retail sites can be straightforward if you start with a good plan, don't bite off too much, and go for quality. Once you develop a concept and a few good templates, sites comes together quickly. Consistent, distinctive table structures, colors, and typography brand a site, giving it a memorable signature without relying too heavily on images. Consistency also makes site construction and maintenance relatively easy.

I think it's important for mail-order companies to get onto the Web sooner rather than later. Building net equity is hard; the best way to distinguish yourself from the competition is by offering quality. In my experience, people are quite willing to type a credit-card number into a web page to get something they want easily. List your distributors, put up a Frequently Asked Questions page, solicit feedback, and read and respond to e-mail. I recommend testing the waters with a small, well-presented offering and seeing what happens.

Test your ideas on prospective surfers, both on paper and in Photoshop, before committing to HTML. Because sites take a lot of work to make and can be expensive to maintain, business owners should take small steps by laying a strong foundation and adding features as time goes on.

Visit the Jimtown site for yourself and tell John and Carrie what you think (www.jimtown.com). Just click on the mailbox!

Application

This general approach works for any storefront. Small business owners like to save money. Here is a way to work existing materials into a compelling site. If you have a quality storefront photo, you can make it into an image map as I've done here. Rather than putting boards in the windows, you can "etch" the words into the glass using Photoshop, or you can make whatever signs are appropriate for the business. *(The Book Site maintains a list of quality retail sites — come on by!)*

```
<TD><A HREF="../jimtown/core.html"
TARGET="_parent">
<IMG SRC="../jimtown/home.gif"
ALIGN=TOP WIDTH="74" HEIGHT="60"
BORDER="0"VSPACE="2"></A></TD>
```

8.29 The return navigation button takes people back to the core page. Note the use of TARGET="_parent" to make the frames disappear.

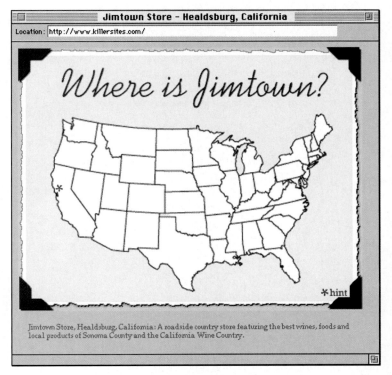

8.30 An entry blurb tells search engines and borderline visitors what's behind the curtain.

Using Quotes

Earlier versions of Netscape were lenient with people who forgot to use quotes around file names and arguments. Recent versions are more strict. Always use quotes on target and file names. This also goes for colors and other tag specifications.

155

## CHAPTER 9

A Hotlist

What you'll learn in this chapter:

Hotlists vs. directories

Foreground vs. background images

Using script type

Making drop shadows

Creating a metaphor

Advanced table tricks

Image inflation

Appropriate button

Women's Resources on the Web

Location: http://www.dsiegel.com/women/women_home.html

Women's Resources

Sites

WomensNet
Voice of Women
Women's Studies
Women's Gallery
AWID
Women on the Web
Beijing NGO site
Virtual Sisterhood
Women Artists
Women's Wire
UNIFEM
CARAL
NOW

Links

Euronet
WomensNet
Social Cafe
Jim's List
Cheryl's List
Jessie's List

The improvement of women's health and status

in society

is Vital to

the improvement of the quality of life

on the planet for all

Be more than a beacon.

Be a builder of beacons.

(If this page has no background or funny white dots, please reload. If your font are really big, the list will be longer than the spotlights.)

Go back to David Siegel's home page

9.1 A, B Matthew Butterick's hotlist (TOP) is focused, while Women's Wire's Directory (ABOVE) is an example of a professionally maintained resource.

A GOOD WEB PAGE doesn't try to do everything. Hotlists are no exception. A hotlist with five sites on it probably isn't worth maintaining, but if your hotlist has 20-50 good sites on horse jumping, there's an excellent chance the equestrian crowd will find its way to your door. If your hotlist has 200 sites, who has time to choose? The role of an editor is to show us the best – a small number says quality. If you have 200 links, maybe you really want a directory.

What's the difference? A hotlist is usually maintained by one person for the benefit of those with similar interests [**9.1 A**]. Hotlists are one person's slice across the Web. A directory is a larger listing, often maintained by an organization. A directory solicits and adds new entries continuously. "Women Architects on the Web" is a hotlist. Women's Wire's "On the Web" page is a directory [**9.1 B**]. In this chapter, I will design a hotlist.

Because of certain technical considerations, much of the material in this chapter stretches the capabilities of browsers available today. I'll discuss some alternative approaches at the end, so be sure to read through the entire chapter before starting.

Strategy

My hotlist points both to *sites* containing interesting women's information, and to *links* – which in this case is short for directories I think are well maintained by members of the Women's Movement. Because there are so many good "lists of links" available on the Web, my list can be small, yet powerful. My goals are to make an impression, recognize these outstanding sites, and guide people who might otherwise be lost in a sea of links. I want to shed some light on women's issues, so I decide on my theme: "Spotlight on Women's Issues." The spotlight metaphor works for almost any subject, but I particularly like the idea of bringing women's issues out of the darkness and into the light.

The overall strategy is to make one background image big enough so that all the type on the page won't cause it to tile, even once. In this way, I'll fool the browser into presenting a single background and put my text links on top of it.

Because of the large background GIF, some visitors might complain about this page being slow, but in this case, I'm going for a visual tour-de-force. I present another method of producing this page in "An Alternative Approach," later in this chapter.

The Background

I begin with a new 1200 × 1600-pixel document. I fill the page with a dark color from the color cube to avoid dithering. By playing with Photoshop's Lighting Effects filter on a new layer, I can get some very convincing spotlight images [9.2 A].

These gradients are so subtle that they dither horribly on systems that display only 256 colors [9.2 B]. Without dithering, you get banding, which ruins the effect [9.2 C]. Gradients also don't compress well as GIFs. So, I decide to use white ellipses for the spot, feather the edges a few pixels,

9.2 A These full-blend spotlights look good...

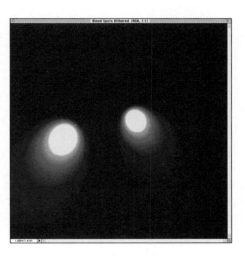

9.2 B But in color-cube colors they dither...

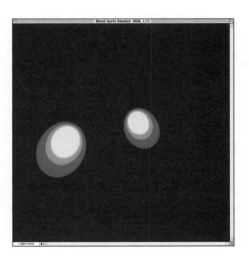

9.2 C Or show banding.

159

9.3 Solid white ellipses load faster and don't dither.

Spots, no beams (RGB, 1:2)

2.05M/1.49M

and rotate them. The spots must be large enough to fit several fairly wide names. They should each be on their own layers, with two translucent pixels around the edges (anti-aliased) [9.3].

Now they look like eggs. I decide to use crossing light beams to reinforce the illusion of spotlights on a stage or writing on a wall. Because one screenful for a small monitor is about 500 pixels wide by 400 pixels high, I'll leave a little less than that for my title. I put these spots and the list texts below, so visitors with larger monitors will see everything, while those with smaller screens will get the immediate impact of the lettering, then scroll down to the main attraction.

Once I have the spots where I want them, I make a layer for each light beam. The trick to making the light beams is to know that the lasso tool can do segmented (straight-sided) shapes and will operate out of the picture boundary. I Option-click the lasso tool three times to make this shape,

with one of the clicks off the picture [9.4]. I then make some small adjustments necessary to get the beams tangent to the ellipses.

The Handwriting on the Wall

The flowing script used for "Links" and "Sites" is a prototype of a new typeface I'm working on, called Zettina. It is based on the handwriting of the calligrapher and type designer Hermann Zapf. I could also have used a nice connecting script like Künstler or Shelley, or Kris Holmes' lovely ITC Isadora – if these had been too light, Galliard Italic or even Tekton would work. In the absence of a type library, I'd choose Palatino Italic.

I open the color cube in Photoshop, choose a foreground color from it and type the word "Sites" using the Type tool. I want the letters to look joined, but I have to join them myself. This is a matter of selecting each letter, hiding the selection marquee, and moving the letters into position. Then I use a fine brush to finish the strokes between the individual letters [9.5]. I make sure everything is perfect with this word before moving on.

Next, I create another layer and call it "Links." I choose a new foreground color from the color cube and repeat the same sequence, adding the necessary strokes to complete the word.

I add shadows to reinforce the spotlight metaphor, because they go off in different directions from their associated words. Each shadow goes on its own layer. To make the Links Shadow layer, I grab the Links layer and drop it onto the "new layer" icon. This duplicates

160

the layer, which I name "Links Shadow." I then use a select-and-fill approach to changing the color.

Two things to keep in mind when making shadows: Make them from darkened shades of the surface the shadow falls on – in this case gray – rather than unrelated colors, and make sure the edges stay soft (anti-aliased).

By selecting the entire layer and using the arrow keys, I move the shadow around precisely until I like its position beneath the layer above. I love this part, because at one point you get the impression that the top letters really are casting a shadow. The distance between letter and shadow determines how far off the page the letters appear to float. I make sure both the "Links" and the "Sites" layers float the same amount.

Put the Foreground in the Background

I incorporate the headline into the background, so the entire page loads as one image. Only the links and the text at the bottom will be in the foreground.

I happen to have a nice version of Andy Warhol's mother's handwriting from a project I did, which I use for the large headline. Or I could use a font like Remedy, by Emigre, or any of the interesting typefaces from FontShop. A narrow script font would work here also, but I don't think I'd use the same font as I have for "Links" and "Sites."

First, I type all the words in one color on a single layer just to get a look at the big picture. This lets me choose the font and size that works in the space I've chosen. I turn off all the Links and Sites layers, leaving only the background visible.

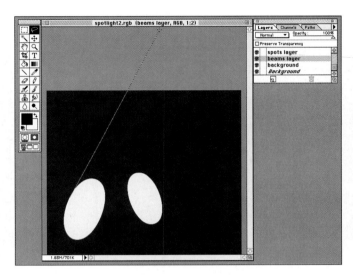

9.4 Make the light beams by holding down the Option key and using the lasso tool.

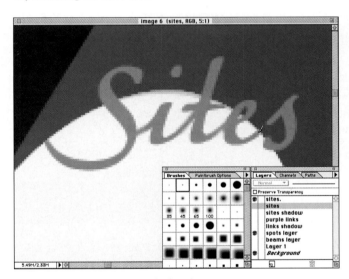

9.5 Connecting script letters by hand.

Small Screen

A Macintosh freeware utility called Small Screen draws on-screen rectangles showing boundary lines of smaller screens for those hobbled by larger monitors. Get it at the Book Site!

9.6 Keeping characters on separate layers helps me position them easily to overlap the swashes.

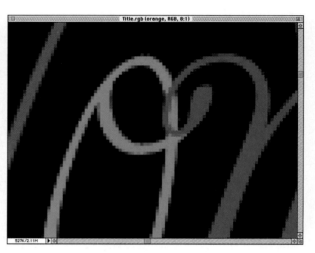

9.7 Photoshop automatically generates intermediate colors for every color transition.

Color Combinations

Books like the *Color Harmony* series (see the bibliography on the Book Site) are quite helpful when choosing colors. They contain multitudes of professionally selected color combinations useful for any graphic application.

From Objects to Bitmaps

If you use Adobe Illustrator, you can lay out the letters for a page like this as objects, size them appropriately, and then open them in Photoshop. Don't judge colors in Illustrator – they don't do well in the CMYK-to-RGB conversion; wait until you convert to pixels in Photoshop to do the coloring.

Now that I know which font and size to use, I start laying down the characters in the different colors. I vary the size and rotation of each character somewhat, balancing the overall look. Note that I make a separate layer as necessary. I want characters next to each other to be on different layers, so I can move them around and on top of one another **[9.6]**. Once I get the characters down, I overlap some of the letters' tails for a custom look.

When I'm done, I save everything. Then I do something interesting: I take all the letters I just arranged for the "Women's Resources," flatten the layers, and flip the image upside down. This makes it impossible to read, but it enables me to see any gaps or imbalances in the overall composition I might have missed otherwise. I often make small adjustments after seeing a page from a new perspective like this. In this case, I like the result. I select Revert to return to the saved version before reducing this image.

How Many Colors?

Now that I like everything, it's time to make the file as small as possible. As always, the first thing I do is save the design as a new file to protect me from myself. I don't want to overwrite my RGB file with an indexed one accidentally. Because web-related software tends to be unstable (in particular, Netscape Navigator and Photoshop seem not to get along well), I routinely save my work every 30 seconds or so.

To see how many colors there are, I choose Indexed Color. A quick look at the dialog box shows me there are more than 256 colors in this image. The majority appear in the anti-aliased

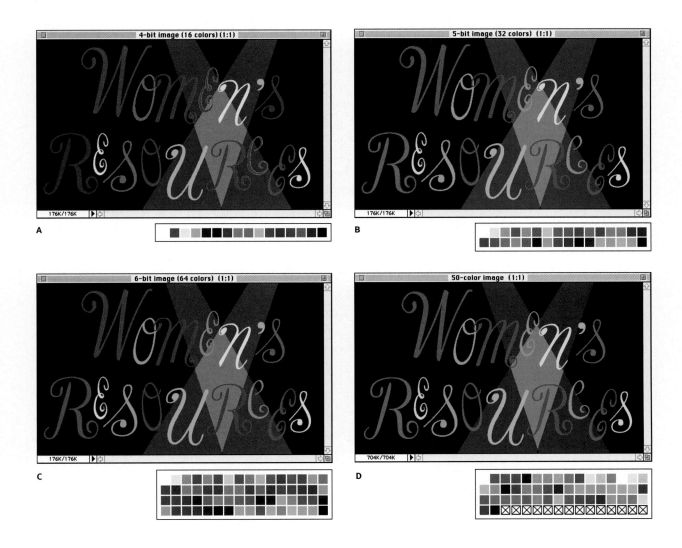

9.8 A-D Reducing the palette: 4 bits (A) was too few, 5 bits (B) was still not enough, but 6 bits (C) was more than enough to capture all the main colors in this image. Fifty colors (D) is barely acceptable – which is what I had in mind.

edges of all my colored type as they blend into the background *(see "Anti-Aliasing" in Chapter 3)* **[9.7]**.

Even though all the main colors come from the color cube, the intermediate colors don't, because Photoshop has no way of anti-aliasing using a given palette.

I must now reduce the number of colors. In Photoshop, I undo to return to RGB mode, and then index the image using an adaptive color palette. *(See "Reducing File Size" in Chapter 3 for more information and an important note about a bug in Photoshop.)*

In either case, I always start with the smallest number of colors and work up. For this image, I start with 16 colors (4 bits); it doesn't work **[9.8 A]**. Thirty-two colors (5 bits) doesn't look very good either **[9.8 B]**. Sixty-four colors (6 bits) does the trick **[9.8 C]**. The curves on the letters all look smooth.

Now I'm in the ballpark. I save the 6-bit image and notice that it is 35K. This is my fallback version. Can I squeeze it down even more? If you've been through the previous chapters, you know I'll try.

Because there's a difference of 32 colors between 5- and 6-bit images, I do some experiments to see how few colors I can actually live with. Influencing the histogram *(see "Influencing the Histogram" in Chapter 3)* won't help with an evenly colored image like this. I find that 55 colors is acceptable and 45 colors looks bad. So I choose 50 colors (barely acceptable) **[9.8 D]**.

I look at the color table *(see "Eyeballing the Palette" in Chapter 3)*. The table has no long streaks of similar colors – the colors are distributed in even groups. If there are too many intermediate colors, the horizontal runs will be too short and won't compress well.

Why do I care about reducing from 64 down to 50 colors? It doesn't reduce the size of the palette. The palette will have 64 places in it, even if only 50 have meaningful colors, because palettes only come in sizes 2, 4, 8, 16, 32, 64, 128, and 256. By reducing the number of colors in an image to the minimum, I maximize the lengths of the horizontal runs, so the image compresses as tightly as possible. Now that I have the right palette, I export the graphic as an interlaced GIF that weighs 32K.

The Foreground

If you take out the Photoshop and table work, making web sites is easy. Some day, designers will be able to create advanced sites like this in the browser window. For now, we type in cryptic instructions and numbers, save the file, and run to the browser to see whether anything has happened. If we're lucky, something has.

In third-generation site design, the HTML work consists of setting up tables and moving elements around in one-pixel increments until they are *exactly* where you want them. During this phase, turn on the table borders and use a colored single-pixel GIF, rather than a transparent one, to see what you're doing.

The Text Links

First, I make a table with three columns, put some site names in them, and space them down using the VSPACE attribute of the <IMG> tag. I guess at some initial values for the table widths and turn on the border, so I can see how close I came [9.9, 9.10].

Trial and error moves them into position. I move the tables so the left border is as close to each spotlight as possible.

Remember from Chapter 4 that you get the thinnest border with BORDER=0 CELLSPACING=0 CELLPADDING=0. I could have used cellspacing or cellpadding to get my vertical space (rather than VSPACE), but that would have moved the contents laterally too, which I don't want. It is important to make both cellspacing and cellpadding zero, so your table borders will be thin.

My Links list has enough sites so that if I need one more or less, I can add or subtract to accommodate the design. I can also make the spots bigger if necessary. In each cell, I take a guess at the first entry and type it in. During this phase of development, I use a colored single-pixel GIF, rather than a transparent one, so I can see what I'm doing [9.11].

Eventually the words start to go into the right places. *(See "Horizontal Space" in Chapter 4 for details about using* HSPACE *to control single-pixel* GIFs.)

I simplify the names of the organizations and place them strategically so the longest ones appear in the widest part of the spotlights. Keeping my eye on the distance from the right edge of the type to the right edge of the ellipse, I order the names to give the most room for expansion.

Because I'm moving these names horizontally in two-pixel increments

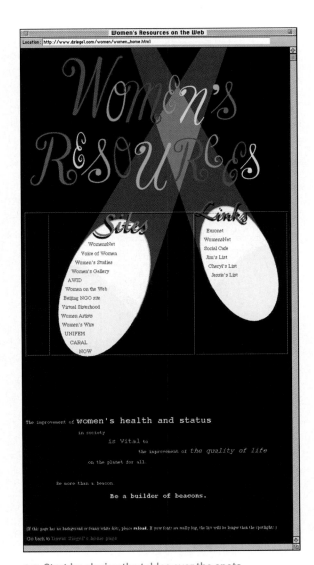

9.9 Start by placing the tables over the spots.

Photoshop Layer Management

You can see more layers in Photoshop's layers palette by turning off the thumbnail in the Palette Options dialog box, which is found on the menu at the upper right corner of the layers palette itself. Many of my Photoshop documents have two dozen layers or more. It helps to have at least 24 MB and preferably 32 MB of RAM for documents like this.

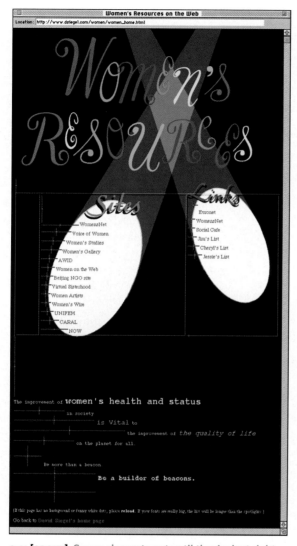

9.11 [ABOVE] Space elements out until they're just right.

9.10 [FACING] The VSPACE and HSPACE parameters move the contents of table cells around. *(Only the code for the "Sites" cell is shown.)*

```
<HTML><HEAD><TITLE>Women's Resources on the
Web</TITLE></HEAD>
<BODY BACKGROUND="resources/spotlight2.gif"
TEXT="#FFFF00" LINK="#993300" ALINK="#FF6600"
VLINK="#993300">
```

9.12 Use color cube values for link and text colors.

(HSPACE and VSPACE use two-pixel increments, WIDTH and HEIGHT use single-pixel increments), I can even compensate for letter shapes. For example, an entry that starts with a "W" might be spaced differently from one that starts with an "A."

Next I set the HTML colors. I set the page's background color to one that matches the background of the graphic, so it turns dark before the background image loads. I'm pretty unscientific about text colors. To get colors out of the color cube, I use the formula RRGGBB to specify hex colors, always duplicating the pairs. If you remember from Chapter 3, the values for R, G, and B must be either 0, 3, 6, 9, C, or F [9.12]. I choose a text color that matches the surrounding dark area, reinforcing the shadow effect. I make visited links the same color – the list is so small that people will easily remember where they've been.

I set the text for the bottom of the page, striving for impact through varying sizes and controlled breaks, rather than settling for a plain line of text. [9.13]. When adding text at the bottom of the page, make sure it doesn't exceed the 1600-pixel vertical boundary of the background image even if visitors use large fonts. If it does, the background image will automatically tile. I turn off the table borders and check the final result [9.14].

Adding the Button

I still have to make a link to this page from my home page (see Chapter 7, "A Personal Site"). I must make an icon button for this page. A button

```
<TABLE BORDER=1 CELLPADDING=0 CELLSPACING=0 WIDTH=587>
<!--beginning of row-->
 <TR>
 <!--empty cell to establish left margin-->
 <TD WIDTH=60><BR></TD>
 <!--cell for sites-->
 <TD WIDTH=325>
 <!--adds some vertical space-->
 <IMG VSPACE=30 SRC="../resources/dot_peri.gif"><BR>
 <!--vertical and horizontal white space control-->
 <IMG VSPACE=2 HSPACE=40 SRC="../resources/dot_peri.gif">
 <A HREF="http://www.igc.apc.org/womensnet/">WomensNet</A><BR>

 <IMG SRC="../resources/dot_peri.gif"><BR>

 <IMG VSPACE=8 HSPACE=32 SRC="../resources/dot_peri.gif">
 <A HREF="http://www.voiceofwomen.com/">Voice of Women</A><BR>

 <IMG VSPACE=8 HSPACE=25 SRC="../resources/dot_peri.gif">
 <A HREF="http://inform.umd.edu:86/Educational_Resources/AcademicResources
    ByTopic/WomensStudies">Women's Studies</A><BR>

 <IMG VSPACE=8 HSPACE=21 SRC="../resources/dot_peri.gif">
 <A HREF="http://www.asu.edu:80/wwol/">Women's Gallery</A><BR>

 <IMG VSPACE=8 HSPACE=17 SRC="../resources/dot_peri.gif">
 <A HREF="http://www.core77.com/AWID/">AWID</A><BR>

 <IMG VSPACE=8 HSPACE=14 SRC="../resources/dot_peri.gif">
 <A HREF="http://www.eskimo.com/~susan/girls.htm">Women on the Web</A><BR>

 <IMG VSPACE=8 HSPACE=12 SRC="../resources/dot_peri.gif">
 <A HREF="http://www.iisd.ca/linkages/women.html">Beijing NGO site</A><BR>

 <IMG VSPACE=8 HSPACE=10 SRC="../resources/dot_peri.gif">
 <A HREF="http://www.igc.apc.org/vsister/vsister.html">Virtual Sisterhood</A><BR>

 <IMG VSPACE=8 HSPACE=9 SRC="../resources/dot_peri.gif">
 <A HREF="http://www.sonoma.edu/library/waa/">Women Artists</A><BR>

 <IMG VSPACE=8 HSPACE=10 SRC="../resources/dot_peri.gif">
 <A HREF="http://women.com">Women's Wire</A><BR>

 <IMG VSPACE=8 HSPACE=13 SRC="../resources/dot_peri.gif">
 <A HREF="http://www.ingenia.com/unifem">UNIFEM</A><BR>

 <IMG VSPACE=8 HSPACE=19 SRC="../resources/dot_peri.gif">
 <A HREF="http://www.matisse.net/politics/caral/caral.html">CARAL</A><BR>

 <IMG VSPACE=8 HSPACE=29 SRC="../resources/dot_peri.gif">
 <A HREF="http://now.org/now/home.html">NOW</A><BR>
 <!--end of sites cell-->
 <!--end of row-->
</TR></TABLE>
```

```
<!--adds some vertical space-->
<IMG VSPACE=66 SRC="../resources/dot_peri.gif"><BR>
<TT><!--tells browser to use a typewriter-style font, like courier-->
The improvement of <FONT SIZE=+3><B>women's health and status</B></FONT><BR>

<IMG VSPACE=9 HSPACE=55 SRC="../resources/dot_peri.gif">in society<BR>

<IMG VSPACE=9 HSPACE=88 SRC="../resources/dot_peri.gif">
<FONT SIZE=+2>is Vital</FONT> to<BR>

<IMG VSPACE=9 HSPACE=122 SRC="../resources/dot_peri.gif">
the improvement of <FONT SIZE=+2><I>the quality of life</I></FONT><BR>

<IMG VSPACE=9 HSPACE=66 SRC="../resources/dot_peri.gif">
on the planet for all.<BR>

<IMG VSPACE=22 HSPACE=30 SRC="../resources/dot_peri.gif">
Be more than a beacon.<BR>

<IMG VSPACE=14 HSPACE=90 SRC="../resources/dot_peri.gif">
<FONT SIZE=+2><B>Be a builder of beacons.</B></FONT><BR>

<IMG VSPACE=22 HSPACE=90 SRC="../resources/dot_peri.gif">
<!--end typwriter font-->
</TT><BR>
```

9.13 I have fun playing with font sizes and weights at the bottom of the page.

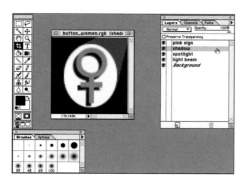

9.15 I exaggerate the circle size because the whole symbol will be small.

9.16 This design reflects what you'll find when you click on the button.

with two small spotlights on it doesn't work: The lights will look like two little eggs. I decide to combine a metaphor with a symbol.

I have only 74 × 74 pixels to do this – the size of the other icons on my home page. First, I create the symbol shape, then I copy it (on the Mac, I grab the layer bar and drop it over the new layer icon), and turn it black for a shadow. I use the same technique as before to make the light beam, so this image takes five layers to make [9.15].

Finally, I use the pencil tool to run around the edges and make the beveled effect. While I don't normally use beveled edges, this single-pixel border carries its weight on the buttons of my home page. I reduce to 32 colors, do a

168

little final editing, and add the button code to my home page **[9.16]**.

An Alternative Approach

This hotlist has been on my personal site since July 1995. Occasionally, I get complaints that it loads and refreshes very slowly. The large background can cause GIF inflation problems for people surfing with low-end machines *(see "Image Inflation" in Chapter 3)*. In fact, this large background image, although it compresses nicely, inflates to over 1.5 MB on most client machines. There is no perfect solution, but I want to present an alternative.

You'll recall that the background image size is 1200 × 1600 pixels. This is to prevent it from tiling in the browser window. Because I can't put layers in the foreground, a more practical approach is to make this entire image into an image map and put it in the foreground.

If I were to go back to the Photoshop RGB file, I could make a new layer with the names of the sites set in an attractive font and structure the whole top portion of the page as a GIF image map over a single background color **[9.17]**. Since I wouldn't have to worry about tiling any more, this new foreground image would be much smaller, and therefore easier for low-end machines to digest.

This image map method also has the advantage of not being sensitive to visitor font sizes, because the type is set into the image. The disadvantage is that you can't get the foreground image to reach the edges in Netscape Navigator, (see "Offsets" in Chapter 4), so

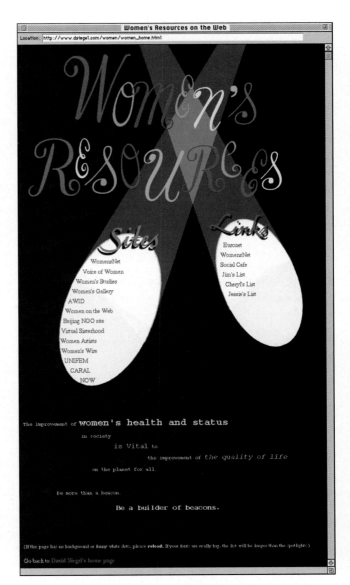

9.14 The final page: If cellspacing and cellpadding have been set to zero, nothing will move when you turn off the borders.

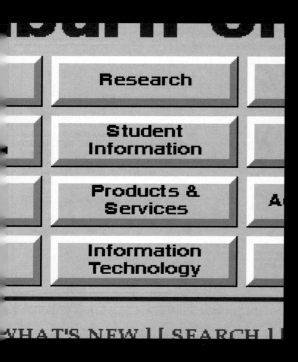

Deadly Sin Number Five

Illegal Use of the Third Dimension

Bevels and drop shadows have taken over the Web. Buttons, type, tables, interfaces: Everything has beveled edges. I call it downloadable chrome. It fills up space. It makes buttons look clickable. It makes programs look like VCRs and the Web look like an arcade.

I recommend not using the beveled, 3-D look unless it's absolutely essential, which means I use it with drop shadows when necessary and single-pixel bevels in rare circumstances.

the light beams are cut off, and that's unattractive. It's also harder to update the links if you have to go through Photoshop every time.

If you're designing for Internet Explorer, you can set the offsets to zero. In this case, the page looks good because the light beams reach all the way to the top. *(See the end of Chapter 6 for a discussion of this solution.)*

Summary

This chapter shows some of the trade-offs involved in designing a third-generation site. GIF inflation makes a large background image difficult for many of today's surfers, while the alternative approach is more difficult to update. In the future, we will be able to make sites that load in layers from the front to the back *(see Chapter 14, "Beyond HTML").*

Making hotlists can be fun. You don't need a fancy background to create a metaphor, and setting your links in a simple shape (like a moon on a dark background) will make them look great. This chapter is also a good primer on rendering script fonts and controlling table elements carefully.

Application

You can make a simple hotlist using the principles of this chapter, without the huge background image. To make an astrology hotlist, I played with the position and length of links until I got the shape my client wanted. I use a dark, tiling background that hardly gets in the way, and put the graphic in the middle – rather than as a banner at the top. This page took three hours to

9.17 A foreground image map helps solve the GIF inflation problem but introduces others.

9.18 Here I've used single-pixel GIFs to lay out a hotlist.

build, from start to finish, because I made it, links and all, in Photoshop before going to my text editor. The HTML involves three cells in two rows of one table. I leave it as an exercise to figure out exactly how I arranged the table cells and rows [9.18].

```
amble.html"><img border=0
ght=5..." SRC="animations/d1.gif"></    td>

amble.html"><img border=0
ght=5..." SRC="animat   s/    gif"></    td>

amble.html"><im             0
ght=5..." SRC="ani          1.gif"></    td>
n -->
img BORDER=0  id
="do   black          d>

0 0f  table
```

## CHAPTER 10

A Gallery

What you'll learn in this chapter:

Putting animated GIFs in tables

Simulated randomness

Directory structure

Preloaded images

Setting expectations

Creating a contact-sheet metaphor

Image processing above the color cube

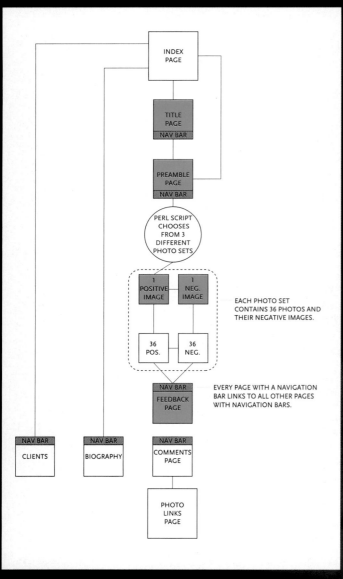

Site diagram

DOUG MENUEZ is one of the country's most versatile and interesting photographers. He was a photojournalist for *Time* and *Newsweek* during the '70s and '80s. He's done editorial and documentary work, as well as fashion and advertising photography. For ten years he's been shooting life on the digital frontier, documenting people in high-tech companies across the globe.

Doug came to my studio in search of a cutting-edge, provocative site, combining words and images to bring his view of the digital revolution to surfers interested in photography and photojournalism. He wanted to show the disparity and similarities between the digital *haves* and *have-nots* – the people who use whiz-bang technological innovations and the people who make them in far-away places.

Doug's primary concern was image quality. We decided to optimize this site for visitors with 28.8 kbps modems and systems that display thousands of colors. We specifically decided not to worry about the color cube and web surfers who could see only 256 colors; that would limit black-and-white images to very few shades of gray, and the photo quality would degrade.

"Content on every page!" as the famous magazine designer Roger Black would say. As Doug and I talked, it became clear that the photographs themselves should be the site, rather than an entry door followed by an antechamber, then several gallery spaces. We wanted a metaphor that was understated, not architectural or literal.

We end up agreeing on a loose interpretation of a contact sheet, enhanced by animated GIFs at the entrance and a different group of photos each time you visit the site.

This fairly technical chapter is much more effective if seen on the Web before continuing – it uses animated GIFs and a Perl script running on the server to present random images (www.menuez.com).

Strategy

Digital Moments is a linear journey with a dramatic entrance, a simple intro page, 36 images, a behind-the-scenes parallel universe, and a closing page that gives visitors a chance to express their comments on the exhibition and its meaning.

I choose the number 36 as a theme, to take visitors through 36 images as though they were in Doug's private gallery, looking at a contact sheet. In fact, there are 56 images total, but I want visitors to see a "roll" of 36 at a time. This site will use a random script to present 36 different images per visit. There's no reason for them to choose which photograph to see next. I want to show the photos in the order I choose.

Advertising the number 36 at the beginning tells visitors how long the journey is, setting expectations for the trip. There is no way to see all 56 total images. They can go through again if they want to see another selection of 36 taken from the total.

The impact of this site relies on randomness, on giving the feeling of a random walk. To set the tone up front, I take an idea from Ray Guillette's animated-GIF title page for his groundbreaking site, "Sound Traffic Control."

To give the feeling of the contact sheet, I use an abstraction of the frame markers on film as a navigational element. As an added feature, visitors can click on the large images, taking them to the other side: a flipped, negative version of the image with the photographer's notes on the circumstances under which the shot was taken. This parallel universe enriches the site and creates an unusual behind-the-scenes view. I got this through-the-picture idea from Suza Scalora's enchanting "Mythopœia" site *(all sites mentioned are listed at the Book Site).*

Entry, Exploration, Exit

This site has a *greeting page* that tells you a bit about the gallery, warns you of the upcoming download, requests that you turn off underlining, and entices you to enter. The next page, with the animated GIFs, is the *title page.* I want it to make everyone who sees it send the URL to her friends. More than just a nice entry, this page also serves as a strong image for magazines and other media to use when reporting on the site. It also allows me to put up a short cut, for those who want to miss the title page and get right into the exhibit. This is helpful for visitors who've already seen the title page but want to go through the photographs again.

The next page is the *preamble,* where I put up a short statement from a curator's point of view. The *exploration* section is the journey through the 36 photos. There is no random access – no way to take a shortcut to the end page – you must go through the entire sequence to get to the end.

The *feedback page* should be worth reaching. I want the equivalent of the

10.1 A-D These three images and the black rectangle will become the layers of the animated GIFs.

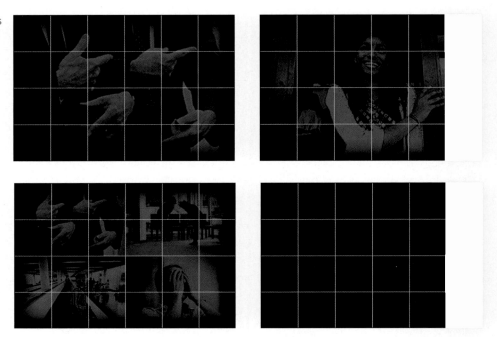

big finale at the end of a fireworks display. I decide to make the 36th photo in full color – an unexpected surprise. To finish, Doug would like an area where visitors can post their impressions for everyone to see. This is a way to build community and get reactions to the site.

The Title Page

The first thing to do is make the site work statically, without the random selector script. As usual, it's best to get into Photoshop to see what works and what doesn't. If I can make the first page and one of the gallery pages, I know I'll be in business. I like to do the hard stuff first, so I start with the title page.

Most of the tricks (discussed in other chapters) to reduce to 256 colors won't work here, where fidelity to the

original is more important than being faithful to the color cube. Although I can assume visitors will view this site with thousands of colors, I don't assume they have blazingly fast net connections or huge monitors.

I start with 70 of Doug's images on a Kodak PhotoCD. The high-resolution versions of each image are very good – certainly good enough for my purposes. To use Doug's images on web pages, I must reduce the size and resolution of these large files. I choose and process a batch of 40 images, giving me enough to play with *(see "Processing Photographic Images" on page 183)*.

The Animated GIFs

To create the animated effect, I first make the title page in Photoshop using plenty of layers. I need only three main images (two complete images and one

176

made of four smaller shots) that will be cut up to make the grid elements. I set up the grid on yet another layer, giving each image enough area to show something, but not too much. I also tune the images to give them more contrast, which helps make the files smaller later. I must also make them lighter than normal, remembering that PCs will show them darker than on my Macintosh screen. I add a fourth layer, containing a plain black rectangle, to the mix to break things up – the squares will seem to disappear occasionally on the black page background. Working with a large black background really helps show this page the way I intend it to look [**10.1 A-D**].

Doug likes the idea of blurring the edges, which makes me wish I could make animated JPEGs, because JPEG is the best way to store a photographic image, and blurry JPEGs really compress well. Unfortunately, animated JPEG images are not possible today.

A quick grid size experiment on a separate layer tells me I should use a 6 × 4 grid, in which each cell is 55 pixels square – the smallest square that still carries enough of the image to be worthwhile.

I cut the images into squares using the grid as a guide and a 55 × 55-pixel fixed-size rectangle marquee. I do the same for the black rectangle.

Ray's trick is to place the type into the six images, so that it appears to float in front while the images change in back. The effect is quite three-dimensional and dynamic [**10.2**].

I have chosen a typeface called DIN Neuzeit Grotesk Bold Condensed. It anchors the page and has a Bauhaus/retro look. I choose a pale green from the

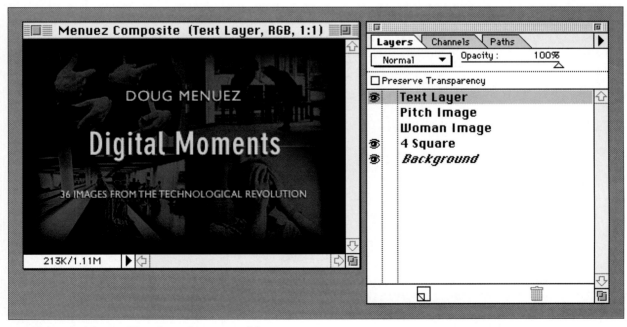

10.2 Make a type layer with as few colors as possible.

10.3 Slicing and dicing to make animated GIFS. Make them all the same size.

10.4 Preparing images for animation: Make them the same size and use the same palette. The three main images have a common (reduced) palette of 40 colors.

color cube to set it off. The subtitle is set in Gill Sans caps (I love the caps, but I rarely use the lowercase). I put the type on a front layer and make a separate drop shadow layer, which I move around until I get the effect I want.

When I have everything the way I want it, I build the animated GIFS (see "The GIF Format" in Chapter 3). I want to save each 55 × 55-pixel square as a PICT file and let the GIF-building program make the GIFS, for a high degree of consistency in processing the images.

I flatten each image and cut it up, each time making the same sized cuts. I set the dimensions of the rectangle tool to a fixed size when making these files. Unless you have some particular effect in mind, it's a good idea to make every GIF in an animation the exact same size [**10.3**].

Now I build all the animated GIFS before locking them together in a table. For each animated GIF, I load all the PICT images into the GIF-building program and choose an adaptive palette setting of 40 colors for the common palette.

Why does the common palette for these images have 40 colors? I did some experiments, trying to influence the histogram at 32 colors, and I couldn't get the images to look perfect. I had to go up to 40 colors to get enough tonal range to prevent banding and other artifacts [**10.4**]. I could have indexed in 16 colors with dithering, but dithering would create distracting visual noise.

Once I have these files made, I give them different delay settings, randomizing the timing. I make sure to give them all different cycle times, so the whole show keeps going but doesn't look like it's in a loop [**10.5**].

Unfortunately, the total weight of all animated GIFs is just under 100K. After considering several options – including a redesign – I throw out one of the master images and use two photo layers, rather than three. That means I have to build every single animated GIF over again. How could I have avoided this? By measuring the size of each GIF and multiplying by 24, I could have determined that each animated GIF must be under 3K. The files I have are around 4K each.

Fortunately, throwing out a layer is just a matter of rebuilding the animated GIFs; it doesn't take long. Now the page is under 60K.

The 4 × 6 Table

Now that I have all the elements, the only way to test them is to build the table and try the effect. I'll need a table with six columns and four rows, plus an extra column to space it over. The key is to get the cells to butt right up against each other (See "The Invisible Table Trick" in Chapter 4) [**10.6**].

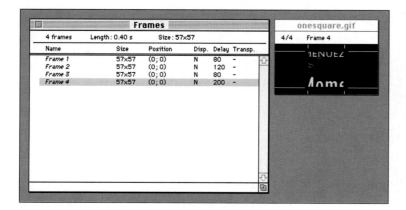

10.5 Different delays make the changing of the squares look random.

This page has four rows in one large table. Each row has a left margin cell (a black single-pixel GIF), six cells containing animated GIFs, and a right margin cell. I link each animated GIF to the preamble page, so visitors enter the exhibit no matter where they click. I center this table in case people have large monitors.

To keep things organized as the project grows, I put all 72 JPEG images into a folder called images, with logical names like images/tokyo95.b.jpg. The negative version of this photo is images/tokyo95.w.jpg. The slash means "get it out of the images folder." I make another folder, called titles, where I store all 112 title GIFs [10.7].

After a little debugging, it actually works. It's great to see this page come together on my screen for the first time [10.8].

The only drawback is that the animated GIFs don't load simultaneously, giving away part of the secret. I make sure the GIF cycle times are fairly long,

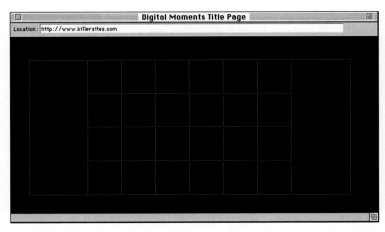

10.6 Position the table and add make each cell 55 pixels wide.

so the images can continue to load even as the first few GIFs start asking for the client computer's attention. (Internet Explorer 3.0 solves this problem by downloading all animated GIFs before starting the show.) I do some careful spacing to make sure the entire page shows up in a 640 × 480 space.

Green Means Go

Throughout the site, I want green to be the navigation color. Anything green is a link that takes you to the next page. After they've watched the main animation, a small green arrow fades in to pull visitors into the site. This is done with a six-frame animated GIF.

I place the text and the arrow into a separate layer over a black background, then I save six identical copies. Leaving the first copy as is, I work back through the other copies, progressively applying the Gaussian Blur filter and decreasing saturation. The last frame must be completely black. Rather than going linearly, I make the blur transitions to the title *nonlinearly* – in small steps

Broken GIFs

Unfortunately, with so many animated GIFs on a single page, there is a chance they won't all load. A snappy server well connected to the Web really makes a difference. If this site sits on a shared server with a lot of traffic, there will be more than a few broken GIFs at lunch time. Reduce it to a 3 × 3 or 2 × 2 grid if you get too many broken GIFs.

10.7 If your files have logical names, it's easy to put them in order.

```
<!-- Page Parameters -->
<HTML><HEAD><TITLE>Digital Moments Title Page</TITLE></HEAD>
<BODY BGCOLOR=#000000 TEXT=#999999>

<!-- Blank Vertical Spacer -->
<IMG BORDER=0 WIDTH=524 HEIGHT=30
 SRC="resources/dot_black.gif"><BR>

<CENTER>

<!-- Begin Title Table -->
<TABLE BORDER=1 CELLSPACING=0 CELLPADDING=0 WIDTH=524>

  <!-- Start Row 1 Of Table -->
  <TR VALIGN=top>

    <!-- Left Margin -->
    <TD WIDTH=97 ROWSPAN=4><IMG BORDER=0 WIDTH=97 HEIGHT=1
     SRC="resources/dot_black.gif"></TD>

    <!-- a 1 -->
    <TD WIDTH=55><A HREF="preamble.HTML"><IMG BORDER=0
     WIDTH=55 HEIGHT=55 SRC="animations/a1.gif"></A></TD>

    <!-- b 1 -->
    <TD WIDTH=55><A HREF="preamble.HTML"><IMG BORDER=0
     WIDTH=55 HEIGHT=55 SRC="animations/b1.gif"></A></TD>

    <!-- c 1 -->
    <TD WIDTH=55><A HREF="preamble.HTML"><IMG BORDER=0
     WIDTH=55 HEIGHT=55 SRC="animations/c1.gif"></A></TD>

    <!-- d 1 -->
    <TD WIDTH=55><A HREF="preamble.HTML"><IMG BORDER=0
     WIDTH=55 HEIGHT=55 SRC="animations/d1.gif"></A></TD>

    <!-- e 1 -->
    <TD WIDTH=55><A HREF="preamble.HTML"><IMG BORDER=0
     WIDTH=55 HEIGHT=55 SRC="animations/e1.gif"></A></TD>

    <!-- f 1 -->
    <TD WIDTH=55><A HREF="preamble.HTML"><IMG BORDER=0
     WIDTH=55 HEIGHT=55 SRC="animations/f1.gif"></A></TD>

    <!-- Right Margin -->
    <TD WIDTH=97 ROWSPAN=4><IMG BORDER=0 WIDTH=97 HEIGHT=1
     SRC="resources/dot_black.gif"></TD>

  </TR>
  <!-- End Row 1 Of Table-->

</TABLE>
```

near the title, increasing the blur as I approach the black, so the fade-in accelerates when played [**10.9**].

In GifBuilder, I assemble the five frames in reverse order, setting the delay for the first frame at four seconds. This helps (although it doesn't guarantee) that the title will appear *after* the main image loads.

Finally, I add a simple navigation bar at the very bottom of this page. The navigation bar is made of seven text images set in Gill Sans. Following my rule, the clickable links are green, but the current page is always grayed out. By making all 14 images in advance, I have everything I need to make the navigation bars around the site (see the diagram at the beginning of the chapter) I make sure they are below the first 480 vertical pixels of the screen, so most people don't even notice them.

The Entry Page

Because the title page is big, it makes sense to put up a small greeting page at the front of the site, instructing visitors to turn off underlining, to enlarge their browser windows, and so on. In fact, I decide to let them enter the exhibition either by going to the title page or taking a short cut around it, in case they can see plenty of colors but want to skip the big title page. People who've visited before and want to see more pictures don't need to see the title again. The greeting page also gives them a chance to go to Doug's information page or his client list, in case anyone wants to go straight there and not visit the gallery. *(You can see this page yourself at the Book Site.)*

10.8 Get the animated GIFs running and make any adjustments to timing.

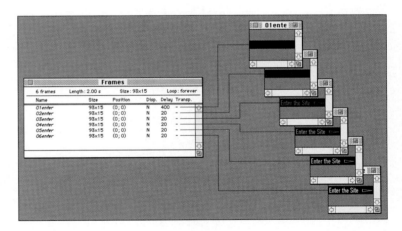

10.9 A gentle reminder fades in gradually and gets brightest right at the end.

The Preamble Page

Doug wanted a preamble page to play the role of the words normally silk-screened onto the wall as you enter a gallery space. I make the page with a single image of type set in DIN Neuzeit Grotesk. After reducing colors (see Chapter 5, "Rendering Type"), the entire image weighs only 16K. I added the extra image at the bottom to tell visitors they are entering another world [10.10].

I want to remind visitors they are about to see 36 images, so I started the navigation graphics on this page. The

arrow again fades in to beckon you on.

Finally, there is a little dot in the lower-left corner of the page. I hope you have to look closely to see it, because you're not supposed to notice it. It's actually the main image on the next page, reduced to one pixel square. Unfortunately, WIDTH=0 doesn't make it smaller. The code for this image is:

```
<IMG HEIGHT=1 WIDTH=1 SRC=
"images/tokyo95.b.img.jpg">
```

While visitors read the preamble, this image quietly loads onto their hard disks. When they click to go to the next page, the image flies onto their screen immediately. As they look at the first page, the images for both page 2 and the reverse of page 1 load, in that order. Whichever way they go, they always have the next images waiting for them, so there is never a wait. With any luck, they won't notice. They'll just think I have the world's fastest server.

This is called a *preload*. It is one of the most user-friendly features you can put into a linear site like this. Preload included, this page weighs less than 34K, and you're reading the preamble while most of it loads. Because of the preloads, it's important not to interlace any of the images on this site.

The Interior Pages

Each of the 35 interior images follows the same format (the final image is a surprise; you'll have to see it for yourself on the Book Site). Each page has a high-quality image that loads quickly, a title GIF, and an ASCII text caption in gray [10.11].

10.10 After reducing this large image to 8 colors, it is 16K.

Image Processing

My first concern on each of these interior pages is to get the main images as small as possible while retaining the subtle details. I decide on a width of 298 and a height of 215 pixels. 215 pixels is as tall as I can comfortably make an image in a browser window that might be full of menu bars. The 298 was necessary to preserve the aspect ratio of the film.

After resizing an image, always apply the Unsharp Mask filter (a sharpening operation). Unsharp masking reinstates the fine details blurred during resizing. It's important to use this filter to correct, not manipulate – overdoing it will make the image look edgy. If I'm reducing an image by a large percentage, I reduce and sharpen in steps, preserving delicate details as I go.

Grayscale images require a full range of tonalities. In particular, I want the blacks to be completely black ("#000000"). Because some images have black at the edges, I decide to use a thin gray 50% border to denote the edge of each photograph. This will also help on the reverse side, where blacks turn to white. I save them as JPEGS, using a medium quality setting.

Now I make the title GIFS. I set each title in DIN Neuzeit Grotesk, using a light gray, so as not to compete with the navigation color.

Contact-Sheet Navigation

The contact-sheet numbering scheme builds anticipation, displaces the usual Forward and Back buttons, and gives a familiar feel to the exhibit. The small

Processing Photographic Images

Making images look good on the Web is a lengthy process; I've covered palettes, reduction, and other related issues elsewhere in this book. But photography and fine art images present a special challenge. Because fidelity is more important than download speed, I sometimes opt for better quality (larger file size). Here are a few hints to obtain the best results:

When scanning, capture the best tonal range you can. Guard against washout in highlights and shadows filling in. You'll never be able to salvage a bad source file, so it's worthwhile to pay attention and use your scanning software to get the most out of the original.

Scan sensitive images as large and at as high a resolution as possible. Color correct at a large size, then resample them down to the final physical size and resolution.

Generally use Unsharp Mask after resizing or resampling (changing resolution) to preserve detail and crispness.

As a general rule, highlights shouldn't burn out to full white unless they are highlights in shiny objects like chrome or point sources of light. Conversely, shadows tones shouldn't be completely black until you get to the darkest areas in a photograph (near-blacks are very hard to see on screen).

By using Curve and Level adjustments in Photoshop, correct images to display proper midtone values prior to processing them for the Web.

Keep cross-platform color issues in mind. When color correcting on the Macintosh, I recommend regularly switching your monitor settings to simulate the darker Windows screen representation.

When color fidelity is of primary importance, using the standard color cube and GIF format will change the colors unfavorably; use JPEG instead. JPEG distorts fine details, but the color stays substantially truer to the original scanned art.

10.11 A typical interior page. Note the preload at the bottom of the screen.

In their excellent book, *Wayfinding in Architecture: People, Signs and Architecture* (McGraw Hill, 1992), authors Paul Arthur and Romedi Passini point out that people need three kinds of signs: 1) you are here, 2) how to get where you want to go, and 3) you are on the way. Most web pages have the first two by default. The third sign, confirmation, is very helpful when taking people on a journey through your site. If your site has five main areas, you might want to make sure visitors know where they are (area and page) at all times.

Site designers should use this kind of sign, a *confirmation*, more often. In the gallery site, the frame numbers under each picture indicate how far along you are. This information can be invaluable to surfers, who unconsciously use a technique called *cognitive mapping* to get their bearings within your site. I highly recommend this book to anyone doing interactive design.

triangle images are reminiscent of those found on contact sheets. I make the triangles into separate GIFs, so there are only two green triangle graphics to keep track of, and the frame-number graphics can be reused. I make the frame numbers into GIFs using a font called Interstate, which is reminiscent of the lettering used on film. The forward and back images, being links, are green, while the current frame number is gray, since it won't be clickable. While I have them in Photoshop, I change the color of all green GIFs to a dark red (the negative color of my navigation green) and flip them horizontally to get the reversed numbers to use on the behind-the-scenes page.

Centered Tables

I decide to use a centered table to hold the picture on the page. First, I use a single-pixel GIF to space down 30 pixels, giving me a consistent top margin. I create a table with a blank cell on the left and just enough room for the image on the right. I then center the entire table. This assures me of a solid left margin, while giving the image more breathing room if people have wider screens [**10.12 A-C**].

This centered table with a firm left margin works wonderfully and is an excellent alternative to the four-column table for laying out text (see "Horizontal White Space" in Chapter 4). I use the centered table trick on every page in the site [**10.13**].

The last set of commands on the page preloads the next two images. Notice I preload the next black image first, because that is the more likely next page. Then I preload the negative version. This ensures the best possible performance as they traverse the site.

The bad news: Surfers can have simultaneous connections that cause these two images to load concurrently; this could also delay my navigational elements. Another reason to have made the green arrows as separate images – they are already cached and load immediately.

Building this site requires a lot of repetitive work. While it's not difficult, I must keep a chart of all the file names to avoid lots of debugging later. (I tape it to my monitor to help me remember where everything goes.) The interior pages are quite easy to link. I use the first HTML file as a template, copying it for each new page and changing the numbers so they all hook together. After copying, I must change the following items in each file: the back link, the forward link, the names of the GIFs that show the previous, current, and next frame numbers, the name of the file that contains the photo, the through-the picture link, the name of the file that holds the GIF for the title, the actual text caption for the photo, and the two preloads.

The first interior page links back to the preamble page, while the last page links to the feedback page. The only tricky part about this whole operation is getting the reverse-image HTML file linked up so it works backwards.

10.12 A-C Adding a blank cell to a table and centering the whole thing ensures a left margin while opening up the left side if viewed with a larger screen.

10.13 A centered table makes a nice template for the interior pages. Notice the two preloads at the end.

```
<!-- Page Parameters -->
<HTML><HEAD><TITLE>Digital Moments - Doug Menuez</TITLE>
</HEAD>
<BODY BGCOLOR="000000" TEXT="999999">


<!-- Top Margin Vertical Spacer -->
<IMG BORDER=0 WIDTH=1 HEIGHT=30
 SRC="../resources/dot_black.gif"><BR>

<CENTER>

<!-- Begin Image Table Table -->
<TABLE BORDER=1 CELLSPACING=0 CELLPADDING=0 WIDTH=524>

  <!-- Start Row 1 Of Table -->
  <TR VALIGN=top>

    <!-- Left Margin -->
    <TD ROWSPAN=7><IMG BORDER=0 WIDTH=112 HEIGHT=1
     SRC="../resources/dot_black.gif"></TD>

    <!-- The Picture For The Page -->
    <TD COLSPAN=5><A HREF="22.w.html"><IMG BORDER=0
     WIDTH=300 HEIGHT=217
     SRC="../images/tokyo95.b.img.jpg">
    </A></TD>

    <!-- Right Margin -->
    <TD ROWSPAN=7><IMG BORDER=0 WIDTH=112 HEIGHT=1
     SRC="../resources/dot_black.gif"></TD>

  </TR>
  <!-- End Row 1 Of Table-->


  <!-- Start Row 2 Of Table -->
  <TR VALIGN=top>

    <!-- Blank Vertical Spacer -->
    <TD COLSPAN=5 WIDTH=300><IMG BORDER=0 WIDTH=1 HEIGHT=3
     SRC="../resources/dot_black.gif"></TD>

  </TR>
  <!-- End Row 2 Of Table-->


  <!-- Start Row 3 Of Table -->
  <TR VALIGN=top>

    <!-- Previous Image Button -->
    <TD ALIGN=left WIDTH=55><A HREF="21.b.html">
     <IMG BORDER=0 WIDTH=24 HEIGHT=13
```

186

```
 SRC="../navigation/all.b.lt.gif"><IMG BORDER=0 WIDTH=24
 HEIGHT=13 SRC="../navigation/21.b.ltrt.gif"></A></TD>

  <!-- Blank Filler -->
  <TD><IMG BORDER=0 WIDTH=89 HEIGHT=1
   SRC="../resources/dot_black.gif"></TD>

  <!-- Image Frame Number -->
  <TD><IMG BORDER=0 WIDTH=26 HEIGHT=13
   SRC="../navigation/22.b.ctr.gif"></TD>

  <!-- Blank Filler -->
  <TD><IMG BORDER=0 WIDTH=89 HEIGHT=1
   SRC="../resources/dot_black.gif"></TD>

  <!-- Next Image Button -->
  <TD ALIGN=right WIDTH=55><A HREF="23.b.html">
  <IMG BORDER=0 WIDTH=24 HEIGHT=13
   SRC="../navigation/23.b.ltrt.gif">
  <IMG BORDER=0 WIDTH=24 HEIGHT=13
   SRC="../navigation/all.b.rt.gif"></A></TD>

</TR>
<!-- End Row 3 Of Table-->


<!-- Start Row 4 Of Table -->
<TR VALIGN=top>

  <!-- Blank Vertical Spacer -->
  <TD COLSPAN=5 WIDTH=300><IMG BORDER=0 WIDTH=1 HEIGHT=10
   SRC="../resources/dot_black.gif"></TD>

</TR>
<!-- End Row 4 Of Table-->


<!-- Start Row 5 Of Table -->
<TR VALIGN=top>

  <!-- Image Title Cell -->
  <TD COLSPAN=5 WIDTH=298 ALIGN=middle>
  <IMG BORDER=0 WIDTH=80 HEIGHT=30
   SRC="../titles/tokyo95.b.txt.gif"></TD>

</TR>
<!-- End Row 5 Of Table-->


<!-- Start Row 6 Of Table -->
<TR VALIGN=top>

  <!-- Blank Vertical Spacer -->
  <TD COLSPAN=5 WIDTH=300><IMG BORDER=0 WIDTH=1
   HEIGHT=6 SRC="../resources/dot_black.gif"></TD>
```

```
    </TR>
    <!-- End Row 6 Of Table-->


    <!-- Start Row 7 Of Table -->
    <TR VALIGN=top>

      <!-- The Text for the Page -->
      <TD WIDTH=298 COLSPAN=5 ALIGN=middle>Japanese women
      bow in traditional greeting in the lobby of Apple
      Computer's Headquarters.</TD>

    </TR>
    <!-- End Row 7 Of Table-->

</TABLE>
<!-- End Table -->

</CENTER>

<!-- Bottom Margin Vertical Spacer -->
<IMG BORDER=0 WIDTH=1 HEIGHT=15
 SRC="../resources/dot_black.gif"><BR>

<!-- Preload for Next Image -->
<IMG BORDER=0 WIDTH=1 HEIGHT=1
 SRC="../images/zurich90.b.img.jpg"><BR>

<!-- Preload for Negative Image -->
<IMG BORDER=0 WIDTH=1 HEIGHT=1
 SRC="../images/tokyo95.w.img.jpg">

</BODY></HTML>
```

The Reverse Side

Once I have each positive image optimized for look and load, I simply Invert and Flip it in Photoshop. It takes very little extra time; the impact is well worth the effort [10.14].

The structure of the page and HTML are the same, but I must remember to link the photos backwards, so people move to the left to go forward (toward frame 36) and right to go back. I work with Doug to get the comments for each photo to be the same length as the caption, so when you go to the back side, you see the same amount of gray text for each photograph. I love the fact that it takes a second before you realize there's something new to read back here.

The preload for this page first loads the next (left) image, assuming people will want to keep progressing down the line, then the main image for the opposing positive page, in case they arrived at that negative page from another negative page.

The Final Frame

Without showing the 36th page, I want to show you what happens when you get to the end of this site. Doug wanted visitors to see others' comments and to be able to leave comments if they wanted. I came up with a film-credits-style presentation that puts visitors' comments opposite their names [**10.15**].

My navigation bar goes at the top, with a gray word to give status information.

The Feedback Form

Contrary to the fill-out form in Chapter 8, this feedback form is direct and simple. No need to make it span the page or include several fields. Just a comment and an e-mail address are enough. I design it so that visitors know they are still in the gallery, not yet back out in the world of default page design. They give their reactions first, then they can see what other visitors have said. On both pages, I give them a chance to go to the information pages or go back to the entrance.

I never make a form from scratch. I always copy one and work with it. There are plenty of good forms on the Web to copy. (See the Book Site for a good list. The Book Site has information on setting up the Perl script that runs this form.) This file is called feedback.html, and the final file for presenting the selected comments will be called comments.html [**10.16**].

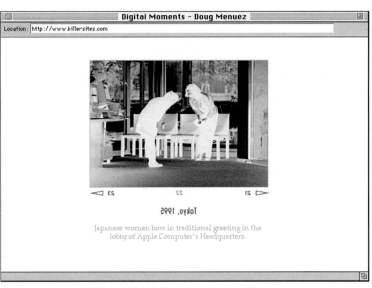

10.14 The reverse pages add another dimension to the exhibit.

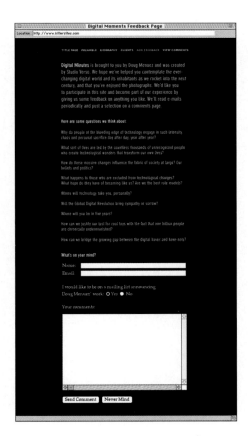

10.15 A form mock-up. I actually mock up the forms in Photoshop, to play with layouts without being influenced by HTML.

10.16 This particular form doesn't do anything fancy. It just sends Doug e-mail and lets him decide what to post on his comments page.

```
<!-- Begin Form -->
<FORM METHOD="post" ACTION="email.cgi">

<!-- Begin Form Table -->
<TABLE BORDER=0 CELLSPACING=0 CELLPADDING=0 WIDTH=524>


  <!-- Start Row 1 Of Table -->
  <TR VALIGN=top>

    <!-- Left Margin -->
    <TD ROWSPAN=12><IMG BORDER=0 WIDTH=85 HEIGHT=1
     SRC="resources/dot_black.gif"></TD>

    <!-- Top Margin -->
    <TD COLSPAN=2><IMG BORDER=0 WIDTH=354 HEIGHT=1
     SRC="resources/dot_black.gif"></TD>

    <!-- Right Margin -->
    <TD ROWSPAN=12><IMG BORDER=0 WIDTH=85 HEIGHT=1
     SRC="resources/dot_black.gif"></TD>

  </TR>
  <!-- End Row 1 Of Table-->


  <!-- Start Row 2 Of Table -->
  <TR>

    <TD ALIGN=left WIDTH=60>Name:</TD>

    <TD WIDTH=294><INPUT TYPE="text" NAME="namefield"
     SIZE="50" VALUE=""></TD>

  </TR>
  <!-- End Row 2 Of Table-->


  <!-- Start Row 3 Of Table -->
  <TR VALIGN=top>

    <!-- Blank Vertical Spacer -->
    <TD COLSPAN=2><IMG BORDER=0 WIDTH=354 HEIGHT=10
     SRC="resources/dot_black.gif"></TD>

  </TR>
  <!-- End Row 3 Of Table-->


  <!-- Start Row 4 Of Table -->
  <TR>

    <TD ALIGN=left WIDTH=60>Email:</TD>
```

```
   <TD WIDTH=294><input type="text" name="emailfield"
   size="50"><br></TD>

</TR>
<!-- End Row 4 Of Table-->


<!-- Start Row 5 Of Table -->
<TR VALIGN=top>

  <!-- Blank Vertical Spacer -->
  <TD COLSPAN=2><IMG BORDER=0 WIDTH=354 HEIGHT=20
   SRC="resources/dot_black.gif"></TD>

</TR>
<!-- End Row 5 Of Table-->


<!-- Start Row 6 Of Table -->
<TR VALIGN=top>

  <TD COLSPAN=2 WIDTH=354>I would like to be on a
  mailing list announcing <BR>Doug Menuez's work:
  <INPUT TYPE="radio" NAME="list" VALUE="unknown"
  CHECKED>Yes
  <INPUT TYPE="radio" NAME="list"
  VALUE="no">No</TD>

</TR>
<!-- End Row 6 Of Table -->


<!-- Start Row 7 Of Table -->
<TR VALIGN=top>

  <!-- Blank Vertical Spacer -->
  <TD COLSPAN=2><IMG BORDER=0 WIDTH=354 HEIGHT=20
   SRC="resources/dot_black.gif"></TD>

</TR>
<!-- End Row 7 Of Table-->


<!-- Start Row 8 Of Table -->
<TR>

  <TD COLSPAN=2 WIDTH=354>Your Comments:<BR></TD>
</TR>

<!-- End Row 8 Of Table -->


<!-- Start Row 9 Of Table -->
```

```
   <TR VALIGN=top>

     <!-- Blank Vertical Spacer -->
     <TD COLSPAN=2><IMG BORDER=0 WIDTH=354 HEIGHT=5
     SRC="resources/dot_black.gif"></TD>

   </TR>
   <!-- End Row 9 Of Table-->


   <!-- Start Row 10 Of Table -->
   <TR>

     <TD COLSPAN=2 WIDTH=354><TEXTAREA NAME="otherinfo"
     ROWS=15 COLS=53></TEXTAREA></TD>

   </TR>
   <!-- End Row 10 Of Table -->


   <!-- Start Row 11 Of Table -->
   <TR VALIGN=top>

     <!-- Blank Vertical Spacer -->
     <TD COLSPAN=2><IMG BORDER=0 WIDTH=354 HEIGHT=15
     SRC="resources/dot_black.gif"></TD>

   </TR>
   <!-- End Row 11 Of Table-->


   <!-- Start Row 12 Of Table -->
   <TR>

     <TD COLSPAN=2 WIDTH=354><INPUT TYPE="submit"
     VALUE="Send Comment"><INPUT TYPE="reset"
     VALUE="Never Mind"></TD>

   </TR>
   <!-- End Row 12 Of Table -->

</TABLE>
<!-- End Text Table -->

</FORM>
<!-- End Form -->
```

Engineering

The software engineering for this site presents challenges beyond the realm of the average graphic designer. While you may not be completely at home with the material that follows, the basic ideas should be clear. *I don't write the programs that go on my server. I work with my webmaster to achieve the effect I want. The better I understand what goes on behind the scenes, the more I can look for solutions that are technically feasible and robust.*

Pseudo-Randomness

Once I have the site built with 36 interior images all hooked up, I test it out on several friends. This test gives me the idea for adding the short cut to the entry page, giving people a chance to avoid the heavy title page if they want to, especially if they've already been there once and want to go through the main exhibit again. I could stop here and save a lot of work, but the idea is to make it look like the exhibit is always changing, with a different 36 images each time you visit. To do this, I'll devise a way to show 36 images chosen from a total of 56, seemingly at random.

There are two ways to present random pages at a site like this: really random and pseudo-random. *Really random* involves a Perl script that runs every time someone gets to the front page, spitting out a temporary site they can visit one time only. The *pseudo-random* way is to prebuild a set of sites, enough that most people won't realize there's a limited number of them.

This approach works well in situations where it's preferable to do extra

HTML work in lieu of programming. Think of it as building several trains and using a switch to put a new train on the track every minute. This "poor-man's random" strategy is not only easier on the designer, it's easier on the server (fewer CPU cycles) and the support staff, since it requires less maintenance and debugging [10.17]. In this case, I'll build three trains from a total of 56 images. If I want to, I can always make more.

Now that I have one train working, it's time to make three trains.

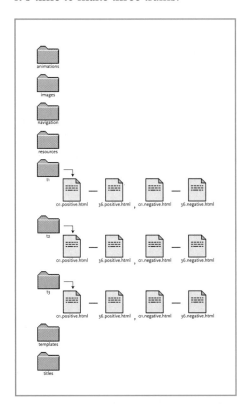

10.17 The directory structure for making three trains.

Directory Structure

I like to run a flat file system on the server. No matter how complicated the site, I generally use only one level of directories (directories and folders are equivalent). I put the resources directory and any other holding tank directories at the top level of a site, along with any second-level logical directories the site will need. For example, if there are five main areas of my site, I might have five main directories. I try not to have any directories deeper than this, unless they store a large group of images particular to the HTML for that directory only. **I never put HTML files more than one level down in the hierarchy, because of the time wasted in debugging file references.** I keep almost all HTML files one level down from the top.

Photographs are in the images directory, but they are called by HTML files one level down, in the different train directories, so each tag in the HTML file looks something like:

```
<IMG SRC=../images/
tokyo95.b.jpg>.
```

The "../" means "up and over" in the directory structure. It works with the folders right on my machine as well as when I put it on the server later. I must refer to the title gifs by typing ../titles/ rather than titles/ before the file name.

Because I'm working one directory down, I also have to add "../" to my resources folder references, or they won't work:

```
<IMG VSPACE=x SRC=
"../resources/
dot_black.gif">
```

▷ 📁 animations
▫ biography.html
▫ clients.html
▫ comments.html
▫ feedback.html
▷ 📁 images
▫ index.html
▷ 📁 navigation
▫ photolist.html
▫ preamble.html
▷ 📁 resources
▷ 📁 t1
▷ 📁 t2
▷ 📁 t3
▷ 📁 templates
▷ 📁 titles

Building railroad cars. I want to make sure this idea works on my desktop before moving it to the server. After preparing another 20 images, I have 56 to work with (and Doug has supplied 56 captions and photo notes). I make the positive and negative versions of all the photos, and I make the title GIFs for each page, including their reversed counterparts. Once I have all the ingredients, it's a matter of putting them all together.

All the images go into the images folder with logical names like tokyo95.b.img.jpg and tokyo95.b.txt.gif as before. This folder now contains all 112 images. I make another folder, called titles, where I store all 112 title GIFs.

I make another directory on my hard disk, called templates. There I make the HTML template for each picture and its negative counterpart. It's important to give each file a logical name, like tokyo95.b.html and tokyo95.w.html. I must put all 112 HTML files in place before taking the next step. It's important to associate the names of images and title GIFs with the right narrative text. This takes the most attention to what I'm doing, but I will do it only 112 times. There is much more linking to do, but it involves less thinking and more repetition.

I link each HTML page (railroad car) to its negative (but not evil) twin, but not by name. Because I don't know the names of the Back and Forward files, or which number each one will be, or which number the negative counterpart HTML file will be, I leave an "xx" in the code in these six places (you'll see why in a minute).

To make room for all the trains, I

create three new directories (folders), called t1, t2, and t3. For each train, I will build railroad cars out of the template HTML files and fill up a new directory with a different combination of template files.

To make the first train, I open the templates folder and copy the 36 HTML files I want for that train (and their negative counterparts) into the first train's folder. Now here's the important part: As I copy each HTML file, I change the name from tokyo95.b.html to 01.b.html or 22.b.html, or whatever number is next in the sequence. This leaves the logical names behind and sorts them in order of appearance in the folder. (Using the 01-09 prefix will ensure that my files alphabetize properly in the folder.) I keep adding these files and changing their names until I get to 36.b.html, which is one of the three special color versions I've made. Notice that I'm only copying HTML files here, not images, so the amount of data duplicated is quite small.

Now I have made all the cars for one complete train. The next thing to do is hook them up.

Hooking up the trains. Now that I have the HTML templates for that train in place, I hook them together by changing the links. This is repetitive, but it goes very quickly. I select 20 files (the first ten pages and their negative counterparts) and open them all at once in my text editor. Searching for "xx", I can replace the numbers of each file without much thought. For file number six, for example, I put "06" into the "xx" part of the file name of the reverse file,

"05" into the previous link and the back button's GIF file name, "06" into the text that shows which file this is, and "07" into the forward link and its GIF file name. I close the file and do the same to the negative version (remembering to switch the "05" and the "07" links so they point backwards). Finally, I switch the preload file names. This takes a little thinking. I do all the front pages in a group, then link the reverse pages. All together, each file has eight items to change [**10.18 A, B**].

10.18 A (B, next page) Inserting the proper numbers hooks the trains together.

```
<TR VALIGN=top>

  <!-- Previous Image Button -->
  <TD ALIGN=left WIDTH=55>
    <A HREF="05.b.html"><IMG BORDER=0
      WIDTH=24 HEIGHT=13
      SRC="../navigation/all.b.lt.gif">
    <IMG BORDER=0 WIDTH=24 HEIGHT=13
      SRC="../navigation/05.b.ltrt.gif">
    </A></TD>

  <!-- Blank Filler -->
  <TD><IMG BORDER=0 WIDTH=89 HEIGHT=1
    SRC="../resources/dot_black.gif"></TD>

  <!-- Image Frame Number -->
  <TD><IMG BORDER=0 WIDTH=26 HEIGHT=13
    SRC="../navigation/05.b.ctr.gif"></TD>

  <!-- Blank Filler -->
  <TD><IMG BORDER=0 WIDTH=89 HEIGHT=1
    SRC="../resources/dot_black.gif"></TD>

  <!-- Next Image Button -->
  <TD ALIGN=right WIDTH=55>
    <A HREF="06.b.html"><IMG BORDER=0
      WIDTH=24 HEIGHT=13
      SRC="../navigation/07.b.ltrt.gif">
    <IMG BORDER=0 WIDTH=24 HEIGHT=13
      SRC="../navigation/all.b.rt.gif">
    </A></TD>

</TR>
```

I change links in groups of 20 files. It takes about five minutes to link 20 files, so each train takes about 20 minutes to assemble. After everything is in place, I hook up the first and last files. The Previous link of file 01.b.html and the Next link of file 01.w.html is ../preamble.html, while the Next link of file 36.b.html and previous link of 36.w.html is ../feedback.html. Note that I have typed "Digital Moments - Doug Menuez" into the titles of all the interior pages, so as to avoid any extra work labeling pages.

10.18 B (A, previous page)

Now there's one last detail. The preload on the preamble HTML page. If you recall, it points to a file called images/tokyo95.b.img.jpg. That means the first "car" of every train should be the page that contains the tokyo95 image. There are complicated (script-based) solutions to let me vary this image from train to train, but to preserve my navigation scheme and keep things simple, I decide that the best solution is to use the same image for the first page of each version. It's a little disappointing, but the preload is more important than avoiding repetition. After the first train, the randomness starts.

After testing this train to make sure it works, I go through the same process to hook up the other two trains. I can mix and match the order of the photographs as I please, building each train from page 1 to page 36. I go through all three folders, making trains and hooking them up.

Putting the trains on the track. To get

```
<TR VALIGN=top>

  <!-- Previous Image Button -->
  <TD ALIGN=left WIDTH=55>
   <A HREF="21.b.html"><IMG BORDER=0
    WIDTH=24 HEIGHT=13
    SRC="../navigation/all.b.lt.gif">
   <IMG BORDER=0 WIDTH=24 HEIGHT=13
    SRC="../navigation/21.b.ltrt.gif">
   </A></TD>

  <!-- Blank Filler -->
  <TD><IMG BORDER=0 WIDTH=89 HEIGHT=1
   SRC="../resources/dot_black.gif"></TD>

  <!-- Image Frame Number -->
  <TD><IMG BORDER=0 WIDTH=26 HEIGHT=13
   SRC="../navigation/22.b.ctr.gif"></TD>

  <!-- Blank Filler -->
  <TD><IMG BORDER=0 WIDTH=89 HEIGHT=1
   SRC="../resources/dot_black.gif"></TD>

  <!-- Next Image Button -->
  <TD ALIGN=right WIDTH=55>
  <A HREF="23.b.html"><IMG BORDER=0 WIDTH=24
   HEIGHT=13
   SRC="../navigation/23.b.ltrt.gif">
  <IMG BORDER=0 WIDTH=24 HEIGHT=13
   SRC="../navigation/all.b.rt.gif"></A>
  </TD>

</TR>
```

Aliases and Shortcuts

On the Macintosh, make an alias by selecting a file and choosing Make Alias from the File menu. In Windows 95, you can make a shortcut to a file by right-clicking it and selecting Shortcut. With Windows 3.1, you can't make an alias. You will either have to upgrade or put everything on the server to test your work.

the trains running, I mock up the behavior of the server script on my local machine. Because the title and preamble pages never change, I just need to change the link for 1.b.html at the top level. The link inside the preamble points to this file, but right now it doesn't exist. I go to one of my trains (inside one of the train folders), click on the file 1.b.html, and make an alias, which I bring up to the top level. By calling it 1.b.html, the preamble now links straight to that train. The whole site works.

Now that I have several trains, I simply replace 1.b.html with the alias of the first file of each train, simulating track switching. Each file tests out fine, from beginning to end. I'm ready to go to the server.

Uploading to the Server. Moving the site from my desktop to the server means setting up symlinks and getting the script running *(see "Cron and Crontabs")*.

After recreating my file structure exactly on the server, I set up a symlink that points from 1.b.html to t1/1.b.html. By going to the site with my browser, I get the intended result: Train 1 works fine. I switch the top-level symlink a few more times and check a few trains at random. Everything tests out.

To automate the switching of the symlink, make a cron table with one entry. The cron table says to run my Perl switching script, switch.pl, every minute. The script simply automates what I've been doing by hand all along: making the symlink point to t1/1.b.hmtl, then t2/1.b.hmtl,

Cron and Crontabs

Throwing the switch to change the tracks involves a special system program called *cron* (by UNIX enthusiasts everywhere). **Cron** looks at a special table, called *crontab*, that tells cron what to do and when. In this case, I set up a crontab entry that tells cron to run a certain script every minute. The script throws the switch by changing a symlink. A *symlink* on a UNIX server is the equivalent of an alias (or a shortcut). *(See your webmaster or a book on UNIX for details on setting up cron events and symlinks.)*

The symlink points to the first file in one of the trains at first, then **cron** comes and tells a program called **switch** to change the link to point to car one of train two. A minute later, it calls **switch** again, pointing the symlink to car one of train three. After another minute, it gets switched back to train one and starts over. The **switch** program keeps track of the state of the symlink, while **cron** keeps track of the time.

It sounds complicated, but it's actually quite straightforward. There are two parts: the crontab entry and the script, each of which is discussed in the text. (This discussion covers how to set these up on UNIX-based servers. If you are running another operating system, ask your webmistress for the best approach.)

interval	crontab event
* * * * *	/usr/local/bin/perl switch.pl

Each asterisk stands for "repeat during every time interval": minute, hour, day, month, day of week. See this script on the next page.

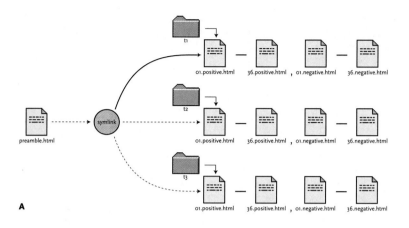

A

then t3/1.b.hmtl. When it gets to t3/1.b.hmtl, it should reset and begin again at directory t1. Because it changes every minute, it will take many tries for anyone to detect the pattern [10.19 A, B].

The crontab event calls the script every minute. The script is quite simple. All together, it's easy to debug, and it should be very easy to maintain. It's exciting to go to the server and see it switching in my browser. I make sure it really works before calling Doug and sharing the news. He's delighted with the results; I hope you will be too.

Summary

I look for solutions like the poor-man's random, where I can prebuild things and not have them running dynamically, because there is so much less to go wrong. This train-switching approach lets me focus on design, not programming. In this case, I simply make enough trains to make it feel random and add more if necessary later. The preloaded image trick works perfectly in a linear exhibit like this, provided people go down the one-way street the right way. Going against the grain of the preloads makes for slower surfing.

Though it is a complicated site, the HTML is very simple. Most of the work is in Photoshop. The hours are long, and the work itself is dull as toast. In the end, though, it pays off, because the site lets the photographs do the talking. I hope I've done justice to Doug's excellent material. It's now up to the visitors to tell us whether we're on the right track.

```perl
#!/usr/local/bin/perl
#
# Cron calls this script every minute. It looks
# at a temporary variable, then changes a sym-
# bolic link. Keep this script in the directory
# above t1, t2 and t3 or change the file names
# that being symlinked.

$VARIABLE_FILE = "tmp.var";   # this is the tem-
                              # porary variable

# looks to see if this is the first time this
is being run
if (!(-e $VARIABLE_FILE)) {
  open(NEW,"> $VARIABLE_FILE");
  print NEW 1;
  symlink("t1/1.b.html", "1.b.html");
  close(NEW);
  exit(0);
}

open(VAR,"+< $VARIABLE_FILE"); # open the file
flock(VAR,2);
$_=<VAR>;
seek(VAR,0,0);
$_++;                     # increment the variable
if ($_ == 4) {            # cycle it if it's over
  $_ = 1;
}
print VAR;
unlink "1.b.html";       # delete old symlink
symlink("t$_/1.b.html","1.b.html");
flock(VAR,8);
close(VAR);              # close up the file
```

10.19 A, B The cron event triggers this Perl script to switch the symlink.

Application

If you're making a gallery, another idea for the captions would be to use a form tag as a design element. This can be a clever way to present information, like a caption, when you don't want it to show at first. In this case, I've put the title at the top of a pop-up menu and added the caption as several lines of options in the pop-up [**10.20 A, B**]. The form doesn't do anything. It just gives me the pop-up element [**10.21**]. It might make a nice variation or give you an idea for making a gallery with a different theme but a similar structure.

10.20 A, B Using a pop-up as a design element adds another tool to your toolkit.

```
<FORM>
<SELECT>
<OPTION SELECTED>
T O K Y O ,   1 9 9 5
<OPTION>Japanese women bow in traditional
<OPTION > greeting in the lobby of Apple
<OPTION > Computer's Headquarters.
</SELECT >
</FORM >
```

10.21 Pop-ups are easy to add to any page.

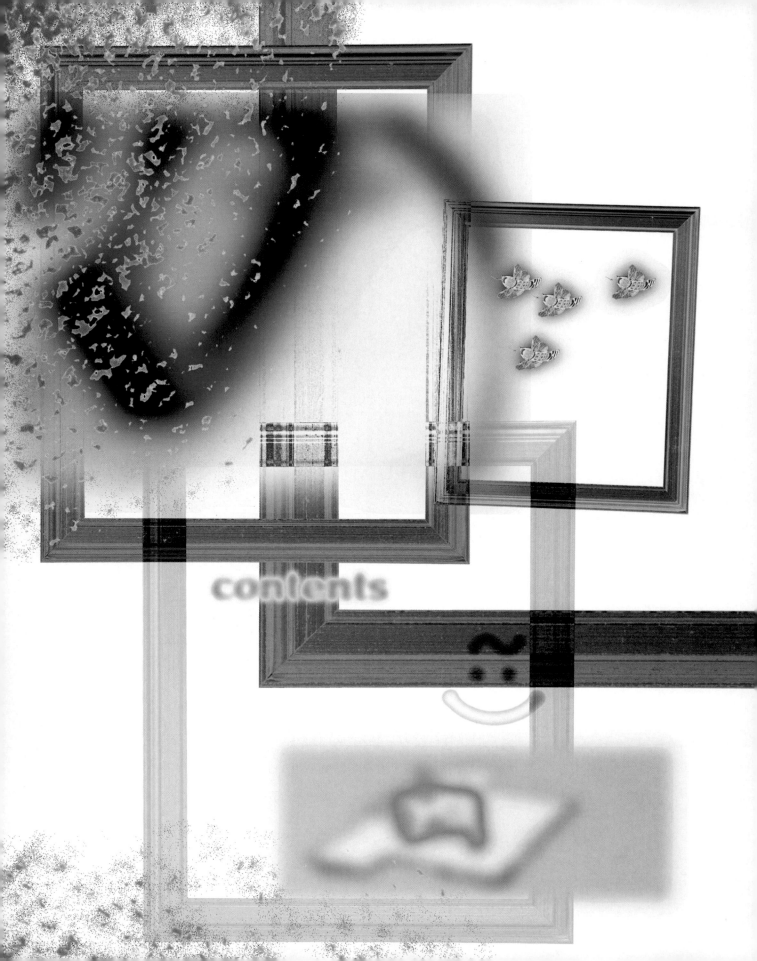

contents

## CHAPTER 11

Creative Design Solutions

In this chapter, I want to present eleven solutions I think are worth noting. Six of these sites earned my High Five award (www.highfive.com) for excellence in site design. These examples show how to use the power of metaphor and theme to bring your web pages alive, plus the little secrets of the Web's leading designers. Three are from sites I've done. Each has a particular tactic you can apply to your projects to achieve an effect or solve a problem.

Dennett's Dream
Matthew Lewis

www.cgrg.ohio-state.edu/~mlewis/
Gallery/gallery.html

Matthew Lewis finished his wonderful exhibition, *Dennett's Dream*, just as the Netscape 1.1 extensions arrived to give him a black background for presenting his work. It shows a number of paintings he did for a multimedia project at Ohio State University. The site won a High Five and much recognition from other award givers. Matt gives us two versions, a high-bandwidth and a low-bandwidth site. The high-bandwidth site is really engaging. He uses a set of ephemeral navigation arrows to provide a familiar interface.

This gallery shows an alternative version of the linear gallery structure of Chapter 10. Matt gives us two ways to walk through the space: either by advancing and turning, or by stepping sideways. No matter how you go through the space, each page gives you hints of where to go next. You never look at a full painting all by itself. You can see small parts of each painting to the left and right. These visual cues keep us moving toward the end, which is a U-turn that sends you back to the entrance. If you take the hint at the beginning and sidestep down the left side, you'll follow the paintings around the U, coming to the big finish at the end. It's an excellent example of a linear exhibition space with a beginning, middle, and end.

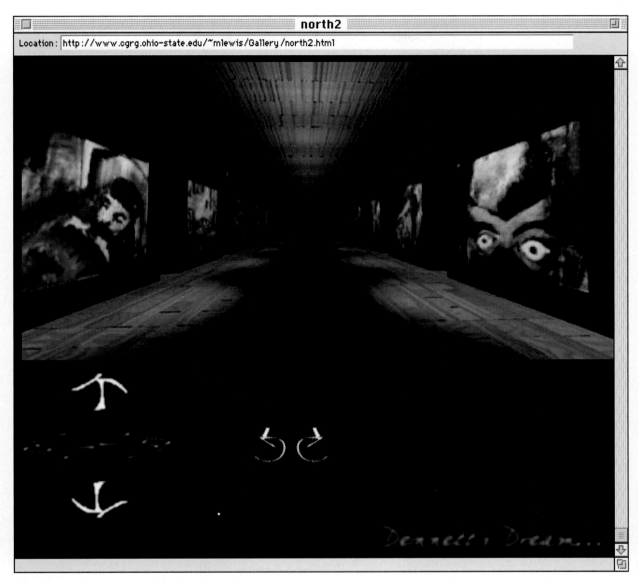

Dennett's Dream: You can walk down the middle or you can sidestep down
the left side, make the turn, and come back up the right.

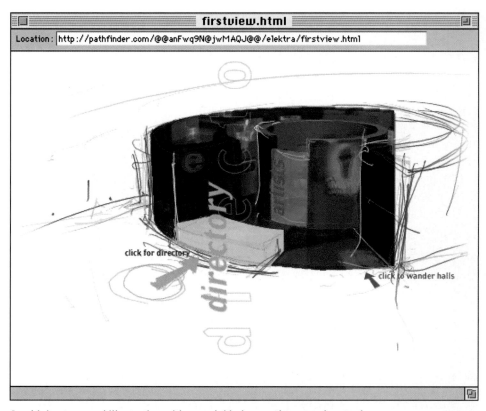

Combining type and illustration with a model balances theme and metaphor.

Elektra Records
Avalanche

www.elektra.com

Avalanche's site for Elektra records is a killer example of how to achieve a metaphor without being too literal. Combining a 3-D building metaphor with type and other 2-D gestures, the site achieves a balance of information and spacial representation. Who needs beveled edges? The depth of this site comes from the excellent combination of color, type, and shadow.

The first screen sucks you in. Wandering around is easy; the graphics color-code the space, and the hallways don't take up much bandwidth. Each room is informative, with a casual host who tells you what's going on.

Note that the building is in the shape of a CD (or a record, whichever you prefer), and the heart of Elektra is the artists. The staff forms a protective shell around the artists, which have their own individually designed home pages. The metaphor melds with their sophisticated use of type to create a virtual space that is truly appropriate.

204

The metaphor is light and graphic; the plan view serves as a core page. The pop-up gives you direct access to all artists' home pages. The "try again" button is unnecessary.

Roger's clever trick: using a table to mortice four static images around one dynamic one.

Big Healeys
Roger Los

los.com/healey/big.html

Don't try this at home! Roger Los, an independent designer (and English sports car enthusiast) in Seattle, has created a very sophisticated frame-based site, using nested frames and JavaScript to keep the frames behaving well. Roger is a site designer with a rare blend of visual and technical acumen. The showpiece of the site is the speedometer dial that tells you what number visitor you are. Many sites have rotating counters; this is the only one I've seen that uses them well.

It's a simple enough trick: Take a photograph of a speedometer, cut it up, and replace the odometer with an active access counter. Doing it well is something else. Each digit is a separate GIF. A special program corellates the number to be displayed with the proper GIFs, spits out the HTML, and the whole page serves up dynamically. Go try it and see for yourself.

Locating Graphic Elements

On the Mac, to see how a page is built, click on individual graphic elements with your cursor, and move the mouse around slightly. You'll be able to "pick up" an image and move it around, pulling its outline out of place on the page so you can see how it fits with other elements. You can also use the View › Document Info command in Netscape Navigator to dissect a page.

The odometer on this dial really works!

Dial It
Peter Horvath

mindlink.net/ph/tv_2.html

Peter Horvath is part of a two-person design team (along with Sharon Matarazzo) called 6168. Peter's design for a TV dial is an excellent way to couch a pop-culture exhibition in a pop-culture metaphor. The TV dial plays center stage, evoking memories of *Gilligan's Island* and *Dragnet*. To flip channels, select a hotlink. The links turn dark as you hit them, so you keep coming back to the dial for the pages you haven't seen yet.

This is simply a tour-de-force of table work; with the tables turned on, you can see how it all works. Rather than put the code here, I encourage you to see the 6168 site and view the source *in situ*.

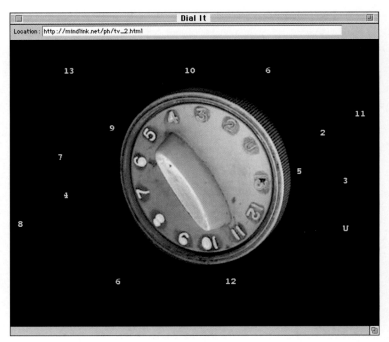

Can you see the table structure of this page?

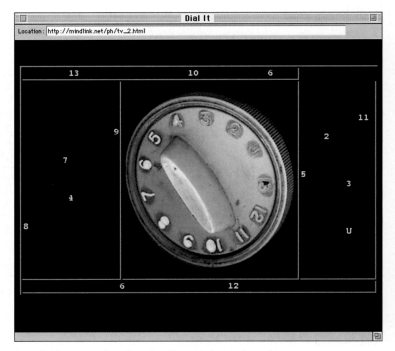

A TV dial is a great interface for dissecting popular culture.

The Throne of Drones
Ray Guillette

www.wilder.net/stc/sombient/throne/
index.html

Site designer Ray Guillette's work
on the promotional site for the *Throne
of Drones* CD by Sombient Records
earned him a High Five. Ray took the
CD's cover art and created a beehive
metaphor with an inner sanctum that
is one of the most appropriate pages
on the Web. When you get to the site,
you see an enticing entry screen with
bees flying into a metal hive.

The core page carries the metaphor
beautifully. Even though Ray had to
use the chrome lettering that came
with the CD, his design of the page
overcomes the extrusion with a sub-
lime interpretation of the metaphor.
The background is a small repeating
element that loads quickly. Looking up
at the top portal gives you the feeling
of having just entered through the top
hatch. As you scroll down, the shadows
of the bees change incrementally,
giving you the feeling of sitting on a
curved surface. This shadow trick,
combined with the angle of the top
and bottom portals, nails the metaphor
without using a huge background
image that takes three days to load.

Ray Guillette's core page
uses shadows to create a
3-D effect.

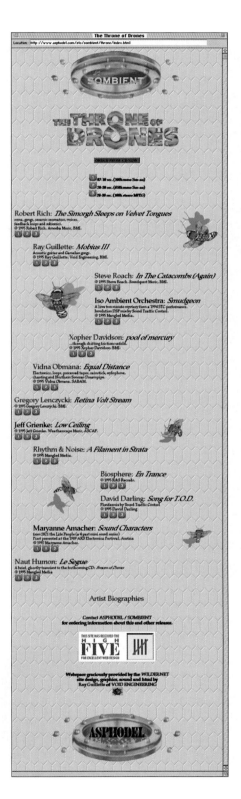

The entrance sets expectations high.

Mercedes-USA
Magnet Interactive Studios

www.usa.mercedes-benz.com

The Mercedes North America site, designed by Felipe Del Corral of Magnet.com, has an excellent use of offsets that is quite clever. The entire site is excellent, but I want to point out two specific solutions I think are excellent. First, the feedback. Wherever you go in this site, the dots tell you where you are. The horizontal dots denote which section, and the vertical dots denote pages within sections. The circle elements reflect the Mercedes symbol and reinforce the circle theme woven delicately throughout.

Any time you have a feedback mechanism like this, you must do extra work to make all the necessary versions. Each graphic needs a different version, one for every position of the dot. A simpler way to indicate status is to use a small element that floats next to your graphics or text indicating status. My GIGAWEB conference pages use a triangle that points to the current area. This separate element is easy to code, update, and maintain.

This two-tiered approach lets you go either to any particular page in this area, or off to any other area. It's not true random access – it is too complicated to link every page from every other page – it gives visitors two levels of choices, which is just right for most sites. You either walk around your local neighborhood, or you go to another neighborhood and start at the top. In this way, you can slice through the site either by model or by category (main, dealer, leasing, index).

The second feature is the way the site deals with offsets *(see Chapter 4, "Laying out Pages")*. Notice that the foreground aligns perfectly with the background, which is a skinny horizontal image. How do they do it? Two ways. First, they have a script running on their server that detects which browser you have and serves you one of two backgrounds: the one with an 8-pixel horizontal offset or the one with a 10-pixel horizontal offset. Having corrected for the horizontal offset problems, the only offset variations are now vertical. The vertical format accounts for that, letting the front images "slide" up and down along the background. The alignment is perfect and the page looks great to all who enter.

The only bug here is that some browser programs (i.e., Internet Explorer) can *cloak* themselves, telling a site upon arrival that they are a Netscape browser, not who they really are. As it turns out, these browsers also have different offsets from Netscape browsers (which are themselves all different), so this page will misbehave in certain situations. Won't it be great when all browsers have zero offsets?

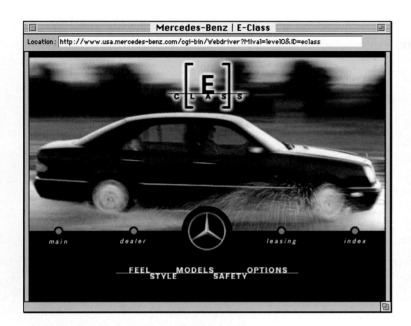

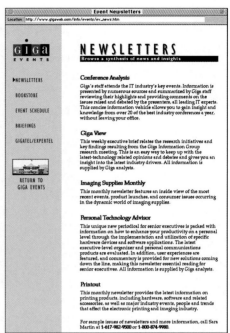

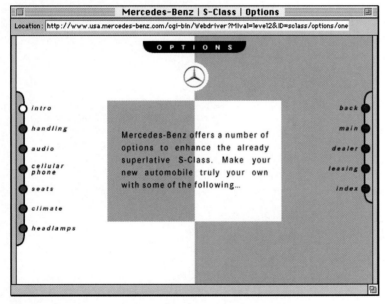

The Mercedes site by Magnet is sleek and efficient. Both Mercedes-USA and GIGAWEB sites tell you where you are with a status indicator.

Zoloft Intro Page
Josh Feldman

www.spectacle.com/zoloft/initiation/letter.html

This clever page was designed by Josh Feldman of Prophet Communications for his interactive adventure, Zoloft. The amazing wood panel back image was made from a scan and made into a seamless JPEG in Photoshop. This page makes excellent use of the LOWSRC argument to the <IMG> tag. An image can have two sources, the *low source* and the so-called *high source*. The low source loads first. It is meant to be a proxy for those with slower connections, so the user gets an idea of what is to come. If the user waits, the higher-quality image loads on top of the low source image. In this case, Josh has made two separate images, the first a torn-open envelope, the second an open letter. Note that he has copied a piece of the envelope, to preserve conti-

nuity after the transition to the high-source image. This is a brilliant use of the LOWSRC option. You occasionally see it used well, but rarely this well.

This page has an extra little gift. There is a Shockwave movie preload that loads the exterior shot of the church for the next screen while you're reading the letter. It's scaled into a small image in the upper left corner. Then, when you go to the next page, there are many images to load, and this one is already in the cache. This image is couched in a Shockwave file, but it could have been a GIF instead.

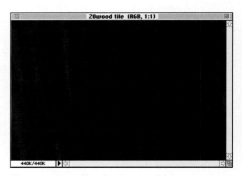

The amazing tiling background image.

The background, the low source, and the high source.

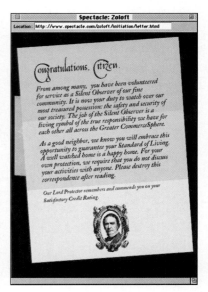

Urban Diary
Joseph Squier

gertrude.art.uiuc.edu/ludgate/the/
place.html

Joseph Squier is an Assistant Professor at the University of Illinois at Urbana-Champaign, teaching photography and electronic media. Joseph's site, called The Place, has received critical praise from around the world. I learned to turn off underlining from this site, just a few days after I first started surfing. Joseph is responsible for opening the eyes of hundreds of thousands of visitors who find his site refreshing and visually stunning.

This page from his piece, the Urban Diary series, is one of several image maps using photographs of graph paper to display an entire page. This page, while somewhat memory-intensive, is perhaps the first page on the Web to really break the grip of HTML. The numbers at the bottom tell you which page you are on, almost everything links to something interesting, and every time you come back you discover something new. Visit the rest of The Place to see what may have been the world's first third-generation site.

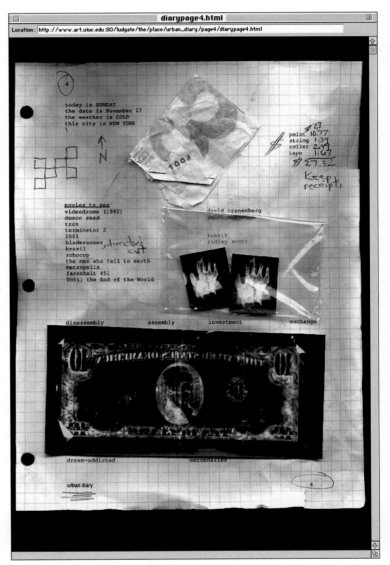

Joseph Squier's Urban Diary uses a metaphor that sets the standard for third-generation designers.

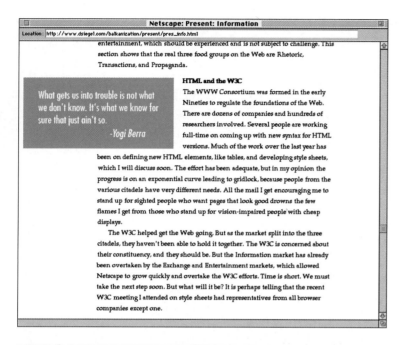

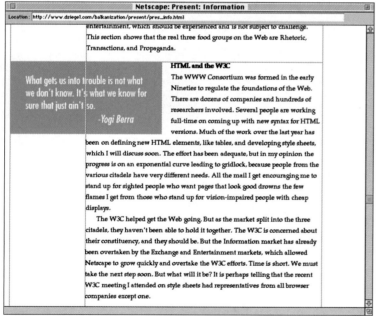

Pull quotes with tables: Amaze your friends!

The Balkanization of the Web
David Siegel

www.dsiegel.com/balkanization/

In December of 1995, I wrote an essay called "The Balkanization of the Web," discussing how the market affects the future of HTML. I wanted to use pull quotes on my pages, and I wanted them to penetrate the table margin I was using for my text. I wanted the text to run around my pull quotes, set in a font called Futura.

After some brainstorming, I came up with a solution that almost solves the problem. By splitting the images, I was able to hang half the image in the margin. Now I had to make sure they would line up, not float away. They had to be at the top of a table cell, which meant I could place my pull quotes only at the beginning of a new section. This way, no matter what font size people have, the text flows around the bottom edge of the left-aligned GIF and continues on.

What I like about this trick is that you don't really notice it. It's stunt html without calling attention to itself. The pull quotes look familar and don't stop you as you go. The rule of thumb here is to make each pull quote no taller than about 350 pixels, so people don't have to scroll just to finish the quote.

GFOZ Home Page
David Siegel

www.gfoz.com

I made this site for my brother-in-law Gary Foster, who is a film producer. Among others, he produced *Sleepless in Seattle* and *Tin Cup*. Gary wanted a simple, elegant, understated home page. To give his page an entry feel without a separate URL, I put his name on a GIF up front, then I made an animated GIF that fades in after it all loads. The animated GIF goes through several color-cube colors, starting out dark blue and ending in a golden list of categories. I made the Courier type aliased, both so it would load quickly and to give the effect of HTML fading in, which everyone knows you can't do. Then I made it an image map, so the links would be operational. The timing on the fade-in is critical. It takes about five seconds total. I worked with several different timing schemes to come up with the final numbers. If I had not restricted myself to the color cube, I could have made the transition effect much smoother, but in this case I end up with a page that weighs in under 10K.

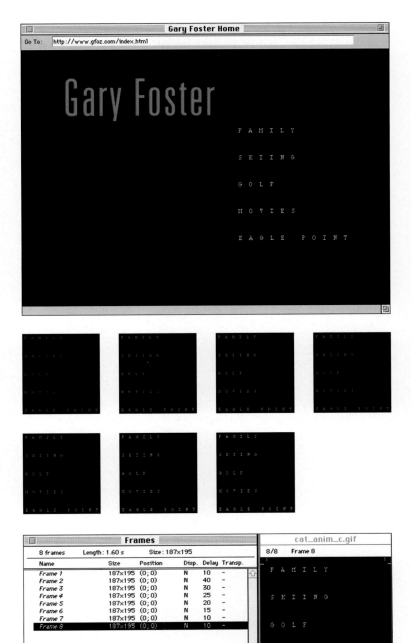

Gary Foster's home page starts with a name and fades in.

Exit Tunnel
David Siegel

www.dsiegel.com/exit/index.html

I like to give people a little rush as they leave my site. It's good for word of mouth, and it leads to my inevitable list o' links. Use this technique any time you want a clickable slide show effect without using Shockwave. The user arrives at a page and, after a slight delay, sees an image. She thinks this is the only image in the file, but when she clicks on it, a second image appears immediately – no waiting. The images present themselves in the same place on the screen each time, for a slide show presentation. They have all been preloaded, because they are all on the same page. The two tricks here are the use of individual tables and the NAME tag.

The NAME tag enables you to designate a place elsewhere in your HTML file to which a link can point. Any book on HTML will tell you about it, but it's important to know that tables block it. If you use tables, you must end the table, give the NAME reference, and then start the next table.

I'd like to take this opportunity to say that most people use the NAME tag badly. They always use it right next to the item they want presented, so the item appears jammed up against the top of the browser window. It's nicer to leave a little vertical space (at least a <p> tag) before the item, so it's set off a bit and easier to read.

Using single-pixel GIFs, I make sure there's a margin above the images as you make your way down the file. This approach works no matter how large the visitors' monitors are.

In essence, the links are playing a game of leap frog, pointing to the next numbered one down. Numbers don't matter, of course, as long as the names are unique; they can be anything.

This method enables you to load any number of images, then surprise your visitors with lightning-fast response. Of course, you don't want people to wait too long for the initial load, so if you have more than about six large (but highly compressible) images, you will probably want the final link to go off to a new file and start over.

<A NAME="one">

<A NAME="two">

<A NAME="three">

<A NAME="four">

<A NAME="five">

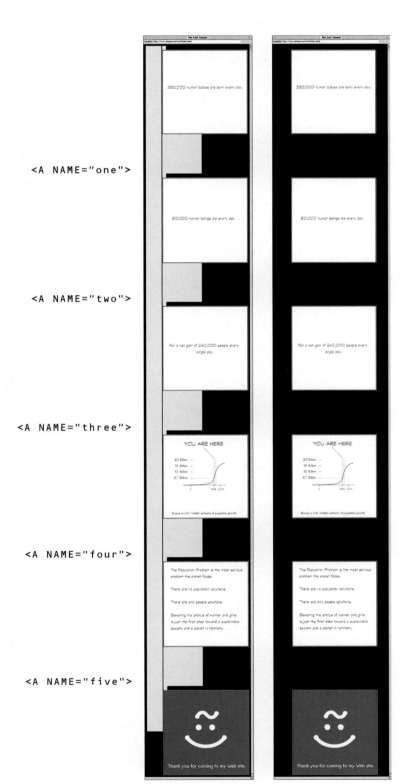

The exit tunnel with and without the GIFs turned on.

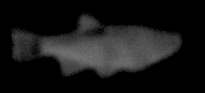

Part III

A PDF Primer

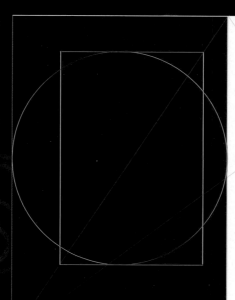

In themselves, experiments are not art. Infinite amounts of energy are wasted because everybody feels he has to make his own start, his own beginning, instead of getting to know what has already been done. It is doubtful that anyone who doesn't want to become an apprentice will ever become a master. To respect tradition is not at all historicism. All historicism is dead. . . . We have to return to the great traditions of the Renaissance and the Baroque book, study the originals and fill them with new life. Here alone is the measuring stick by which we should methodically judge faulty books. Experiments aimed at creating something "different" may be fascinating and entertaining, at least for the experimenter. But a lasting tradition will not spring from experiments. Only the legacy of true mastery can provide this.

Jan Tschichold, 1964

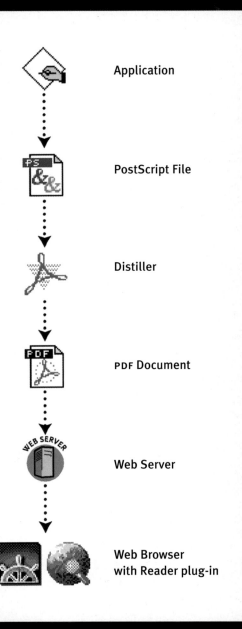

Application

PostScript File

Distiller

PDF Document

Web Server

Web Browser
with Reader plug-in

12.1 Making PDFs is as easy as printing to a PostScript printer.

In 1993, Adobe Systems introduced the Portable Document Format (PDF) as a way to distribute fully formatted, print-quality documents electronically. PDF is now on the Web, rapidly developing into a powerful complement or alternative to HTML. Using familiar desktop publishing software and the Adobe Acrobat family of products, you can publish a single PDF file as an entire Web site, featuring the most sophisticated layouts and typography, all without writing one line of code or indexing a single GIF. Alternatively, you can mix PDF with HTML on a site to take advantage of the unique qualities of each.

Earlier generations of the Adobe Acrobat product family (2.1 and before) required surfers to download entire PDF files before they could open them. This limitation and a plague of poorly designed PDFs on the Web has led to the unfair perception that PDF is an awkward, large-file format. Acrobat 3.0 addresses the first problem, allowing PDF pages to download one at a time and appear quickly, right in the browser window. This *streaming* feature makes it possible to surf a PDF-based site just like an HTML one. In addition, text now anti-aliases automatically, for vastly improved legibility at smaller type sizes. While it's still just as easy to design poor PDF files as poor HTML-based sites, the potential for rich visual design is much greater in PDF. What's more, PDFs designed with proper attention to bandwidth issues compare very favorably to HTML-based sites in total file size.

This chapter introduces the PDF format and tools, while Chapter 13 explores the design challenges and potential of publishing in PDF with a real-world example: a mail-order product catalog.

What Is PDF?

PDF is essentially a compact, special form of PostScript – the language computers send down the wire to most printers. Unlike HTML, PostScript is a *page-description language,* offering total graphical control of fixed-size pages. Designers have as much control over PDF as over paper, but with many of HTML's interactive features as well. Because it's largely a *vector* format, PDF is *resolution-independent,* or *scalable.* You can zoom into a PDF page in any increment up to 800%, or view it at smaller than actual size, with excellent design fidelity. Finally, PDF is a fixed *output format.* Like hard copy, you can mark up, rearrange, add, or delete pages, but it's not practical to edit their contents substantially.

How Publishing in PDF Works

Virtually anyone can view, search, or print PDFs with the free Acrobat Reader software, which includes a plug-in for integration with Netscape and Internet Explorer. Making a PDF, however, requires either Acrobat Distiller or PDFWriter (which isn't currently free). PDFWriter is suitable for simple documents like word-processed files, while Distiller is the more powerful, flexible program. Included with both of these is Acrobat Exchange, which can view and modify existing PDFs. I will concentrate on Distiller, because it's more appropriate for higher-end work.

In stark contrast to the painstaking processes described in Parts I and II of this book, cranking out single pages or large sites in PDF is easy. Any print publishing tool – PageMaker, Quark-XPress, even Microsoft Word – can "print" PDFs to the Web.

You begin by preparing a document as though you were printing to a Post-Script printer. Instead of printing, you save a PostScript file to your hard disk, then process the file with Distiller. A few seconds (or minutes) later, a PDF file appears on your disk. You can then copy this file to a Web server just as you would an HTML document [**12.1**].

Of course, I'm simplifying. As it turns out, most documents designed for print are unpleasant to read on screen, and there are many fine points of design and execution separating good PDFs from bad. As you develop a feel for the medium, you learn to design PDFs for the screen right in your desktop publishing program.

Preparing the Document

The first step in preparing a document for output to PDF is to decide whether to format it for print, or for on-screen reading, or to attempt a compromise. While PDF is a great way to distribute print documents, this book covers designing PDFs for the screen, where much of your audience might have only a few hundred pixels horizontally (and fewer still vertically) to view your pages.

A good starting point is to pretend you're designing a small, landscape-format booklet with single-sided pages. This will minimize the need to zoom and scroll around in the PDF. As a de-

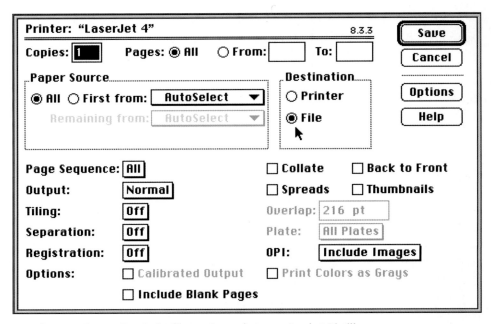

12.2 Once you have a PostScript file, you're ready to use Acrobat Distiller.

signer, fixed-size pages are either your friend or your enemy – if your audience can't read whole pages without zooming or scrolling, your layout becomes meaningless, and page breaks become a nuisance *(see Chapter 13 for more detail on design)*.

Once you've designed and proofed your document, you must write a PostScript file. This is not the same as saving an *Encapsulated PostScript* (EPS) file. You save a PostScript file through the Print dialog box of your publishing application [12.2].

Acrobat Distiller

Distiller makes your PostScript file portable. PostScript files tend to be big, especially if the document has many images. It also requires that any fonts used in the document be available to

the target printer or system. Distiller overcomes these portability problems by means of *compression, downsampling,* and *font embedding.*

Distiller can compress both the text and images in your document. How much compression occurs depends on your settings and on the nature of the document. Distiller lets you specify separate methods and degrees for each kind of image. JPEG compression is the default for most images, with lossless methods available as well.

In addition to compressing your images, Distiller can downsample them, limiting their resolution (DPI). If you expect your PDF to be viewed at 100% magnification and are willing to sacrifice some quality if the document is printed, set Distiller to downsample to 72 DPI for the greatest file size savings. If you want people to be able to zoom in on an image to see more detail, downsample to a higher resolution (multiplying the magnification factor you want to support by 72), but remember that higher-resolution images translate to significantly larger file sizes. Both image compression and downsampling occur on a job-wide basis, meaning that all images of a given type will undergo the same process.

Between image compression and downsampling, you have a great deal of control over the image quality and size of your document. Hundreds of megabytes of PostScript can sometimes compress to less than one megabyte in PDF, which might amount to just a few kilobytes per page. In most cases, a given amount of text and graphics can be significantly more compact in PDF than in HTML, though it's difficult to generalize about such very different formats.

Distiller can embed in your PDF all the fonts it requires. Your fonts can be Type 1 or TrueType, Macintosh, Windows, or UNIX (one PDF will work across all of these platforms). Adobe's embedding scheme makes it legal to distribute PDFs containing commercial fonts by all major vendors. Distiller can also embed *font subsets*. If your document contains only the word "birdboy" in a particular font, only the six necessary characters will be embedded.

Each style variant of a complete embedded font (roman, bold, italic, and so on) typically adds 20-50K to your PDF. In a document of several hundred pages, this isn't significant, but for smaller PDFs, it can account for the majority of the file size. If a document contains many fonts, you might want to embed only those most critical to its appearance.

When you choose not to embed a certain font, Acrobat performs a trick: Distiller takes a few key measurements (*metrics*) of the font's characters and records them in a *substitution table* in the PDF. When either Acrobat Exchange or Reader opens the PDF, it refers to this table to generate a substitution font for the missing originals. These substitute fonts might not look too much like the originals, but because the metrics are the same, they won't affect your original layout [12.3].

Acrobat Exchange

After Distiller creates a PDF, you can open and edit it using Acrobat Exchange. With Exchange, you can mark up, rearrange, crop, rotate, add or delete pages, but not edit their contents. The non-editable part of a PDF is called the *document layer*. The editable part is called the *annotation layer*. It's beyond the scope of this book to document the very rich (and extensible) set of enhancements available in the annotation layer. What follows are only a few of the most relevant for Web work.

Exchange's *Link Tool* lets you draw hot areas on pages, which you can link to various actions. Among them are the *Go to View* and *Open* URL links. *Go to View* lets you specify a destination and magnification or a particular area of a PDF, for example: "go to the next page" or "go to page 78, showing only the lower right-hand corner of the page at 359% magnification." *Open* URL is the equivalent of an `<A HREF>` link in HTML. The target URL can be any

Cheltenham Book	I before E, except as in Deity I before E, except as in Deity
Cheltenham Ultra Italic	*I before E, except as in Deity* *I before E, except as in Deity*
Bernhard Modern	I before E, except as in Deity I before E, except as in Deity
Futura Light	I before E, except as in Deity I before E, except as in Deity
Gill Sans	I before E, except as in Deity I before E, except as in Deity
Tekton	I before E, except as in Deity I before E, except as in Deity
Künstler Script	*I before E, except as in Deity* I before E, except as in Deity

12.3 The substitution faces (shown below the originals) preserve the metrics and overall weight of your fonts, but not necessarily their design.

document on the Internet, including another PDF.

Exchange also lets you specify a document's *open attributes;* that is, how the document appears upon being opened. Examples include "open to page 5," "open at 675% magnification," or "open in full-screen mode, scaling to fill all available space." As I show in the next chapter, the last of these provides for a dramatic, windowless presentation of your document.

Summary

PDF is a compelling medium if absolute design control and easy, powerful authoring are your priorities. There's a price to pay for these benefits. The full Acrobat authoring package currently costs a few hundred dollars, and because Acrobat Reader is an extra application that runs alongside the browser, many people don't have enough RAM in their computers to surf PDFS on the Web (16 MB is a practical minimum). This means you limit your audience to some degree when you publish in PDF. The situation will likely improve over time as current versions of Acrobat Reader achieve better market penetration, but serious document design challenges remain with PDF. Its unique qualities relative to HTML – a rigid, page-based document paradigm, scalability, and complete typographical control – can be great advantages or terrible annoyances, depending on how thoughtfully the designer uses them. The next chapter explores these design issues in greater depth.

Deadly Sin Number Six

Aliasing, Dithering, and Halos

Aliasing means you can see jaggies. Think of jaggies as bugs: They creep into your images and eat away at the quality of your site. Although they make images smaller, they also make images look like they've been nibbled by leaf-cutting ants. Strive to eliminate jaggy lines or pixelated areas of images that should be smooth.

Dithering is a form of jaggies, since the pixels are usually noticeable. Dithered images generally look bad, unless they are in photographs, which should probably be JPEGs, not GIFs.

Halos are the biggest symptom of pixel rot. Halos often occur when you assume people have a certain background for surfing (like gray) and anti-alias your images to this background. Visitors with white backgrounds in their surfing preferences see gray halos around all the images.

A Catalog in PDF

What you'll learn in this chapter:

Outputting a QuarkXPress file to PDF

Print design vs. screen design

Building a navigation system

Using Distiller and Exchange

Netscape: klutz.pdf

Go To: http://www.killersites.com/a_catalog_in_pdf/klutz.pdf

The
KLUTZ
Catalogue
Spring 1996

Document: Done.

13.1 The Klutz catalog has a design that would be impossible to reproduce in HTML.

KLUTZ PRESS, proud purveyor of some of the coolest, goofiest kids' books and toys on the planet, has a colorful print mail-order catalog. Klutz also has an HTML version of the catalog on its Web site. Making and maintaining both versions involves a great deal of redundant labor, expense, and bother. This chapter describes the process and design challenges of delivering Klutz's print catalog on-line in PDF.

The Klutz Catalog

The Klutz print catalog is a 50-page booklet, formatted in an 8.125-inch square. It features extensive, full-bleed color photography and illustration, and a playful, highly irregular layout. It uses 21 fonts, ranging in size from 8.5 to 165 points **[13.1]**. A faithful translation to HTML is inconceivable.

Klutz's art department uses Quark-XPress to prepare the catalog, so I'll use it as well to prepare a PDF version. The Quark file is 13.5 megabytes, and ties together several hundred megabytes of image files.

Making a PDF

First, I'll produce a direct PDF translation of the existing format. This exercise will give me a sense of the compressibility of the catalog, so I can make informed decisions about where to economize. It will also highlight many of the difficulties inherent in translating print formats directly to the screen.

After installing all the necessary fonts on my machine and opening the Quark document, my first step is to enter Quark's Page Setup dialog box and select Adobe Acrobat Distiller as my printer type. I enter the actual page width of 8.125 inches into the paper width field, and make sure the page orientation is set to portrait, not landscape.

As this book goes to press, Adobe is announcing new tools to create, publish, and view PDFs on the Web. Some of the procedures I describe here may soon be obsolete. I'm telling you how it works today to illustrate the underlying principles. See Chapter 14 and the Book Site for more PDF discussion.

Next I open the Print dialog box and save a PostScript file to my hard disk. As a single PostScript file, this eats up several hundred megabytes on my hard disk, so I'm going to continue this exercise with only ten pages of the catalog.

With the PostScript file on my disk, I'm ready to distill. I drag and drop the file onto the Distiller icon. After a moment, a PDF appears on my disk. This file is about 1% the size of the original PostScript file. This is an amazing feat of compression, but at about 100K per page, it is still too large for the Web.

I open the PDF in Exchange. On my 1024 × 768-resolution monitor, it looks great, faithfully reproducing the look of the print catalog, but much of the type is too small to read comfortably at 100% magnification, even with anti-aliasing [13.2].

The PDF format is not to blame for these problems; the document's design is. An equivalent amount of graphics and text in HTML would probably be somewhat larger, especially if there

were any attempt to reproduce its typography with GIFS.

I copy this file to my Web server exactly as I would an HTML file. Its URL is the same as for an HTML document, but its file extension is .pdf instead of .html.

What will a surfer with a 640 × 480-resolution monitor sees when she arrives at this page on the Web? Visit the Book Site to see for yourself [13.3].

It's in there somewhere, but the print document does not provide a good browsing experience. Magnifying the page to make the type more legible is not a solution: It merely underscores the failure of the design. I can either redesign the document, or I can buy everyone surfing the Web a 21-inch monitor.

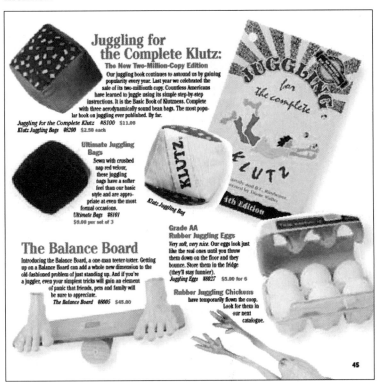

13.2 Distiller reduces this page to about 100K – too big for the Web.

13.3 Too much chrome: The Acrobat and browser interfaces don't leave enough room for the document.

Making a PDF the Right Way

It's best to build a PDF for on-screen reading from the ground up. The ground, in this case, is page size and geometry.

Virtually all computer screens have width-to-height dimensions in a 4:3 ratio, so I favor this proportion for on-screen PDFs. Operating systems, browsers, and Acrobat itself will crowd in unpredictably on this 4:3 area with their own user interfaces (especially in height) but monitor proportions themselves are constant, and the simple harmony of 4:3 makes it worth using. Similarly, the minimum screen resolution in common use is 640 × 480 pixels, so that's my target size for PDFs. Surfers with small monitors will see

pages at somewhat less than actual size, or view them in full-screen mode, without the browser and all the chrome it takes up on the screen. I'll design for either case – this means sizing the type generously and including a navigation system.

I return to my QuarkXPress document and begin reformatting. With some documents, I can begin by changing the page size in the Document Setup dialog box. In this case XPress won't let me: The page elements won't fit on the pasteboard. Instead, I create a new document, 640 by 480 points large (printer's points = pixels). I begin dragging the elements of the old document over into the new one, adjusting their sizes as necessary [13.4]. This is not an automatic process. I am literally redesigning the Klutz catalog, but I'm doing it in XPress, not with single-pixel GIFs.

In general, all elements involving fine detail need to be a bit larger for an on-screen PDF than would be appropriate for print. This is especially true of text, which I generally increase between 10 and 30 percent. Because the type is anti-aliased, I can get away with remarkably small sizes – some faces are legible even at 7 point, without magnification – but the idea is not to see what I can get away with, it's to get the best results.

Fortunately, this document was constructed with *style sheets*. Changing the type specs for the whole document is a simple matter of redefining existing styles. The more rationally a document is built in the first place, the easier it is to reformat. I choose 16-point for the running text, set in Chel-

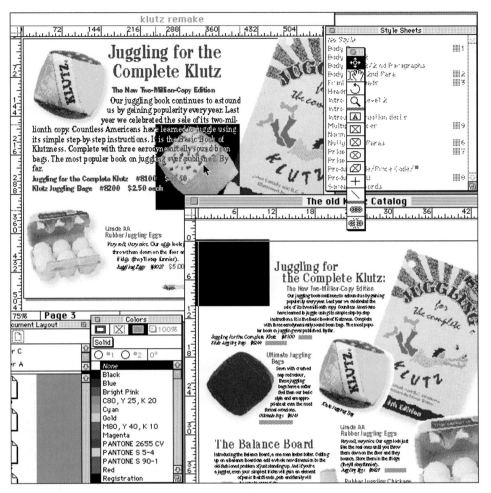

13.4 Adapting a paper-format design to a screen format.

tenham Condensed. Acrobat's serif substitution font mimics the Cheltenham family especially well, so I will choose not to embed Cheltenham when I distill the PostScript, for a savings of about 100K in the final PDF.

With larger type and less total page area, there isn't room for a one-to-one page translation. I could downscale all of the graphical elements, but I'd lose too much detail. Instead I include images selectively, and cover only one item per page [**13.5**].

In general, the fewer elements you arrange on a page, the fewer lines of code will be required to describe them in PostScript, and the smaller your PDF will be. As in HTML, clean construction and a considered use of images translates to a better browsing experience.

Before I go through the same process for the rest of the document, I want to address a structural problem. The printed Klutz catalog has no table of contents; it's meant to be flipped

13.5 Formatted for the screen, fewer items will fit better on the page.

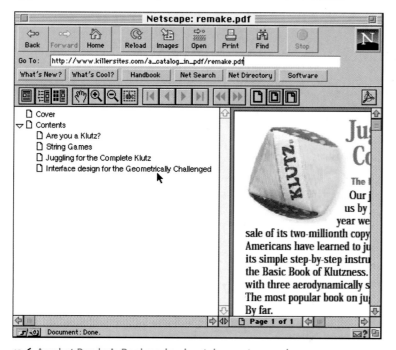

13.6 Acrobat Reader's Bookmarks view takes up too much screen space.

13.7 Let chickens in the document layer show you the way.

through. This works for a slim, printed catalog. It doesn't work for a PDF, where every page flip can take a few seconds. I need to build a navigation system allowing random, non-sequential access to the catalog's pages.

Acrobat Exchange lets me build a *bookmark* directory for any PDF, but relying on it will require surfers to sacrifice too much screen space [13.6].

I want to use as much of the screen as possible for the document, so my only choice is to build navigational help into the pages themselves. A functional document-based navigation scheme lets me dispense with Acrobat Reader's toolbar, gaining even more screen space.

While Exchange will let me add hyperlinks to a PDF's annotation layer, these links will either be invisible or simple rectangles with colored borders. If I want anything more distinctive (like rubber-chicken buttons, for example), I have to place them as art in the pages themselves (the document layer).

I pick a juggling bean bag and two plump rubber chickens from the artwork and arrange them into a compass of sorts. I'll put this at the foot of every page. The bean bag will link to a directory page, and the chickens will link to next and previous pages [13.7].

I design a directory page. I want it to be very simple – just a list of products and a legend for the chicken-bean-bag device. This will be page 2 of my document [13.8]. When I'm done with the directory, I generate a PostScript file as before.

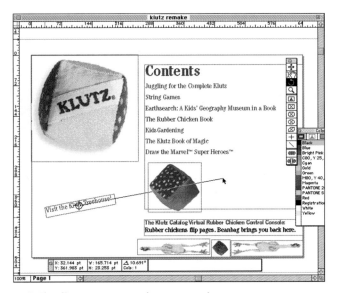

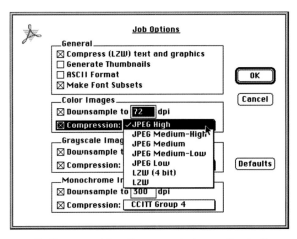

13.9 Do it once and for all – every choice applies to the entire document.

13.8 The directory page under construction.

Distiller Settings

Before processing the PostScript file, I make my image compression and font embedding choices.

Most of the catalog's artwork is pretty robust. To keep the file size manageable, I will downsample to 72 DPI with maximum JPEG compression; this is the lowest quality [**13.9**].

Upon review of Quark's Font Usage report, I decide to embed only one of the document's 21 fonts. Acrobat's substitution fonts will do an adequate job of representing most of the faces, especially the Cheltenhams. The only really critical face is Gorilla, used on the cover. This is used in the Klutz logotype. Only the five characters of the name need be embedded – a trivial addition to file size.

Markup in Acrobat Exchange

With the document layer finished, I move on to the annotation layer in Acrobat Exchange. While the most obvious need is to add directory and navigation links, it is crucial to set the document's Open attributes.

Open attributes determine how the document presents itself when it's opened. You set them through the File menu's Document Info submenu.

For this document, I choose Full Screen as the viewing mode and Fit Page as the magnification [**13.10**]. Full screen will cause the document to display in the browser window without Acrobat's button-bar interface. This button bar takes up too much space, and because I provide navigation within the document itself, users don't need it – better to take all the screen space I can.

13.10 The Open Info dialog box is accessible through the File menu.

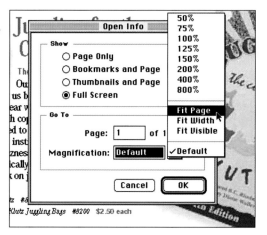

13.11 Creating hyperlinks in Acrobat Exchange is a simple process.

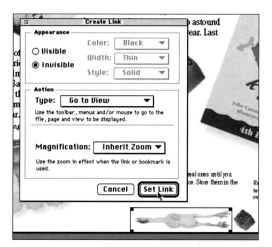

After making a PDF, deactivate or deinstall all the fonts used in the document from your system. Then open the PDF in Exchange to confirm that the font embedding or substitution is working properly. If you leave your fonts active at the system level, you might never see what most of your readers will see.

Fit Page causes the document to scale bigger or smaller as necessary to show the entire page at once. Because my navigation system is built into the pages, and I'm hiding Acrobat's user interface, it's especially important that none of the page ever be obscured.

All of my choices for this document – page geometry and size, type size, and open attributes – work together as a unit. If your document is designed differently, different open attributes might be appropriate. My choices are not a recipe, but rather an illustration of a design process you should go through for each document. Do what works.

Creating the directory and navigation links is easy. Using Exchange's Link tool, I draw rectangles around the hot areas, assign destinations, and test the links **[13.11]**. I make my links invisible, letting the artwork and text indicate what's hot. The cursor changes to a pointing finger when over a hot area. To establish the idea that this is a hot, clickable document, I make the entire cover page a link to the directory page.

One point of finesse here: I nearly always choose Inherit Zoom as the magnification; this respects whatever magnification choice the reader might have specified. For example, a reader with a 21-inch monitor might prefer to view the document at 100% magnification, rather than the very large default in this case (full-screen, fit page).

I can link any part of this PDF to documents on the Web. Using the Weblink tool, I simply draw a rectangle for a hot area and enter a URL.

This manual linking process in

Exchange can be tedious. For larger, more complex PDFS (those that might serve as complete Web sites) there is a smarter approach. Using a language called PDFMark, it's possible to place hotlinks right in the creating application. By placing my PDFMark-enhanced chicken buttons on a master page in Quark, I could spare myself the trouble of linking every page in Exchange. See the Book Site for more detail and pointers to examples.

Surf this PDF on the Book Site for yourself. Then save it to disk, and open it directly using Reader. Now you understand why I made the document in a 4:3 ratio and chose fit page/full-screen modes upon open! Just press the escape key to leave.

Summary

Designing PDFS for the screen as an alternative to HTML is an infant art; as Acrobat's interface matures, and more designers and surfers tune in to the possibilities, we're sure to see a lot of exciting work in PDF on the Web.

Is PDF a win over HTML? The answer depends on your goals and publishing environment.

If typography and sophisticated layouts are your goal, and you have a substantial investment in desktop publishing, PDF might be for you. If printability is important, PDF is *probably* for you. More and more people are picking up Acrobat Reader; Apple and IBM ship it on every machine they sell. If you start from scratch, you can, with a reasonable amount of work, make one file that is both a four-color catalog and

a web site. Unfortunately, on-screen design and print design are so different that the idea of killing two birds with one stone is tenuous at best.

If complex interactivity, universal access, and flexibility are important, HTML will continue to provide solutions, even if they are imperfect. HTML and its tools will get easier, and more people will be able to make good-looking HTML pages. If cost is a concern, HTML tools are less expensive, but the hand work is much more involved.

As we head into the next generation of site design, PDF will be significant for layout-oriented designers who want to capitalize on a familiar design model without the pains of coding. As I will discuss in the next chapter, both PDF and HTML are changing to accommodate the needs of designers who want to do high-quality, low-bandwidth design.

Serving PDFs

Note for Webmasters: To serve PDFS, make sure the extension .pdf maps to the application/pdf MIME type, and that Adobe's free, small byteserve CGI script is installed; this is available for download from Adobe's web site at www.adobe.com.

## CHAPTER 14

Beyond HTML

What you'll learn about in this chapter:

Structured layout

Style sheets

The future of PDF

New image formats

Superpalettes

Alpha channels

Authoring tools of the future

IF YOU'VE MADE IT THIS FAR, you're probably wondering what the future holds for site designers. Trying to predict exact events is like trying to read swirling tea leaves. In this chapter, I hope to give you some idea what is coming down the info-pike and at the same time influence the histogram of browser design by describing which tools are important to designers.

Structured Layout

By now, you're convinced there will be a head-on collision between third-generation site designers and the information purists. Because I have advocated the guerrilla-terrorist approach to site design – throw out all those ugly HTML tags and think visually – it looks like things couldn't be more polarized. I promised an answer to this question, and here it is: Believe it or not, the two trains will soon be headed in the same direction.

Structured layout is coming. If there is an overall message to this book, it is that third-generation site designers are using workarounds to get results, but when structured layout comes to the Web, we will finally be able to do appropriate on-line design. Sites as we know them will change considerably.

There are two ways this will happen: Structured languages like HTML will get many more layout features, and layout-based approaches like PDF will get many more structural features. These two approaches start from opposite ends of the spectrum. Whether they will meet in the middle to become one common language is not possible to say. Though each is headed toward the center, which approach will be more useful to site designers? *That* is the 64-Gigabyte Question.

Style Sheets

From the structure side, the most important development is the advent of *style sheets,* proposed and now promoted by the World Wide Web Consortium (W3C), the governing body of HTML. Style sheets will be implemented by both Internet Explorer 3.0 and Netscape Navigator 4.0. Whether style sheets will become ubiquitous is impossible to say.

Style sheets separate an HTML document into a declaration section and a body section. While the body is similar to today's "orthodox" HTML, the declarations define the behavior of the various elements in the body (similar to a game of bridge, where you agree on the conventions before playing the hands) **[14.1]**.

The declaration section defines the rules of behavior for the tags that will follow. You can keep adding definitions to a single tag, so if you're defining a header, say `<h2>`, you can say it is bold, 18-point, dark green, italic, etc.

A style sheet may contain any number of rules to define the actions of today's tags (`<H1>`, `<P>`, etc.) and new tags you care to define yourself (`<HANGING INDENT>`, `<INSTILL FEAR>`, etc.). When you use those tags in the body, the rules take effect, according to a predetermined hierarchy of precedence. Style sheets give site designers many useful typographic tools: font changes, leading, spacing control, run-arounds (eventually), font colors, margins, and more. You can also combine style sheets; the current document uses all styles available in all included style sheets. Furthermore, style sheets can have URLs, so they can live anywhere on the Web. You can just refer to them and they will stay in your disk cache as long as you need them, then they'll go away when you start using a different set of style sheets.

To prevent people like me from telling others exactly what they should see, style sheets can *cascade*. If one style sheet isn't right for some reason, another style sheet fills in. I can specify a style sheet for a document, but a visitor to my site may override that style sheet and use her own. I can say I don't want her to do this, but she has the last word – the power stays with the browser. In practice, this works out well. It lets me define several different style sheets for a site, starting with what I would like people with high-end systems to see and working down the hierarchy to the low-bandwidth end of the user spectrum: visitors with small screens, few colors, and who may be color blind or vision-impaired. This could be very useful in presenting my site to someone surfing on TV using a cable modem, for example.

Style sheets will automatically negotiate between browsers and servers, establishing information about the user, her equipment, and how she likes to view the Web. It will be relatively easy to detect whether she has a large or small screen, for example, so the appropriate set of style sheets can be served directly without any questions.

Style sheets provide a much higher level of typographic sophistication than

HTML does today. You can do leading, make margins, embed fonts into your pages, and get more control over the look of the page. Soon you'll be able to do run-arounds and hyphenation. Style sheets are not PostScript, but they will get many more PostScript-like features over time.

Rather than writing their own style sheets, site designers will rely on certain prewritten standard style sheets available on the Web. These will be written and maintained, most likely, by people with little or no typographic training or understanding. I can only hope that a core set of principled, well-designed style sheets emerges as a standard. (Please see the Book Site for pointers to quality style sheets as they

14.1 A style sheet declaration section.

```
# You will need Arena or emacs w3 to decode the style sheet below
h1        : font.color = #900000 ! important
h1        : margin.top = 10
h1.center : align = center

h2        : font.color = #900000
h2        : font.size = 14pt
h2        : font.style = roman & bold

ul        : indent = 20
ul        : margin.left = 30
ul        : margin.top = 4
ul        : margin.bottom = 4
ul        : font.color = #000000

dl        : margin.left = 30

/h1 p/    : font.style = bold
p         : margin.left = 30

address   : font.color = #008000
address   : align = left
address   : margin.left = 30
address   : margin.right = 30

b, strong : font.color = #598
em        : font.color = #009000
a         : font.color = #0050C0
a         : font.style = italic

h4        : margin.left = 0
h5        : margin.left = 0
h6        : margin.left = 0
```

become available.) There is also the danger of too many style sheets on the Web. I hope to see a few sources of well-made style sheets, without a lot of second-rate ones floating around.

Layout

On the layout side, Adobe has a good chance of providing the functionality web designers need. Adobe's PostScript language has dominated the print industry and led to the development of many sophisticated tools (like QuarkXPress and Adobe PageMaker). Artists are used to a working model called *direct manipulation*. They place artwork and text containers on a page and move them around, overlapping and combining elements visually. These programs let type run around objects, for example, and use a multi-layered, multilevel transparency approach to displaying many objects on a page.

PDF is behind Adobe's strategy for providing complete publishing solutions on the Web. The PDF approach combines vector and raster graphics with a sophisticated display "engine" on the client computer to render pages. As described in Chapter 12, designers can use PDF to send line-art images (type, shapes, objects, blends, etc.) and make web pages that weigh a small fraction of the GIF-laden pages they currently make. These pages would download much faster, take up less memory, consist of many layers, and adapt to any resolution or scale. All the anti-aliasing is done on the client, rather than by the author.

While PDF is not optimal for surfing today, it is excellent for presenting documents with complex layouts and sophisticated typography. It is also far superior to HTML for printing and probably will be for some time. A corporate annual report is an ideal candidate for today's PDF. A catalog with live updated items, prices, and availability is not.

Adobe has been racing to develop its PDF standard as the designer's platform for publishing on the Web. While PDF capabilities and tools are in their infancy, much more will be built on PDF as the Web matures. Today, you can add text links and make invisible hot zones in PDF documents that link to other documents on the Web. In the very near future, the level of interactivity will increase rapidly due to several new developments:

1) Adobe plans to let designers embed PDF documents right into HTML web pages, similar to a Shockwave movie or a GIF. This is significant, because it combines the scalable, layout-based approach (PDF) with the common browsing paradigm (HTML) on a single page. Designers can start adding Illustrator graphics to their web pages without making them into huge GIFs.

2) Adobe also plans to include interactive capabilities in its new "Bravo" rendering engine, which is essentially a multimedia-featured version of PostScript for the Web. Bravo will also be incorporated into the Java programming language as the standard 2-D imaging model. This means that as the Java programming industry matures, many applications will rely on Bravo as the underlying graphics layer. This puts PDF one level down in the hierarchy, in the layer between the operating system itself and the Java applications that run on the desktop.

3) Adobe's new "Vertigo" development environment promises to bring interactive PDF authoring tools to site developers. Using the Bravo imaging model, Vertigo will let authors create artwork in Photoshop and Illustrator, then place them into Vertigo documents with any number of multimedia options. Vertigo will add structure to PDF documents so they can be seen by search engines, render differently on different systems, etc. Think of it as CD-ROM authoring for the Web.

PDF is not the only layout-based format on the Web. New developments like Shockwave, QuarkImmedia, and mTropolis all bring interactive, CD-ROM-style design to site developers. Freehand for Shockwave is a technology that allows vector graphics to be inserted into web pages today – they are light and zoomable. Virtual reality tools are sprouting like weeds. Soon, many people will think of sites as 3-D spaces to navigate and explore. Certainly, interaction will involve movement, animation, time-based events, "actors," agents, spatial metaphors, and avatars (graphical representations of various surfers within a site). All these technologies will become more web-savvy, trying to tie in with the rest of the Web.

Tomorrow's Web Sites

Most sites continue to be driven by technology (what *can* be done, rather than what *should* be done), and these sites are likely to make up the bulk of all URLs for some time. People can't resist the latest whiz-bang toys. While browser manu-

facturers shoot each other with the latest bells and whistles in the feature wars, I would like to offer a few suggestions for the underlying technology of structured layout that could improve the design of sites across the Web.

Superpalettes

People will continue to surf with the ability to see only 256 colors. It's a shame, but it's the way things are going to be. Imagine you have a page with 15 small images on it. If each image has 30 colors, the number of colors on the page could be as high as 450. Since many of these colors are probably close, it's a good idea to define one single palette for the page and take all colors from it. That single palette is called a *superpalette*. I expect there will be two ways to define one.

You can define a superpalette simply by not needing too many colors on any one page. In this case, simply keep track of how many images and colors

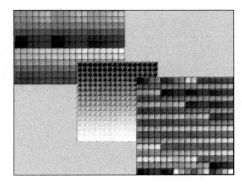

you're using, and don't let the combined total of images exceed 216 (or whatever the system can stand). This is intuitive to designers, but the browser doesn't know what to expect, so there will have to be a way to specify that the

243

palette should come from the page.

The second way is to define a palette ahead of time and choose all your colors out of that palette, the way we do with the color cube today. DeBabelizer is particularly good at analyzing a set of images and creating a superpalette. You can then use the colors in this palette to pick colors for solids and type. Several predetermined palettes should be available (grayscale, lineart, photography, etc.), so you should only have to specify a new one if necessary.

Load Order

If designers can specify load order, they can better control the presentation of their pages. Load order accomplishes many things. It lets designers specify superpalettes, simply by sticking to the first 256 colors that are served, no matter how many images it takes. It lets designers control the timing of events and the experience of arriving at a page. Load order will also help specify the appearance of elements on a page once we have z-axis layering.

Z-Axis Layering

The PostScript model builds a page

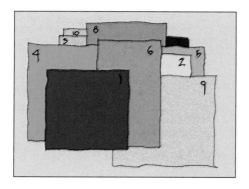

from back to front, with objects being obscured as each element is added. The final image is what you see from the front when it's all done. On the Web, the reverse approach makes more sense.

Z-axis layering goes hand-in-hand with *absolute positioning* of elements to give us a kind of Reverse PostScript Notation, in which we send various page objects to be loaded generally (though not strictly) from front to back, so the user can see the most important items first. By specifying load order, I could design a page with a group of most important images up front, then perhaps navigation and a text summary, followed by a quick sound or voiceover, then some background theme elements, followed by detailed text that runs around a background shape, etc. Imagine the opportunities.

A True Alpha Channel

Animators and CD-ROM developers have been using alpha channels for years. An alpha channel is simply another 8 bits to describe your image, along with 8 bits each of red, green, and blue. Typically, alpha channels denote transparency. Think how much less work it would be if we never had to worry about anti-aliasing! All anti-aliasing should take place on the client system using 8 full bits (256 levels) of transparency [**14.2**].

Better Raster Formats

The next raster graphic format on the Web may be PNG, or Portable Network Graphics Standard (pronounced "ping"). PNG may replace GIF with a superior, patent-free compression method that is as good as LZW or better, platform independence, and greater color range. PNG supports a range of features, including interlacing, color depths up to 48 bits, grayscale depths up to 16 bits, a full 8-bit alpha channel, and file corruption checking, all while remaining open and extensible into the

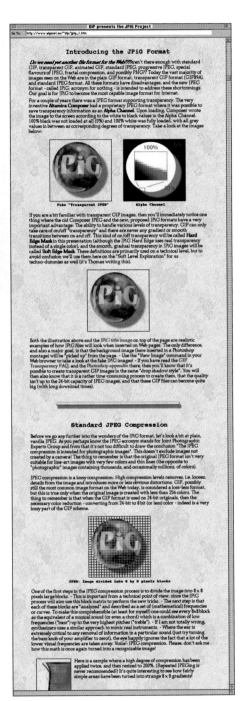

14.2 Several new graphics standards are on the horizon, promising site designers increased functionality and flexibility.

future. If PNG extends to animation with excellent compression, it should be a formidable challenger to GIF.

Remember the problems I had reducing the main image of Chapter 8? The problem with that image was that it had both line art and screen art combined. Do we need an alpha channel for JPEG images? Yes. Do we need a new image format that combines GIF and JPEG? No! We need z-axis layering, so we can send solid shapes and type as vector data, not raster. Leave JPEG alone and give artists the tools they need to present multifaceted pages at low bandwidth.

White Space Control

In desktop publishing, absolute positioning is all you need to specify the layout of a page. On the Web, where pages are as long as days in outer space, designers also need *relative positioning*. White space control will let us space down and over without having to resort to single-pixel GIFs. True white space control, in very small increments, would let us set up design grids and gutters, margins and offsets, all with precision. It would let me guarantee a certain amount of space between

elements, no matter what happens. Once we have white space control, we can make third-generation sites without single-pixel GIFs.

Better Feedback

Today's browsers don't give designers much choice in offering visual and sound cues to users. As sites get more sophisticated, little things will make a difference. Rollovers are a good example. A *rollover* is an effect that triggers a certain event – like a color change – when the cursor is within a certain range. This usually tells you it's "hot" and can be clicked. Rollovers are an important user interface element and should be incorporated into HTML, rather than having to rely on Shockwave or some other third-party solution. Another idea is the visited image. If I use images for navigation – as I have on over half the sites in this book – I would like the browser to present a "visited" version of that image once the page has been seen.

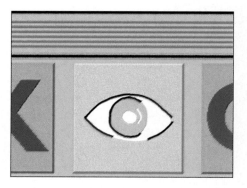

Sound In, Sound Out

Many designers want sound, and so do many surfers. I think sound may be a better way to provide for vision-impaired readers than large fonts and simple screen designs. I also think people will be able to surf by voice command; this will be a big advantage to consumer surfers who don't or can't type. Designers may have to add special commands to their sites so people who surf vocally can navigate easily.

People will want to talk with other surfers they meet in a site. This is possible today and will soon work its way to the consumer. Sound will be a regular part of the surfing experience in the near future.

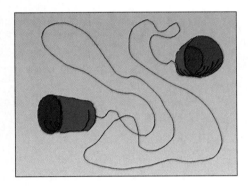

The Third Dimension

Many people are excited about VRML (Virtual Reality Modeling Language), QuickTime VR, and other 3-D surfing paradigms. To keep the quality high, these sites will be much more complicated than their two-dimensional counterparts, requiring more bandwidth than today's consumers can afford. I fear for surfers everywhere that the third dimension will not be a beautiful place. We can look forward to seeing plenty of walls, triangles, and wireframe environments, many of them with the same repeating textures and structural elements. Good architecture and interior design is likely to be years away.

The Fourth Dimension

Web pages will sing, they will dance, they will be alive with movement. I predict that sometime in 1997, when you arrive at the Infiniti car site, a spokesperson will greet you in his black mock-turtleneck, open the door to a car, climb in, start the engine, and drive off-screen. That will be the entry page. What tools will make these pages? I expect these tools to be similar to the Director/Shockwave combinations we have today, though more refined, and more tuned to the Web.

Adding the element of time to sites will be interesting. Rather than leaving all the timed events to Shockwave, I expect HTML (or something like it) will need to coordinate timed events. This will probably be useful to third-generation site designers, who want to have as much control over the appearance and events that happen on their sites as possible.

The 64-Gigabyte Question

Okay, structured layout is coming. Which web page description model will win? Will style sheets gain enough interaction and layout capabilities to entice true designers? Will PDF documents become as ubiquitous as HTML, run animation, let us fill out forms, and serve dynamic data from distributed databases? Will typography give way to interactive posters and 3-D wallpaper? Which standard will emerge to win the hearts and loyalty of site designers around the globe?

The answer is: It doesn't matter. What matters is the software tools designers use to make sites. Hand coding web sites – the subject of this book – is ridiculous. No one should have to do it. The right tool will provide intuitive, easy-to-use interfaces for both the structure and layout of a site, and implement them using whatever underlying technology is available. It will take advantage of anything and everything available, giving designers the choice of which model to use where. Without the proper tools and interface, the majority of sites won't be able to take advantage of all the sophisticated technology the Web can produce.

Yet the day when we can use a sophisticated program to take complete control of our pages using direct manipulation is not in sight. Though parts of the job will become more automated, we will continue to make the best sites by hand until both the underlying models and the tools begin to serve our needs.

PostScript is a stable language. It has only changed once in ten years, and PostScript Level II wasn't much of a change. Tools have had time to mature. On the Web, big, complicated tools have no chance of keeping up with current developments. Following the model of computer graphics over the last ten years, the cutting-edge projects will be done by teams of collaborators: designers, Java programmers, graphics people, story specialists, writers, etc. Small tools will spring up overnight to solve this problem or that. Because it's hard to make money on tiny programs that do one job well, these tools will continue to be unsupported, unreliable, and free.

Most site designers, who can't afford to hire programmers or learn the arcane syntax of CGI scripting, want stable, professional software that helps them solve their problems. Programs like Netscape Navigator Gold, Microsoft FrontPage, and Adobe PageMill are not third-generation design tools. They are merely front-end interfaces for writing HTML, the way HTML was written ten months ago. It takes ten months to get a product like that to market – by the time a new version becomes available, its feature set is obsolete. More important, these programs do not define a paradigm for good web page design. They merely provide buttons and dialog boxes for the current HTML command set.

The authoring tool of the future will be based on the addition of plug-ins – modules that expand its capabilities without rewriting the entire code base. Just as browsers can have plug-ins to enhance surfing capability, programs can have plug-ins that enhance their ability to create new kinds of documents. Plug-ins can be written and distributed quickly, almost as quickly as new plug-ins can be added to browsers. The difference is that, while browsing plug-ins should be free, authoring plug-ins should be paid for.

Only through a lucrative web-based plug-in market can tool development keep up with the pace of change. The flexible, plug-in based tool of the future will allow typographers to add a hyphenation module as easily as they al-low catalog makers to add a search module or architects to add a new shading-and-texture module. The creation of a viable plug-in market for web authoring tools will be a major indication that designers will get what they need to do the job well.

The single-pixel GIF trick is not a hallmark of a third-generation site, but a necessity. Once we have a tool that works the way we think, we won't care how it does the job underneath. It should have everything outlined above, and we shouldn't even notice. Site designers already have to know too much about the production process. Some day, it will be easy to design pages that are structural, beautiful, and fast.

Until then, remember the credo of the third-generation site designer:

QUALITY   BREVITY   BANDWIDTH

Paralysis

Possibly one of the most difficult things to do on the Web is to make a single page as good as it can possibly be. You can always do something to make it better. If you have a site, you know there are places you haven't touched in a long time, and two months is a very long time on the Web.

We all start with horizontal rules and blank-line typography. It's part of the learning curve. As we gain control of our pages, we raise the bar on ourselves, striving for better pages as we add tools to our toolkit. It doesn't get easier, the results just get better.

Possibly the best piece of advice I can give any designer is to roll up your sleeves and dig in. Start pushing pixels and tables around to see what works and what doesn't. I never get a page right on the first, or second, or third try. I'm always rethinking my pages, realizing in the middle of the night how I could have done something more simply or cleanly.

A web site is an adventure. It's like surfing. You pick a goal, you start the journey, you end up somewhere else, but it turns out to be more interesting than where you thought you were going. While I advocate control over your pages, I hope this book has expanded your creativity by freeing you from the narrow, linear thought process imposed by HTML programming.

HTML is not for dummies. It can't be learned in a week. Making great pages is exacting work, and you can always do better. Third-generation site designers work their way up the hard way, sweating the details and using whatever tools are at hand to make balanced, beautiful, communicative pages. I hope that after you make a third-generation site, people you have never met will come visit, enjoy, send you mail, and connect in ways you never expected. Then you will know why it's all worth the effort.

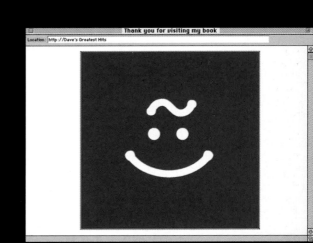

Dave's Guide to Better Surfing

Because I insisted, my publisher let me squeeze in a few notes on surfing. Though it is beyond the scope of this book, I would like to make a few recommendations to increase your surfing pleasure.

Link Colors: Brain Damage on the Infobahn

The Framers of the Web decided to denote links with underlining and special colors. They decided to make unvisited links blue and visited links purple. They avoided using red, probably because they thought red universally meant "STOP!" Also, they might have figured that some people can't see red, and many people (at the time) had black-and-white monitors, so underlining links was a good idea.

At user interface school, they teach us that the color red has a prominent place in the evolution of our visual system. In the jungle, the color red serves as a strong warning of danger. Red is a "flag" color: It shouts. It does not mean "STOP!"; it means "HEY!"

Good designers take advantage of this attention mechanism without overusing it and watering it down. Have you ever seen a blue speedometer dial? The right choice is to turn the "hot" unvisited links dark red and leave the visited links distinguishable, but "cool," receding into the black text [**A1.1**]. Red says, "Over here! Hit me!" Blue says, "Been there, done that." Red jumps out. Blue recedes into the background. Go to a magazine stand and test this hypothesis for yourself.

I want my visited links to become associated with (but distinct from) the text and leave the active (unvisited) links standing out on the page. Hot red and cool blue links should be standard on all browsers, but they aren't. To compensate, I start almost all my pages with the following header:

```
<BODY BGCOLOR="#ffffff"
TEXT="#000000" LINK="#CC0000"
ALINK="#FF3300"
VLINK="#330099">
```

This makes unvisited links dark red, visited links dark purple (which I happen to like better than dark blue – it's a personal preference), and the "active link" color can be almost anything you like, since you see it only while your mouse button is held down. I hope you will use this formula on your pages unless you have good reason to do otherwise. Perhaps if enough people set these colors on their pages, browser manufacturers will change their default ways of thinking.

You may have noticed that not a single site in this book has an image with a blue or purple border around it. While visited and unvisited link colors around images are an integral part of first-generation sites, they are so hideous that most reasonable people banned them long ago. Borders ruin the effect of most photographs. If you are relying on them to tell people something, you should consider redesigning. I always

set my image borders to zero.

I also use these colors while surfing. I will see them unless the site designer has specified otherwise. It's much nicer to surf with these colors; you quickly get accustomed to red items being clickable. Change your browser preferences and surf happily!

Underlining

Underlined links are necessary if you are surfing from a black-and-white monitor, or if you are colorblind. If you can see colors, you should turn underlining off, and you should encourage people who visit your sites to turn underlining off. Maybe if enough people turn underlining off, the browser programmers will stop making it the "default" setting. Then again, maybe everyone who buys a copy of this book should just send email to *webmaster-@netscape.com* and *webmaster@microsoft.com* asking them to turn underlining off at the factory.

Underlining is a traditional typographic "proofreader's mark" that says "make this italic, for emphasis." People using typewriters couldn't do italics, so they used underlining to compensate. In quality typography, underlining simply does not exist. On the Web, if you can see colors, you can safely turn underlining off and live a longer, happier life without it.

Background Colors

Choose anything but gray. As you surf the Web, the best background to use is either white or a very pale shade of a light color. If you think white is too

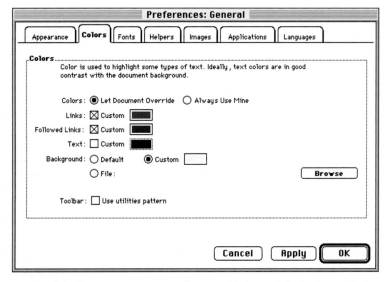

A1.1 Good design starts at your own browser. Make unvisited colors red, visited purplish-blue.

harsh, use an extremely pale "minty green" as your default background color, or my new favorite: "wheat." **[A1.2]**

Please note: I cannot give you an exact recipe for this color, because I don't know enough about your system. If you have 256 colors, you might not be able to get a light enough color. Use your own judgment to come up with a very pale background color that will eventually "disappear" as you get used to it. These colors should be extremely close to white. If you can't get something very light, stick with white. If you try a light background like this, give it a week before changing it back. It will take a little while to get used to, but you'll be happier in the long run.

Don't set a subtle background color like this on your pages. If it's not in the color cube, many people may see it differently. Always look at your pages with 256 colors to verify a background color. Most of the time, white is best.

Many browser manufacturers have finally figured out that white is the best all-around default color and have begun to ship their browsers with white backgrounds right from the factory. Cleaning up the information highway is a dirty job, but if everyone pitches in, we'll get those gray backgrounds in the garbage can, where they belong.

Fonts

Make sure to use high-quality fonts for surfing. Many Adobe fonts work quite well for surfing. I recommend Gill Sans, Syntax, and Melior as possibilities. TrueType fonts should only come from Microsoft, Apple, or Monotype. These vendors make their TrueType

fonts with special hints that adapt the type well to the screen. Other TrueType fonts are not likely to be as well made.

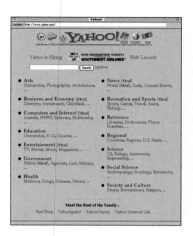

A1.2 Fewer trips to the Advil home page: Set your background to just barely green, or a light neutral "wheat" color. (Quiz: How many deadly sins can you find on these pages?)

The Color Cube

ON THE FOLLOWING PAGES I present my own look at the color cube, mentioned throughout this book (and described in detail in Chapter 3), for your reference. Most graphic representations of the cube show all 216 colors, either laid out in a big table, or arranged as slices through the cube. The problem with these approaches is that they don't show the various color combinations possible when looking at the cube in different ways. Both versions shown are different from other representations in that they have more than 216 entries. They have as many as necessary to show their perspectives. Many colors are repeated, but that's the idea.

I hope you will find these two presentations both stimulating and useful when choosing colors for your images. I encourage you to cut out the extra page provided and tape it to your monitor or near your desk. You should also pick up the color cube graphic from the Book Site, where you can get instructions on loading it into your color picker for easy reference.

Transitions Between Fully Saturated Colors

The first version [A2.1] is a transition table, showing possible transitions between prominent colors. This shows the intermediate steps between each of the colors at the eight corners of the color cube. Transitions between primaries, like the pure red of FF0000 and pure blue 0000FF, in one color and decrement the other by hex 33 for each step. Transitions between secondaries are the same as for primaries. The most complex transitions are those between a primary and a secondary made from the other two primaries. Blue to yellow involves blue decreasing as red and green increase.

The Cube Unfolded

The second [A2.2] is the cube peeled, so you can see the outside layers and the inner core. These groupings can be helpful when choosing colors that go together or making transitions from one area of color to another.

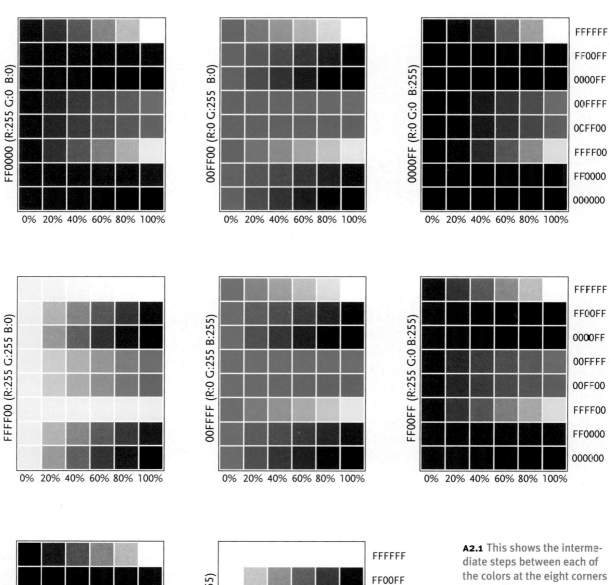

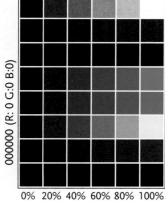

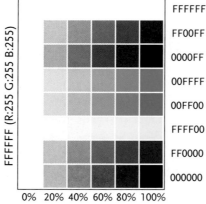

A2.1 This shows the intermediate steps between each of the colors at the eight corners of the color cube.

The outside faces of the color cube are dominated by pure, saturated colors. In the depths of the cube, colors are noticeably murkier. The eight colors in the center of the cube are middle grays and muted tints with little variation.

Converting Hex Triplets to Decimal RGB Values

The hex (hexadecimal) values for each color are shown on the swatch. Use the following table to translate hex to RGB. Example: FF00CC, a hot pink, translates to 255 red, 0 green, 204 blue in the decimal Photoshop palette. 9966CC, a faded plum color, would be 153 red, 102 green, 204 blue.

HEX	DECIMAL
00	0
33	51
66	102
99	153
CC	204
FF	255

A2.2 These groupings can be helpful when choosing colors that go together or making transitions from one area of color to another.

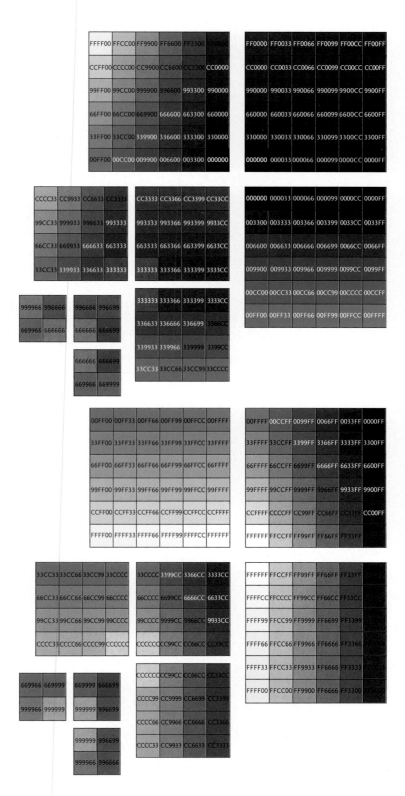

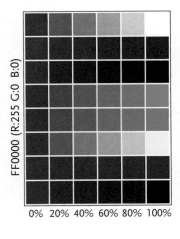

FF0000 (R:255 G:0 B:0)

FFFFFF
FF00FF
0000FF
00FFFF
00FF00
FFFF00
FF0000
000000

0% 20% 40% 60% 80% 100%

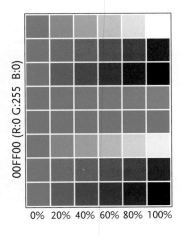

00FF00 (R:0 G:255 B:0)

FFFFFF
FF00FF
0000FF
00FFFF
00FF00
FFFF00
FF0000
000000

0% 20% 40% 60% 80% 100%

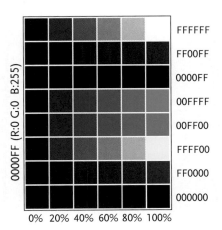

0000FF (R:0 G:0 B:255)

FFFFFF
FF00FF
0000FF
00FFFF
00FF00
FFFF00
FF0000
000000

0% 20% 40% 60% 80% 100%

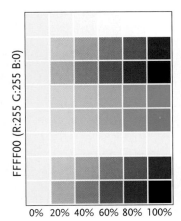

FFFF00 (R:255 G:255 B:0)

0% 20% 40% 60% 80% 100%

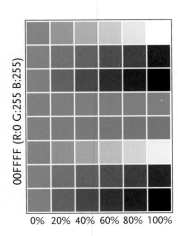

00FFFF (R:0 G:255 B:255)

0% 20% 40% 60% 80% 100%

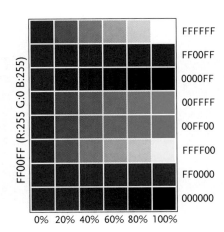

FF00FF (R:255 G:0 B:255)

FFFFFF
FF00FF
0000FF
00FFFF
00FF00
FFFF00
FF0000
000000

0% 20% 40% 60% 80% 100%

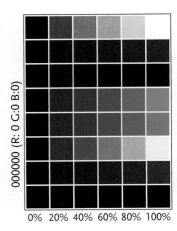

000000 (R: 0 G:0 B:0)

0% 20% 40% 60% 80% 100%

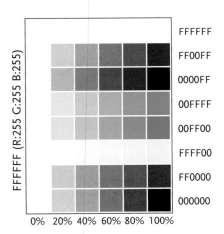

FFFFFF (R:255 G:255 B:255)

FFFFFF
FF00FF
0000FF
00FFFF
00FF00
FFFF00
FF0000
000000

0% 20% 40% 60% 80% 100%

Creating Killer Web Sites

Cut this page out and tape it to your monitor as a handy reference guide.

Index